The GRAMMAR

—— *of* ——

ANGELS

The
GRAMMAR
—— *of* ——
ANGELS

*A Search for
the Magical Powers
of Sublime Language*

EDWARD WILSON-LEE

**WILLIAM
COLLINS**

William Collins
An imprint of HarperCollins*Publishers*
1 London Bridge Street
London SE1 9GF

WilliamCollinsBooks.com

HarperCollins*Publishers*
Macken House,
39/40 Mayor Street Upper,
Dublin 1, D01 C9W8, Ireland

First published in Great Britain in 2025 by William Collins

1

A catalogue record for this book is
available from the British Library

ISBN 978-0-00-862179-7

Typeset in Minion Pro by Jouve (UK), Milton Keynes

Printed and bound in Great Britain by CPI Group (UK) Ltd, Croydon

MIX
Paper | Supporting
responsible forestry
FSC™ C007454

This book contains FSC™ certified paper and other controlled
sources to ensure responsible forest management.

For more information visit: www.harpercollins.co.uk/green

TABLE OF CONTENTS

A NOTE ON QUOTATIONS AND
READING ALOUD

F ollowing early modern practice, direct quotations are given in italics; the source of these quotations can be found in the endnotes. The narrative also contains a number of passages of gibberish, backwards-speak and nonsense, and for a complete understanding of the subject matter the reader is strongly urged to read these passages aloud, insofar as safety permits.

Speech was divided into four parts: that the inspired priests know.
Three parts, hidden in deep secret, humans do not stir into action;
the fourth part of Speech is what men speak.
THE RIG VEDA, TRANS. WENDY DONIGER

انَّ من البيان لَسحرًا
Indeed there is in speech a magic.
SAYING OF THE PROPHET MUHAMMAD, FROM THE HADITH

*Though I speak with the tongues of men and angels, and have not
charity, I am become as sounding brass, or a tinkling cymbal.*
1 CORINTHIANS 13

In great things, it is enough to have tried.
PROPERTIUS, *ELEGIES* II.X.6

I

The 900

It had already been a summer of prodigies by the time Giovanni Pico della Mirandola arrived in Rome in the autumn of 1486. There were reports from the mountains that a blood rain had fallen in the cities of Tagliacozzo and Celano near L'Aquila, and some had brought stones covered in red gore to the city and shown them publicly so that it was believed without contradiction. People might not have needed much convincing after the year just passed. In the endless feud between the Colonna and Orsini clans, the Montagues and Capulets of Rome, a man had been slaughtered one Friday around lunchtime by a poisoned knife and a woman eight months pregnant was murdered by her own stepson. The Pope had issued proclamations against *brigandage, enmities, homicides and criminals*, sending warning through Rome and its environs that all murderers and thieves should void the city under pain of heavy fines or even excommunication to them and those who harboured them in their retinues. But these threats went unheeded, and when the Pope's commissary was sent to abjure the warring sides to peace he was stripped and sent away naked. Even his own cardinals were part of the fray: on the Feast of the Assumption of the Virgin Mary in the middle of August a fight had erupted between a French cardinal's men and a local noble over a prostitute named *La Greghetta*, which is 'The Little Greek', and three men were left dead, while *La Greghetta* herself survived the torching of her premises by sheltering in a window frame more strongly built than the burning timbers of the structure. There were few in Rome who knew what *great peace and felicity it is to the mind when a man has nothing that grudges his conscience nor is appalled by the secret twitch of any privy crime.* When peace was at last concluded between the city's factions, through a contract of marriage between the Pope's son Franceschetto and the daughter of Lorenzo de' Medici, allied to the Orsini, the détente was threatened after Franceschetto and his companions sought to abduct and scandalize some women of good name, both married and not, and were repulsed with great shame and ignominy. *Among all things,* Pico was later to write, *the very deadly pestilence is this: to be conversant day and night among them whose life is not only on every side an elective to sin, but over that all set in the expugnation of virtue, under their captain the devil, under the banner of death, under the stipend of hell.* He could very well have been thinking of those darkening months in Rome.[1]

Yet Pico was a prodigy of a different kind. He had come at barely 24 years old to the centre of Christian Europe for the purposes of defending against all comers a universal philosophy, laid out in 900 propositions or conclusions which in their entirety he claimed to cover *all knowable things.* These *Theses* were printed on the seventh day of December and distributed throughout Italy and he promised to stand the passage of any who wished to come a month later – on the Feast of Epiphany – to challenge any of his assertions. If this appeared an act of supreme arrogance, it was nevertheless in keeping with the aura that had begun to grow up around Pico even at this young date. In this era of wonders that was later to be called the Renaissance, Pico would become the uncontested marvel of the age, and the brokers of compliment emptied their coffers to rise above the usual flattery and express their amazement. The greatest scholar of the day, perhaps of any day, would speak of Pico in terms that sound more like the announcement for a prizefighter than anything, and yet there is reason to believe he meant every word: he was *the one-and-only, a demi-god, endowed with every blessing of fortune, body and spirit that can be had, a young man of near divine beauty and majestical bearing, of the most piercing intelligence, singular memory, and tireless concentration, a clarion of almighty eloquence, as famous for his judgment as his character* – Pico. Della. Miiiiiiiirandola!*²*

Those who thumbed through the programme for the grand debate would have seen that there was indeed a wild profusion of things treated therein, down to the reasons for the saltiness of the sea and why owls struggle to look at the sun, treatments of snub-nosedness and the causes of pallor and corpulence in Germans, on the two kinds of drunkenness and whether God could choose to transform himself into an ass or a piece of wood or a damned soul or even the Devil himself. Many of the propositions would simply have been befuddling or nonsensical, such as one that stated that *By 'Heaven' we should understand the green line that encircles the universe*, and the proposition that there was not just one world but in fact 183 of them, arranged in a triangle. There was, though, also a defence of the nonsensical in the assertion that *meaningless voices are more magically powerful than those that have meaning*. So that the magnificence of his scheme should not be frittered away in mere incomprehension, Pico spent the final months of that year preparing a grand oration that would be addressed to the college of cardinals before the debate began, a manifesto for his vision of concord, in which all disagreements were settled and all contradictions resolved. To accomplish this, he said, required not only the understanding of all existing knowledge but to go somewhat further than that: he had determined, he wrote, *to swear allegiance to no creed, to plumb the depths of every philosopher, to scrutinize every scrap of paper, and to master every kind of thought*, and to push forward past that into such secret things that had not previously been spoken of or even thought. In the final words of this speech he prepared to astonish those few who had not yet been provoked by his conduct: the point of this spectacle was *not so much to show that I know many things*, he would say, dangling a morsel of humility in front of the audience before snatching it away – *but that I know what others do not*.[3]

Pico's road to Rome had not been without incident, and in his trail behind him were the scenes where he had almost been stopped in his course. He narrowly escaped the plague in Perugia, and before that had been briefly imprisoned when the wife of the Medici governor of Arezzo had abandoned her husband to go with Pico and he had been accused of kidnap. He had been forced to leave behind him in Fratta the mentor under whose spell he had spent the previous months, a mysterious Sicilian Jew calling himself Flavius Mithridates, and under whose tutelage Pico had been furiously studying Hebrew and Arabic and even the tongue of the Chaldeans, an ancient language thought lost by many and considered to have been the medium for knowledge of inestimable power. Mithridates himself had mesmerized Rome in a Good Friday sermon five years previously, speaking in a number of tongues that were unknown to those present but in which they affirmed his immense eloquence, and the Pope and his cardinals raised a clamour of his praise that was said to reach as far as the skies. But shortly after that Mithridates had been chased out of Rome under circumstances that were not clear and he was forbidden to return, though had he done so he might have been hard to spot among the influx of *Marranos*, or converted Jews, who were flooding into Rome from Spain and making themselves everywhere indispensable. The associates who remained to Pico in Rome were just as suspect. He was intimate with the presiding spirit of Roman intellectual life, a man named Pomponius Leto, who had founded an academy to revive the glories of Rome and Greece, but an aura of suspicion had surrounded Leto ever since he and his associates had been accused of performing pagan rituals during orgies in the catacombs and of conspiring to overthrow the Pope. Leto himself had been absolved but others of the group known to Pico had fled as far as Poland and even there had been hounded by the Roman authorities.[4]

There were those who attempted to divert Pico from the course on which he was set, and in the months during which he approached Rome he answered pleas that he put aside his philosophical projects and instead take up the active life of a man of consequence, to which he was after all entitled as one of the wealthiest men in Italy and moreover the focus of such extraordinary expectations. All these warnings Pico staunchly refused to heed, insisting that he was more suited to the contemplative life, though he acknowledged that the undertaking was not without risk and there was no sense in which this contemplation was partner to retirement. As he wrote to one friend in October, he was continuing towards Rome, *from whence you are like to hear the echo of all your Pico has achieved*. In another letter he averred that the number of conclusions he had settled upon was a perfect emblem of the inspired poetic frenzy he intended to achieve on that day in Rome.[5]

Those able to understand Pico's conclusions knew that this was not some showman's attempt to wow the crowds with misdirection and inflated claims. As he laid out in his *Oration* introducing the event, Pico asserted that he would unify the two major fields of European thought, showing how to reconcile the meticulous precision through which Aristotle had described the world with the infinite expanse of Plato's philosophy. This had been attempted by many before but so far had been achieved by none. To do so would bring an end to a battle that had been running for much longer than the Roman street brawls and was scarcely less vicious. But this was just a start, and the choice to hold his gathering on the day of Epiphany may have signalled the next place to which his thought was tending: on the day that the Wise Men had knelt down to the infant Jesus, submitting all foreign knowledge to the supremacy of God's truth, Pico would produce proofs even from the most secret writings of the Jews themselves, which would silence the contra-dictions of unbelievers once and for all.[6]

This was not to say that he would push aside all but Christian learning; far from it, the scheme that he proposed was intended to be universal, to include within its sweep all the knowledges of the world and yoke them to his purpose, bringing them together as so many fragments of a shattered mirror and being the first to gaze into its fullness. He even surrendered any claim to the primacy of Christian knowledge, saying that it would not do to leave out the philosophies of the Greeks and Arabs, as *all wisdom passed from Barbarians to the Greeks and from the Greeks to us.* This much was clear when he opened his *Oration* by saying that key to all wisdom lies in رجل, *rajul,* that is, *man,* citing a Muslim philosopher and doing so in Arabic. Following the lead of his model Mithridates, he went further than this, inserting a passage from a text he iden-tified as Chaldean and which went as follows:

በረናሡ ሀ ሐያ ሚጠበ0 ሜሥታኔ ዌናዳደ ሜመሐለጸተ ጋረጣሀ ኮ ወኮ

For those unable to take his meaning, Pico clarified that the key to deriving all possible knowledge from within was first to recognize that *man is a living thing whose nature is ever-changing, many-fold, and unstable.* He was born to be *the go-between of creation, intim-ate with those above and master of those below, a waystation between the stillness of eternity and the flood of time.*[7]

It was at this point that the path laid out in Pico's oration began to move from the merely surprising to the downright strange. He promised that those who followed his method would learn to leave behind the physical dross of their bodies, and even surpass the niceties of reason, becoming like the angels themselves, *transcend-ent beings merely clothed in human flesh.* The method was nothing less than the revival of an ancient and forgotten rite, one which led those *living in the wilderness of the body's solitude* to rise above the mundane and experience eternity in the here and now. *Who would not desire those Socratic frenzies of which Plato sings*, states of ecstasy that cause us to leave our minds, *incited by the frenzy of the Muses to pour celestial harmonies into the ears of our souls*? This path, Pico promises, can lead us even higher than the angels, even to the point of becoming God ourselves. *Stung by unspeakable desire*, he predicts, *we will be driven to ecstasy, moving beyond our bodies like burning Seraphim, and full of divinity we shall be ourselves no longer, but rather we will be Him, the One who made us.*[8]

While Pico's words may seem to our ears just so much hocus-pocus and mumbo-jumbo, these ideas would have been familiar to many of his audience, even if parts of the speech and the theses it introduced would have made them distinctly uncomfortable. Lodged at the heart of many of the traditions of thought known to them – and countless more they had yet to encounter – was the idea that, under certain circumstances, humans could transcend the boundaries and weaknesses of their physical bodies, and indeed that achieving this was the utmost thing to be desired. Ranging across the vast expanse of ancient and medieval thought available to him, Pico would see that there was little agreement on why this happened, how far it could be taken, how it should be used, or what the meaning of it was. But he would also see that there were extraordinary similarities between these many widely dispersed ways of thinking, so much so that one could easily conclude that they were all parts of the same puzzle. Central to many of these connections was the idea that there is an underlying oneness to all existence, that beneath and beyond the many things and beings we encounter there is a level at which they are all part of a shared fabric, and that if only we could access this deeper structure we could overcome the frustrations and limitations of our bounded selves.

Though people had arrived at this conclusion in myriad ways, there was an uncanny tendency for certain things to come up again and again, such as the states of ecstasy or disembodiment, which were understood as the threshold to this hidden reality. These experiences are fossilized in our everyday speech, still living among us, though largely deprived of their erstwhile meaning and power: the idea of being *astonished, entranced, enraptured, amazed, captivated, fascinated, ravished, stupefied, transported, beside oneself* and even *surprised* may now be common banalities, but they carry within them the cultural memories of experiences at once terrifying and transcendent, of being deprived of all control, turned to stone, dumbstruck, and provoked to out-of-body experiences. Some more recent additions to the list may still be fresh enough to retain a trace of their origins, even as they are swiftly decaying into cliché: many will know that to be *hypnotized* by something was once more than simply to be very interested in it, and perhaps some will have a dim sense of the same about the word *mesmerized*. Another thing that came up time and again was the connection of these ecstatic states with various experiences of sound, of rhythm and harmony and spoken utterance. We still speak of being *enchanted*, but few mean that they were brought to this state by *being chanted over* or by *incantation*, and claiming to be *spellbound* is normally not now preliminary to accusations of witchcraft.[9]

For Pico and his audience, however, these were no dead metaphors. The *frenzy of the Muses* and the power of *celestial harmonies* were central parts of a highly sophisticated and widely dispersed understanding of the world, one that had been honed and sharpened and elaborated over much of the duration of recorded thought, and doubtless well before that also. Central to one part of this tradition was the notion of angels, who were commonly understood to be intermediary beings existing between the fragile, isolated and transient bodies of worldly beings and the eternal infinitude of the most fundamental level of existence, which may or may not have been the same thing as God. The widespread fascination with angels was in part to do with the fact that they represented the next step in ascendance, the essence of what it would be like for man to become more than he was. And at the heart of imagining angels were visions of how they spoke and sang. From the choirs of heavenly angels to the Annunciation by which Gabriel stirred the life of an incarnated God within the womb of a virgin, the voices of angels were understood to have qualities and powers that seemed to lie at the very limits of human speech: the ability to blend many things into one, as with voices in a choir, or the power to change the fabric of the world simply by speaking at it. At the angel song heard by the prophet Isaiah, *the foundations of the thresholds shook*, and *the house was filled with smoke* (Isaiah 6: 4). Many believed that angel speech was so powerful that it did not attempt to express thoughts like human speech but, rather, made the thoughts of one angel inhabit another, dissolving the boundaries between the two in such a way as to leave it unclear whether there were still two beings or only one. This opened whole new vistas of enquiry: could there really be said to be more than one angel when they shared the same thoughts? Could angels really be said to *speak* when all boundary between speaker and listener were lost? And could man himself acquire this skill? Some humans seemed once to have had the gift of this preternaturally powerful speech, as with the legendary poets Amphion and Orpheus, whose lyrical voices were so irresistible that not just people and animals were brought under their control but even stones and rivers were said to move at their commands. Orpheus's song indeed had almost brought his beloved Eurydice back from the dead. Pico teased the readers of his works with hints of secret knowledge of how these effects were produced: *I will leave this knot to be untied by the reader,* he said – *that the same serpent who deprived Orpheus of Eurydice was the very one who taught him music.* He concluded: *no-one will discover this secret other than those who have ears to hear.*[10]

If these ideas seem hopelessly archaic, that should not come as a surprise: the cultural movements that began to stir shortly after Pico's time, from the Reformation and the New Science to the Enlightenment, used as their stock-in-trade jokes about their predecessors' fascination with angels. Intellectual endeavours considered to be dry and pointless are still compared to enquiries about the sex of angels, or debates about how many of them could fit upon the head of a pin. Yet the casual mockery of these ideas does little justice to the radical nature of the questions that led to them, questions that began from everyday observations and extended to the very limits of what could be thought. Why is it that beautiful poetry or music can make the hairs on the back of your neck stand up, and how do certain tunes get stuck in your mind? How are we to understand the way that listening to a powerful speech or song can sometimes make you feel like you are being drawn along by it, or even that you are speaking or singing the very words yourself? Think about these things more than a little, and you might begin to wonder whether the boundaries between what is inside you and what is outside you are quite so definite as you had previously imagined. Take this train of thought a little further and you might start to ask what would happen if you amplified the catchiness of the tune, made every speech so captivating. Now you are in the territory of angels. What if the force of a voice is every bit as real as the force of a crashing wave, just more difficult to see – like magnetism? What if to be understood the universe really needs to be seen on the level not of physical things but of these unseen forces, and if at that level the individual existences of these things appear as mere illusions? That level is close to what Pico might have called *undifferentiated matter*. If later thought turned away from these questions, it was partly because of the discomfort that this way of thinking provoked, shaking the foundations of concepts from sin to free will, and the very idea of the individual itself. It was not the first time that European thought had turned away from this beckoning abyss, and Pico's final days were to usher in one of the most dramatic moments in European history, a moment that determined its radical aversion to these ideas.

This aversion also had a profound impact upon how Pico was

remembered, casting a spell of forgetting upon his life for half a millennium. Nineteenth-century historians, who created the idea of the 'Renaissance' as an age of light and reason emerging from the superstitions of the Dark Ages, drew selectively upon the life of Pico to frame him as the emblem of this rebirth, a herald of the human spirit's triumph over the oppressive forces of orthodoxy. In Paul Delaroche's 1842 painting *The Childhood of Pico della Mirandola*, the cherubic Pico and his mother, Giulia, feature as a secular Madonna and Child, she gently fostering his brilliance with an open book while the infant's finger does not bless (as the Christ child's would have) but instead rests upon his lip in contemplation. The message is clear: the divine is being nudged aside by the mortal, heavenly revelation by human genius. Yet while Pico was certainly convinced of the transcendent capabilities of man, the methods by which he proposed to achieve this were far stranger and more deeply imbued with the secret knowledges of the past than this picture would suggest. As more recent scholarship has shown, Pico was not the dewy-eyed poetic figure the Romantics would have had us believe, but, rather, stood at a remove from his age, setting himself against the advocates of mere human elegance in his push to go beyond, into an understanding of the very foundations of being and the nature of existence, along with all the power that such an understanding would provide. At stake in Pico's thought was – and still is – nothing less than the question of whether we could ever be anything *more* than human beings, what that thing might be, and how we might become it.[11]

Pico's tumultuous life, in which the debacle in Rome formed only one crescendo among many, was lived at this precipice of the thinkable, and it was his constant determination to seek out the most astonishing ideas from wherever they could be found, travelling to the great centres of intellectual endeavour and surrounding himself with the most brilliant minds of the age, showing scant regard for distinctions between different religions or races or the respectability of his guides. His one ambition was simply to understand it *all*, to leave no stone unturned and place no thought beyond bounds. In this quest he lived a life that swiftly became legend and reverberated around Europe in the centuries to come. The friend who wrote his epitaph suggested that he must be known not only from Portugal to India but even in the as-yet-undiscovered Antipodes, unable to believe that such a lightning bolt of a life could not have thundered around the globe entire. This book cannot follow Pico into every labyrinth to which his thinking called him, but instead follows a particular path that leads through his life, one which it became clear to him had its origins in the mists of time and which had the potential to change fundamentally the nature of existence, by asking questions that had been asked many times before but never fully answered. Charting this quest, to which he was destined it seems even before he was born, means following Pico and his associates on their exploration in the realms of thought, both deep into the past and up into the heavens; the terms they use will at first be strange, but the experiences they are describing will be surprisingly familiar. That day in Rome, Pico promised to deliver secrets of immense power to his listeners, techniques that would allow them to join the angels, dispense with the apparent laws of nature, *turning the multitude into one*, and what was more to *call forth from the shadows into the light the powers dispersed by God across the world*. To understand what on earth he meant by that, we'll have to begin where he did, only pausing to say as he did, as his speech closed to give way to the debate: *shake hands, and come out fighting*.[12]

II

Ring of Fire

I t was said that in the moments before Pico's birth a sign appeared above the bedchamber of his mother, Giulia, in the form of a circular flame that hovered for a moment and then suddenly disappeared. The story appears first in the biography of Pico by his nephew, the zealot Gianfrancesco – published across the Continent soon after Pico's death and translated into English by Sir Thomas More – who was in no doubt about the omen and its meaning. The circle was the perfect shape, infinitely symmetrical and made of a single line everywhere the same. The greatest magical compendium of the day, the *Picatrix*, called it *the first of all shapes*, and Pico himself would one day go further, comparing it to the *angelic mind returning to its first perfection*, and pointing out that *philosophers of old even called God by the name of circle*. Fire, on the other hand, was the perfect element, the one most apt to rise towards the heavens, growing infinitely as long as it has fuel to burn and converting base, earthly things to intangible luminescence. *Splendid beyond all material bodies*, the philosopher Plotinus writes, it is *the subtlest and sprightliest of all bodies, as very near to the unembodied; itself alone admitting no other, all the others penetrated by it.* When the spirit of God descended upon the Apostles at Pentecost and endowed them with miraculous powers of speech, it came in the form of a flame. The appearance of a circle of flame above the bed of Pico's mother, then, was to Gianfrancesco a clear message that the perfection of his uncle's intellect would be like this shape, that his fame would encircle the globe, that like fire his thoughts would tend ever upwards, and the flames of his eloquence would resemble the blaze of the divine. How the burning circle was interpreted by his mother, Giulia, exhausted from the searing pain of childbirth as the crown of her last child emerged from her into the world, history has not seen fit to record.[1]

In giving Pico extraordinary omens of future glory at the very outset of his life, his nephew was writing him into an established tradition in which the lives of a few are seen to be on a determined path from the beginning. Hercules strangled serpents in his crib as a token of the labours that he was to undertake; the great preacher and musician St Ambrose had bees swarm about his mouth as an infant, a portent that his speech would be mellifluous, flowing like honey and just as sweet. The soaring genius and aeronautic experiments of Pico's contemporary Leonardo da Vinci were thought to be foreshadowed by a bird of prey that landed on his cradle. These were all, of course, examples in miniature of the birth of Jesus, announced by an angel and heralded by the appearance of a new star, which drew the powerful and the wise from afar to kneel before him.[2]

While stories of such omens were only accorded to a select few, showing that they were marked out by fate to play a great role in history and that – from some vantage point, obscure to men but known to bees and angels and raptors – the shape of their lives was visible from the start, these legends also spoke to deeper anxieties about human life that only surfaced in the biographer's art. The question, then, was this: how can we say that a person's life is *one* thing, rather than many? As a character in one of Plato's dialogues puts it, while a *person is said to be the same from childhood until he turns into an old man*, in truth the child and the man are made of different things, with parts passing away and others coming into being. And this was not simply a question of the body: *for none of his manners, customs, opinions, desires, pleasures, pains or fears ever remains the same.* Certain thought experiments helped to clarify the problem, such as the famous matter of the Ship of Theseus. This ran as follows: the celebrated ship on which Theseus sails to kill the minotaur and escape from the labyrinth is kept as a monument to his triumph, but over time the ageing pieces of it need to be replaced, first a rope and then a bench and planks and so on. Eventually no piece of the original ship remains. The question is: is what we have now still Theseus' ship, and, if not, at what point did it cease to be so? And what if the ageing pieces of the original were kept, and a ship built in the same form from them and placed alongside the renovated one. Which one would be Theseus' ship? The same might be said for people: which is the *real* Pico, as his hair, teeth, ideas and beliefs change? How are we to keep any life from fraying at the edges, from disintegrating into so many things that it becomes almost indistinguishable from the maelstrom of what goes on around it? The birth omen is one solution to this: it suggests that from a certain celestial perspective the new life is always and already complete, coherent and unified from the outset. Everything in it is predetermined, and even seemingly contradictory things make sense from the perspective from which the whole is visible. The biography is another solution, attempting to make a picture from the puzzling pieces available, and, given the periods of obscurity and violent changes of direction in his uncle's life, Pico's nephew needed all the help he could get.[3]

The fire-ring is not the only legend about Pico's early life. A few years later one of the great scholars of the day was visiting the family seat at Mirandola, where a learned friend of his was installed as tutor. The visitor recalled how he found Pico's mother, Giulia Boiardo, alone with her youngest children, and how after lunch the girls were trotted out to recite some Latin poetry, and Pico was brought forward in swaddling clothes for general admiration. At one moment, Pico's nurse was heard to ask *whether this infant will follow the path of arms or perhaps of letters?* The scholar took this to be a premonition of Pico's extraordinary genius, even if that

15

seems to us something of a stretch. Other signs, though, were quickly to follow: Pico was soon reciting poetry himself, and it was said that his memory and his capacity for learning were so astonishing that hearing any lines of poetry only once he was able to repeat them ever after, *both forwards and backwards*. This somewhat puzzling claim will become more significant given the curious course of his future interests, though it is charming to imagine the boy Pico wandering about Mirandola and reciting

> Ativ artson id 'nimmac led ozzem len
>
> Arucso avles anu rep iavortir im

as he turned the opening lines of Dante's *Divine Comedy* back to front.[4]

This picture of sophisticated domestic bliss is a tribute to what Pico's extraordinary mother was able to conjure in the most difficult circumstances. Mirandola was and is a desolate kind of place, swept by the winds traversing in uninterrupted fashion the immense Padan plain, and the squat terracotta bulk of the Castello dei Pico is a solid testimony to the authority the family had won over this area as warlords, and which it held from behind fortress walls. If, as Aristotle says, a house begins as an idea in the mind of the architect and only afterwards takes shape in wood and stone, the idea of the Castello was domination. Certain delicate touches were added over time to the terracotta bulk, to give the impression that the lords of the castle were an ornament to the town as well as being its undisputed masters, but no amount of Ghibelline merlons or brick arcading could hide the fact that these were really battlements and buttresses to reinforce the power of those within, who could see in every direction from the deep openings in the wedge-thick walls. Even the esplanade that separated the town from the surrounding countryside was less a place for recreation than a defensive clearing, as advertised by the fortresses that commanded every route into the town, immense and jagged structures designed to give no flat surfaces on which a battering ram could find purchase. Pico's father was the Lord of Mirandola and was very much a soldier of fortune, hiring his services out to other noblemen for their campaigns, and when he died in this service in Pico's fourth year the elder sons Galeotto and Antonmaria showed themselves to be their father's children, immediately launching a bitter and violent feud against each other over the inheritance. Galeotto went so far as to imprison his rival Antonmaria for two years in the dungeon of the Castello, and when their mother pleaded her son's case Galeotto locked her up as well.[5]

Giulia Boiardo was, however, cut from a different cloth, as the Latin education of her daughters suggests. Shortly after the death of her husband she embarked upon a project to change the centre of Mirandola, building a new loggia for the Palazzo della Ragione on the central square, paid for by public funds and supported by *twelve columns of fine marble and set about with large windows*, and overlooking the square a *statue of the Blessed Virgin in marvellous alabaster*. When the project was brought to completion for less than expected, she had the savings returned to the citizens from whom it had been taxed. For all the delicacy of her colonnade and the statue, they have better survived the wars and earthquakes which shattered Mirandola over the centuries than the fortifications, and remain today a defiant statement of civility by their foundress, a challenge to their inauspicious environs. From the same period comes the lucent 'Mirandola Hours', which survives today at the British Library, a prayer book commissioned for the marriage of Giulia's elder son to the learned Bianca d'Este; the frontispiece features an Annunciation set in another delicately columned loggia, and the volume is filled with miniature scenes of women reading and men and children making music. Giulia's nephew was swiftly becoming one of the most celebrated poets of the day in the court at Ferrara, and she was determined that her youngest son would have a career in the relative safety of the Church rather than follow the other men of the family into the way

MIRANDOLA - B. VERGINE DELLA PIAZZA

sul frontone dell'Oratorio della Madonna della Porta
già sul Palazzo della Ragione dal 1468, in alabastro

of blood. If it was indeed possible to prophesy the young Pico's future, it was because the single-minded determination of his mother was not hard to read. Like the alabaster Virgin she commissioned to watch over the public square, who looks demurely aside while hoisting her child upwards on her shoulder, Giulia Boiardo seems to have excelled at the art of cloaking her ambition in modesty. When she moved to have Pico named an Apostolic Protonotary at the age of 10, it was not because children were believed to be capable of vocations and cures of souls so early, but because this post was understood to be the anteroom to the College of Cardinals, the powerhouse of Western Christendom to which many younger sons of the Italian nobility were appointed before they were fully men. Shortly after this he was sent to university at nearby Bologna to study the laws of the Church, and there were reports that by his fifteenth year he had mastered all the papal decrees, gathering them together into his own compendium.[6]

The anecdote about the nursemaid's prophecy fits perfectly within these schemes for advancement, and the letter leaves it amusingly unclear whether the nursemaid was speaking Latin to the infant Pico along with everyone else. This was a matter of no small importance, given the ways in which early childhood was then understood. Nursemaids were believed, by philosophers and doubtless by the illiterate as well, to have extraordinary influence upon their charges; Plato went so far as to compare the hypnotic effect of their humming and rocking upon the infant to the frenzied rituals of ecstatic cults, both infant and worshipper coming under control of the rhythms of chant and movement. It was believed that the nurse, like the cult leader, also often bewitched the infant with mysterious songs whose meanings, if any, were unclear, a playfulness descending into incomprehensibility. (The lullaby – that by which the baby is lulled – is called in Italian the *ninna*

Opposite: Statue of the Virgin and Child commissioned by Giulia Boiardo for the Palazzo della Ragione, Mirandola

nanna, itself a nonsense phrase.) But the nursemaid's power did not end there: the very patterns of language were also believed to be set by these early interactions. Dante had drawn up a scheme in which all the languages of the world fell into two categories, namely the *grammatical* languages such as Latin and Greek, which had unbreakable rules governing their use and could only be mastered after long years of gruelling study; and the *vulgar* tongues, which were constantly changing and varied not just from nation to nation but from region to region and even between towns, and which we acquire (as Dante put it) *without study, merely by imitating our nursemaids*. What, though, if you were immersed in a grammatical language from the earliest years, if you made Latin your mother tongue? Would you not have an intuitive familiarity with the ancient world and its ways of thinking, so much so that you became almost a traveller in time? One of Pico's later rivals was to compose Latin lullabies in an attempt to set the patterns of the infant's language from the outset. Speaking Latin would also have saved the Mirandola children from talking too much like the local Ferrarese, of whose Italian dialect Dante was particularly damning. They spoke abruptly like the Lombards, chatterers without sophistication. *This is why*, Dante noted, *no poets come from Ferrara, Modena, or Reggio.*[7]

Learning to speak by imitation was not just for humans, though: birds also were seen to have their own languages, ones which would become central to Pico's story. These languages were thought by many to be more powerful than the tongues of men and connected to the heavens they traversed, bringing to earth what Plato called *the sacred arts of the vast aether*. Pico's favourite love poet, Guido Cavalcanti, wrote of how at dusk and dawn the birds can be heard to sing *ciascun in su latino* – each in their own Latin. It was unclear whether the language of birds was grammatical or vulgar, whether it had rules or was merely passed from beak to beak and varied between times and places. Medieval composers often used birdsong in their music, repeating single words over and again until they transformed into a dawn chorus, and during Pico's childhood there are the first records of a festival somewhat to the north of his home, the Sagra dei Osei, where pretenders gathered to show off their skills in the mimicry of birdsong. Further south in Assisi, St Francis had been said to speak to the birds and even the cicadas, whose rapt attention was testament to the powers of his speech. This captivation by the language of birds was far from local to the Italians: one of the magical powers given to Solomon in the Qur'an is to speak *mantik al-tayr*, the language of birds, and the Norse hero Sigurd also gains the ability to understand bird speech when he drinks blood from the heart of the dragon Fáfnir.[8]

Yet though the fascination with birdsong was general, there was a particular bird with which Pico shared a special bond, and which he would have known well from the fields and copses surrounding Mirandola. This was the wryneck, a species of woodpecker whose Italian name, *pico tocciolo*, connected it to Pico's family, an association to which close friends often playfully referred (he was also

Woodcut of a wryneck from Andrea Alciati, *Emblemata*

tied to the great speaker among European birds, the magpie, whose Latin name is *Pica*). The wryneck, which would have visited Mirandola each spring in its migration, is no ordinary bird, uncanny both in the writhing of its extended neck in imitation of a serpent's coiling, and in the curious *jinking* cry that it makes, a noise widely understood across the ancient world to have magical powers, as recalled in its Greek name *Iynges* and the word derived from it, still familiar to us in childhood games – the *jinx*. This bird and its cry were believed to wield immense power over those against whom it was used: Aphrodite was said to have taught Jason how to fix the bird to a spinning wheel to enchant Medea, *her mind on fire with the whip of persuasion*, and Chaldean sorcerers recommended the same technique for drawing back faithless lovers. In another twist of fate, then, Pico was tied to one of the most powerful charms of the bird world, a winged creature who (like an angel) could call the minds of listeners to order, bending their will to the purpose of others.[9]

The glimpses that have come down to us of Pico's early life are momentary and were written down later by those who knew what was to come, for whom even these first signs were fraught with meaning. From the time of his youth onwards, legends gathered around Pico like moths to the light, so that often his life can only be seen through the stories that were told about him, making of him the mythical creature through whom others understood the workings of their world. Everyone was in agreement that Pico was destined to live an extraordinary life. The way in which this life would bring together many strange ingredients – birdsong, the magic of languages long dormant and hardly understood, questions of whether a person was indeed one single thing or, rather, many things in succession, or even all at once – was yet to be revealed. In any case, his life was not to be the sedate and respectable life of a churchman as his mother had hoped. She died in his fifteenth year, even as he was performing feats of memory at Bologna, and without her expectations to fulfil Pico soon abandoned his study of church law, moving to Ferrara to focus instead on matters of philosophy.

One more important omen, tied to the birth of Pico, should be mentioned here. Marsilio Ficino, who under the protection of the Medici had become the uncontested sage of the movement later known as the Renaissance, held it to be a matter of destiny that he completed his pioneering translation of the works of Plato from little-known Greek into widely read Latin on the very day and even hour at which Pico later arrived in Florence and, what was more, that he had begun this behemoth task twenty-one years previously in the exact year of Pico's birth. Whatever we read into the alignment of these dates, there was little doubt that Plato would be central to Pico's life, having in a sense begun almost two thousand years before a chain of thought that Pico was determined to bring to its triumphant conclusion.[10]

III

A Light & Winged & Sacred Thing

O ne day Socrates was walking around the outskirts of Athens when he came upon his friend Phaedrus, who appeared to be both rapt in concentration and eager for company. The two of them decided to go out of the city together along the path of the River Ilisus, both men barefoot, walking in the very water itself to keep their feet cool and in search of a secluded place where Phaedrus would share the words he could barely contain. Their conversation forms the subject of Plato's most poetic dialogue, which bears the name of Socrates' companion. Continuing their ramble, the two men reach a plane tree in whose shade they stretch out. Socrates draws attention to the fact that the tree is in full bloom and the smell pervades everything, somehow different in shadow than in light, though there is no visible boundary. They keep their feet in the water, and the slope of the bank behind them rises in such a fashion as to prop their heads even as they recline upon it. Socrates also remarks upon the sound of the cicadas' chorus, the drowsy and piercing shrill that accompanies the somnolescent heat of summer in Athens.[1]

Phaedrus is mad for speeches. Athens is mad for speeches. When Socrates met him Phaedrus had been silently rehearsing a speech he had heard that same morning by the famed orator Lysias. So enamoured was Phaedrus of the words that he had Lysias repeat them over and over again, and still unsatisfied he had taken the written text and recited the crescendos to himself, before taking himself off alone to rehearse them, the runnels of each phrase wearing into his mind like the course of a riverbed. Lysias is a master at weaving his words around his audience, but he is not without competition; Socrates mentions Licymnius the poet and Thrasymachus, who *can put a whole company of people into a passion and out of one again by his mighty magic.* Socrates the philosopher plays along, saying he is also *sick with a love of discourse,* led without resistance by the promise of hearing Phaedrus' recitation, like an animal enticed with a fruiting branch, a willing *partner* (as Socrates puts it) in his *ecstatic dance.*[2]

In truth Socrates is worried: as in the summer ritual of the *Bouphonia,* when the bulls are allowed to wander on the sacred mount of the Acropolis, it is the animal that is first tempted to eat that becomes the sacrificial victim. He tells Phaedrus a story about the cicadas. They were once humans themselves, alive in that age before the Muses came into being. When the Muses arrived and brought singing into the world for the first time, people were so drunk on the exquisite ecstasy of song that they quite forgot to eat or drink, and sang themselves to death without so much as pausing to notice. In memory of this martyrdom to the beauties of music the Muses gave those martyred to melody this gift, to be reborn as cicadas – without the need for food or water, breaking into song the moment they come to life and continuing their chant until the moment of their death, whereupon they return to the heavens to report on who down below has done honour to the Muses. On every tree in Athens Socrates places a reminder of the overwhelming power of musical, rhythmical words, their power to make us forget ourselves and our own interests. The cicadas are not just an emblem of the sickness for speech, but purveyors themselves of a hypnotic noise, and spies for jealous divinities eager to extend their mastery over us.[3]

This is not the only time Socrates was to dwell on this in Plato's writings about him. In a conversation with the rhapsode Ion,

Socrates tried to get to the bottom of how certain people – poets themselves, but also rhapsodes, a curious guild who would recite poetry and expand upon it at fairs and festivals – managed to have such a mesmeric effect upon their audiences. Homer was Ion's particular speciality, and indeed Homer seemed to hold a sway over audiences that was unequalled. It couldn't be that the audiences were captivated by the substance of the poems, as a general or a doctor or a charioteer would be better able to speak upon the wars and wounds and races in the Homeric poems than a mere poet could. It must therefore not be so much the matter as the manner of speaking, and this itself was something not entirely within the control of the speaker. This much was clear (Socrates pointed out) from one-hit wonders, great lyrics written by men who never went on to do anything else. In these instances it was as if the gods themselves were demonstrating that the power lay not so much with the speaker as with them, to be given and taken away on a whim. If, as Socrates said, the poet is a *light and winged and sacred thing*, he or she was also a thing not wholly under its own control. *It is a divine power which moves you*, Socrates told Ion, *like the power in the stone which Euripides calls a magnet, but which most people call the 'Herculean Stone'. This stone*, he continued, *not only attracts iron rings, it also confers on them the power to do the same, that is, to attract other rings, so that sometimes a long chain of rings and pieces of iron, suspended from one another, is formed, the power of them all depending on the stone.* In the same way, the Muses inspire certain speakers, and they in turn attract and inspire others, just as Phaedrus had conned the speech of Lysias, and so a chain is strung out of people *all inspired with the same enthusiasm*.[4]

Strange though it may seem to us, Socrates was trying to understand the hypnotic power of words using two relatively new technologies: the magnet and the chain. As the common Greek name for the magnet suggests, the *Herculean Stone* was considered a substance of immense and irresistible force, and more strikingly one that wielded its power entirely unseen, drawing iron filings towards it without so much as touching them. Both the ancient and the medieval world had used the powers of the magnet to create wonders, as in the Temple at Arsinöe where a statue of a goddess was suspended in mid-air by their means, or the Greek church at Nakhchivan in Persia where the same trick was played. Socrates' predecessor Thales concluded that the way magnets moved things suggested that the magnets themselves had souls; it was as if, as the medieval authority on magnets Petrus Peregrinus was to write, the magnet could simply will things to come towards it, *according to the natural desire of the stone.* If the magnet was capable of action, then the iron filings experienced passion – which means nothing more than the state of being acted upon. The magnet, then, became irrefutable proof of *action at a distance*, of the fact that some things in this world can and do operate upon one another by means other than brute force, without physical contact or so much as the movement of air. Above all, the magnet became a way of thinking about how powerful words work upon us, as when the playwright Euripides said that *He who knows the patterns of men's minds can draw or repel their inconstant minds like a magnet, as suits his purpose.*[5]

Even more inconspicuous to us is the miracle of the chain, which has become so commonplace in our world as to disappear from notice, for all that our lives would not work without it. The chain, which along with the magnet first begins to appear in the Eastern Mediterranean in the centuries before the birth of Socrates and which is one of those vital words shared across most Indo-European languages, demonstrates in extraordinary fashion the power of making many things into one, and having one thing made of many. The drooping chain is just as strong as its iron links but as wondrously flexible as rope, allowing the tethered a feeling of freedom that is never really there, only to show its rigid power when the enchained person tries to stray. Socrates may even have been thinking of the chain as a way of imagining the unshakeable but insensible power of divine things upon us because Homer had

done the same. In the eighth book of the *Iliad*, furious at his bick-
ering family, Zeus tells them that the power he wields over the
earth and sea is like a golden chain and if he wished he could drag
up all the world and hang it all in space to dangle, though the same
chain could never be used to pull him aside even an inch: *by so
much am I above Gods and above men*. Put together, the magnet
and the chain formed a terrifying weapon – flexible, unbreakable,
invisible: just like the power of overwhelming words.[6]

For all our enjoyment of the rapturous effect of poetry, the effect
of such words upon us posed a deeply troubling problem for
Socrates. If a well-handled speech is a way of *directing the soul*,
would that not mean that the listener was deprived of the power to
choose between right and wrong, carried along instead on the
current of speech and helpless to determine the course of their
own actions? If Socrates suggested that the power of intoxicating
speech must be a heavenly gift that moved the speaker, it was in
part because the alternative was too awful to contemplate: if this
powerful tool was not controlled by the gods but merely by the
speaker, it threatened a world in which any skilled orator could
hijack the minds of his audience, leaving it unclear whether or not
they bore any responsibility for what they did in this state. This
was why Socrates preferred dialogues, which allowed the speaker's
enchanting flow to be interrupted with questions and demands for
clarification. For the same reason, Socrates didn't like things to be
written down, as a written text does not provide us with the means
to interrogate its author. He never wrote anything down himself,
and what we know of his words and thoughts comes largely from
his student Plato, who made his writing-shy mentor the central
character in his works, though if he went against Socrates' wishes
with regards to writing, he did at least write him in dialogue form.

The Greeks had long been under the sway of rhythmic sound
and dance, with a succession of cults migrating over from the East
being received variously with suspicion and delight. The worship
of the god Dionysus, or Bacchus, involved various infectious

techniques of ecstasy, from the chanting of the peculiar dithyrambic verse to rhythmic cries and shouts over the sound of a two-barrelled flute called the *aulos,* which was said to bring on mania, turning the gathered initiates into a single, many-headed thing. The legendary poet Orpheus, whose lyrics could make the stones dance and the waters stand still, was seen by many to be the prophet of Dionysus, and a group of songs on Dionysian mysteries were attributed to him, perhaps first by Pythagoras. Plato railed against those who produced a *hubbub of books* from Orpheus by which to perform their rituals, but it seems that even his mentor and idol Socrates was not immune to the lure of this frenzy: there are hints that Socrates himself was initiated in his youth into the *korybantes*, a mystery cult whose central rite involved dancing oneself like a dervish into a state of *ecstasy* – the Greek word meaning transported, bewildered, out of your mind, insane.[7]

The power of spellbinding rhythms was in fact only one of a set of problems that was worrying Socrates, all of which centred on the troubling habit of things to lose distinction, for it to become unclear where one thing ended and the next began, or whether there were really two separate things at all. Was a chain one thing or in fact many things that just happened to overlap in a particular way? This kind of riddling question was the bread and butter of many of the philosophers of Socrates' time, perhaps none more so than the group from the Greek colony of Elea on the southwestern coast of Italy. Their thought experiments spread throughout the ancient world and endured as troubling glimpses into an abyss in which all time and space ceased to make sense. If in a race between Achilles and a tortoise the tortoise has a head start, common sense seems to dictate that Achilles can never catch him: by the time Achilles covers the head start, the tortoise will have gone further, and this process will repeat ad infinitum, meaning that Achilles will have an infinite number of distances to catch up, even if they are very small. Paradoxes like these were trotted out to stun the listener into silence, preparing the way for the grand pronouncement of their sage Parmenides: that in reality all distinctions between things as well as apparent changes such as motion are mere illusions, and in fact *all is one* – there is only one thing, and recognizing this fundamental underlying fact is the key to understanding the universe.

The arguments of the Eleatics had the bewildering and disorienting feel of revelations, a philosophical counterpart to the disorienting dance of the *korybantes* and the chanting of dithyrambs. They also presented a matter of grave concern. Just as intoxicating speech threatened to make it impossible to choose the right over the wrong, so the loss of distinction between things would make it impossible to know about anything or say anything abidingly true about it – given that the thing itself was an illusion, with no real or independent or permanent existence. In response to the dangers posed by this precipice of anarchic indistinction, Socrates was formulating his most brilliant and lasting idea. He reasoned that, while it was true that the things of this world were constantly in flux, always breaking down and decaying and changing shape, *some* things were actually eternal and stable and knowable. Numbers, for instance, and the rules of geometry, didn't change from one place or one time to another. Ideas also were more permanent and unchanging than the fickle things of this world: while a bubble may not last longer than an instant, I can hold the idea of a bubble in my mind for much longer than that. And if my idea of a bubble is more long-lasting and unchanging than the bubble itself, doesn't that in some senses make it *more real* than the iridescent sphere of water? Along these lines Socrates proposed that there was a whole realm of such ideas, above the physical world, where each thing existed in its ideal state eternally. Statements could be made about them that were true or false; they could be known about; their properties could be discovered by reason. In fact, the world we see around us is just filled with poor copies of these ideas, these ideal things, and we are much better off turning away from the transitory physical things around us and focusing our minds on the superior world of rational inquiry, the *metaphysical* world, which is above-the-physical.

Greek philosophy was not alone in formulating this response to the tragic impermanence of earthly things. The Guarani peoples from the region of modern Paraguay also saw it as the great evil of the world that we human beings, who wish to be eternal and remain stable and separate from one another, are constantly changing and melding into one another, a child becoming an adult and an adult decaying into dirt, which is eaten by one thing and it eaten in turn. The fragility of individual existence, and its habit of returning to undifferentiated matter was a source of despair to the Guarani. *Things in their totality are one*, according to the Guarani, *and for those of us who wish otherwise, this is a horror. It is because the things of this world are One and not multiple that evil is written upon the face of the earth.* The anger of the newborn even against his mother's breast is evidence of how sorry we are to emerge into this bodily world. The Guarani held out hope, however, for a world to come in which the individual persists in eternity, an afterlife in which *being is no longer One*, and we assume a divine state of perpetual stability. The role of their priests, known as the *Great Speakers* or masters of *ñe'ẽ porã*, Beautiful Words, was to persuade the gods to allow us to return to our former divine state of being, eternally held in stable individuality. Indeed, as the world became ever more connected, it became apparent that the fixation on the relationship between the one and the many was near-universal, and that the techniques for investigating these boundaries was uncannily similar, a matter of sound and language and rhythm.[8]

Socrates' solution to the challenge of everything merging into one indistinct mass was by no means immune to criticism and objections. Another work of Plato's portrays a confrontation between Socrates and Parmenides over these ideas, each circling the other and prodding at the weak spots in his opponent's armour. Parmenides pokes fun at Socrates by asking whether in his divine realms of ideas there are also heavenly versions of things like hair, dirt and mud, attempting to reduce Socrates' argument to the absurd, and Socrates is thrown for a moment onto the back foot. Could it really be that vile things like these have been enshrined in some stable, eternal form – and what would that form look like, given the amorphous, wobbling nature of mud and slime? Hair is also troubling since, while a single hair is almost nothing, a lock of hair is certainly something, suggesting that many nothings can be made into something and perhaps vice versa. *It would be quite absurd to believe that there is an idea of these things*, Socrates says, pausing: *and yet I am sometimes disturbed by the thought that perhaps what is true of one thing is true of all. Then when I have taken up this position, I run away for fear of falling into some abyss of nonsense and perishing; so when I come to those things which we were just saying do have ideas, I stay and busy myself with them.* In essence, Socrates is admitting the driving force behind his argument: whether or not it is convincing, we *must* accept it, if only because the alternative is literally unthinkable and (to Socrates at least) utterly terrifying. If we deny the existence of ideas that remain in all places and all times the same, he sternly warns towards the end of the dialogue, we will *utterly destroy the power of carrying on discussion.*[9]

On that day with Phaedrus, by the banks of the Ilisus and with his feet in the water, Socrates was to launch an offensive against these dual threats of hypnotizing speech and the dissolution of boundaries between things, and he was to do it in his own inimitable fashion, with a glint in his eye and a keen sense of drama. Dismissing the speech rehearsed by Phaedrus as pretty enough but lacking in substance, Socrates pulled his robe over his head like a priest engaged in secret rites, and seemed to enter his own mystic and ecstatic trance, saying to his companion that the beauty of the place seems to have driven him out of his mind and that he felt he might be divinely inspired, about to break into dithyrambs like Orpheus, priest of Dionysus. Socrates reassured Phaedrus that this divine madness was not something to be afraid or ashamed of, that it had once been held in reverence, especially that kind of *possession and madness that comes from the Muses*, which takes the innocent soul and inspires it to Dionysian ecstasies of song and music. But Socrates had no intention of using his prophetic fit to summon orgies of self-abandonment; instead, he uses the sacred atmosphere created to summon up a vision of the soul in the form of an extended parable.

The soul, he says, was once a winged thing, able to soar within that empyrean realm where all things exist in their perfection, as ideas or ideals. The gods live permanently in this place, capable of flight and eternally surrounded by the true nature of things; but in gaining a body man's soul has shed its wings, and is tethered here below. There are, however, ways for man to regain this lost paradise, using those powerful urges that draw the soul out of the body, like the lightheaded feeling that comes with longing for a lover, or the ecstatic experience of great song and music and poetry. The technique is not without risk. Instead of being winged beings ourselves, Socrates suggests, we are now more like a charioteer in charge of flying horses; if we cannot control them, they will pull us down from the heavens into the swamps of bodily lust and orgiastic pleasure. Yet if we can hold the line, Socrates promises, these techniques will help the initiate to regain their vision of the metaphysical. Working himself into a fury, Socrates recalls when those now living *saw beauty shining in brightness*, and *beheld the beatific vision and were initiated into a mystery which may be truly called most blessed, celebrated by us in our state of innocence, before we had any experience of evils to come, when we were admitted to the sight of apparitions innocent and simple and calm and happy, which we beheld shining in pure light, pure ourselves and not yet enshrined in that living tomb which we carry about, now that we are imprisoned in the body, like an oyster in his shell.*[10]

The game that Socrates was playing was a dangerous one and one that was to have incalculable consequences for what came afterwards. His gamble was that he could divert the powers of ecstatic experience to his own ends, to suggest that those feelings of disembodiment provoked by sexual attraction and by powerful music, language, dance and song were indeed evidence that there was an elsewhere beyond the physical, and that the soul was yearning for it, yearning to shed its bodily form and ascend into the heavens. This elsewhere was for Socrates a realm of stable concepts, a philosopher's paradise in which the elevated feelings created by love and rhythm should be used to power the understanding of the true nature of things. But the evidence that this place existed at all, that there was something above and beyond the fluid and intransigent world of the body, came precisely from those irresistible, irrational urges that posed the problem in the first place. Socrates even made his own that notion, common to the cult members and the speechmakers and Parmenides, that the distinction between things was an illusion and that we were drawn irresistibly towards the One thing of which we are all a part – though for Socrates this was another proof of his metaphysical realm. As all the Ideas were the perfect form of what we experience here, so what unites them is that very state of perfection, making them all simply part of the Good that is the underlying principle of all things. From this primordial unity were all other things formed, unfurling into multiplicity like a frond from a fern, like the sequence of numbers produced by division – one thing split in half becomes two, and split again becomes four, and so on. It was precisely because of these ways in which things were portioned out, in ratio and proportion to one another, that the soul was moved by harmony, itself a blending of proportionate sounds. The soul moved by music was merely remembering its belonging to primal Oneness, and that it was in fact merely a detached part of a larger World Soul.

In tethering the foundations of knowledge to powerful ecstatic experience, Socrates and his disciple Plato were creating an explosive combination, which was to determine the course of more than one civilization in the centuries to come. All of the elements of the conversation with Phaedrus would return in various combinations: winged beings and their ability to move between the earth and the heavens, the power of particular kinds of rhythm to provoke a state of mania, and the effect of certain speeches upon crowds of enraptured listeners. If Ficino felt that his translation of Plato was in some sense tied by fate to Pico's birth and movements, that was in part because Plato had taught him to think about chain reactions, the undiscovered links that determine the course of events, and Pico seemed to hold out a particularly strong link between the things of heaven and earth.

IV

The Philosopher

I n the year that Pico moved to Ferrara a Levant merchant brought from Venice a curious lumbering stranger disguised by a shroud, hiding the marvel from eager eyes so that the duke could be the first to see. A Ferrarese diarist who was there at the unveiling described the visitor as bigger than an ox and heavier, with no neck and no knees, a nose as long as an arm and as thick as a loaf of bread, dark hair and huge eyes, and vast ears the shape of spades. During the closing masquerade of that year's carnival the creature was brought before the duchess and he danced, it was said, *in a most humane and pleasing way*. This was, the diarist recorded, the first time that anyone could recall Ferrara being visited by an elephant.[1]

It is not clear whether Pico arrived in Ferrara before or after Lent in 1479, but either way he would have encountered a parade of novelties. Carnival was the most outrageous moment of the festival year, when citizens in disguise could expunge their longings and frustrations before the long dark vigil of Lent. It was the custom during carnival for both the duke's entourage and the Ferrarese children to pelt passersby with eggs, but that year one man went too far and threw a pail of shit at a citizen's wife. Another man at the closing masquerade, perhaps overexcited at having seen an elephant dance, died after his own cavorting and leaping caused his innards to spill into his scrotum through an abscess. A law student took advantage of the costumed anonymity to stab a Jew to whom he

Woodcut of Ferrara, 1499

was in debt; so many were in debt to the same Jew that this motive did not help narrow down the suspects. When the assailant was finally caught, the duke was inclined to forgive him, being of a good family; but when the Jew died, the duke was obliged by his own indebtedness to the Jewish community to act, and the law student was hanged from the window of the palace, chained at the ankles and dressed as a Turk, like a macabre theatrical backdrop to what happened on the public square. For all that carnival gave way to particularly outlandish behaviour, the border between pageantry and violence continued to be fluid at all seasons. Later that year, two bakers were pilloried in the public square because they were caught adding lye to their flour to make the bread softer, and for kneading the dough with sore-covered legs. Many others were caught in the same acts, but only these two could not afford the fine. It was probably in this heady atmosphere of theatrical vengeance that Pico first met Girolamo Savonarola, the young Dominican firebrand who was making a name for himself in Ferrara, and with whose dark ascendency Pico's final days were to be closely intertwined.[2]

The settling of scores during festivals tied the life of the city to the cycle of seasons, making the periodic outbreaks of anarchy and the return of order as regular as blossom and leafdrop. This was nothing new: in the miraculous sculpture cycle that once surrounded the Porta dei Pelligrini at the cathedral, figures for each month undertake their annual tasks, each in its stout Romanesque proportions presenting itself as the idol of its particular season. February is pruning, April is hunting, July is threshing and September is picking grapes. The month of May is on horseback and carries a shield, a monument to the campaigning season that was part of the rhythm of the year in northern Italy. The current duke Ercole d'Este was a master of the concertina of powers that existed between the many small states of the peninsula, constantly shifting alliances from one party to another to make sure that none of them became strong enough to crush him. Ercole had been bred to conflict. His father had sired so many children the locals affectionately joked that *around and about the river Po / we're all the sons of Niccolò*; one of Niccolò's bastards became the stuff of legend when both he and his stepmother were beheaded after a tumultuous affair. All the siblings were named after classical or Arthurian heroes, but Ercole (Hercules) had risen to the top, and was remarkably successful at holding his vast territories against the surrounding powers. Like most of the petty Italian lords, he also made efforts to soften the violent nature of his domination with displays of culture and learning, and Ferrara would have seemed immensely cosmopolitan to Pico after the backwater of Mirandola. Ferrara was a town of windows and loggias, all open to the spectacle and prosperous display of the town. Ercole, to whom Pico was related by marriage, also maintained a prestigious circle of intellectuals and had one of the most celebrated collections of newly unearthed antiquities in northern Italy. Yet as the carnival violence against Jews and the executions in Turkish costume suggest, the tensions and anxieties being confronted during the festal suspension of rules were ever more complex and global. The following March the Pope granted a special indulgence to anyone who would visit all four of Ferrara's great churches – Santa Maria degli Angeli, San Nicolò, San Andrea and Sancto Spirito – to raise money for the defence of Rhodes, key to holding off Ottoman advances in the Mediterranean. These emergency measures fell short, and in August 1480 the Turks took the southern Italian town of Otranto, giving them their first stronghold in the heart of mainland Europe.[3]

This attempt to spread the costs of military operations was a response to desperate circumstances. International credit networks increasingly determined not only the size of campaigns but also against whom they were directed, and were even making the cycle of boom and bust, of profligacy and insurmountable debt, part of everyday life. Small-scale Jewish moneylenders, who as outsiders were allowed to lend in ways which were in demand with Christians but also forbidden to them, became the convenient scapegoats for processes of which they were largely the instrument.

In the following year news reached Ferrara from Treviso of fifteen Jews who had been arrested using the perennial anti-Semitic weapon, an accusation of *blood libel*: the purchase of a Christian child for sacrificial purposes. The letter purportedly found on one of them, and the only evidence to support the charge, was depraved in its clumsiness, a creation of those who knew the wider public colluded in the attack. *My dear brother*, it opened in a caricature Jewish voice, *the God of Abraham and Jacob keep and maintain the law of Moses, Son of Israel, and damn and confound all other laws, congregations, and faiths, especially the Christian faith and its false followers.* It closed by exhorting the recipient to pay his share of the blood money – *and don't delay, as this money is not your own, but from the Christian dogs, gained by usury. So let us make war using their own weapons. Signed Samuel Rabbi of Messia.* It is all the more surprising, given the fear and distrust that were sweeping Italy, that Pico was eventually to place Hebrew and Islamic learning at the heart of his theory of *all knowable things*.[4]

Pico had come to Ferrara after his mother's death to study philosophy, and for Pico as for all others of the period that meant starting not with Plato but with his pupil Aristotle. Just as the scriptures were 'The Book', Aristotle had become 'The Philosopher' in the centuries prior to Pico's birth, and his dominance of late-medieval thought was almost complete, as was his rejection of the central principles of Plato's system. Aristotle was deeply unsatisfied with Plato's model of a realm of ideas compared to which the physical things of this world were only fleeting shadows. What, The Philosopher asked, was the relationship between these things, between the eternal concepts and the tangible embodiments of them? The Platonic answer to this question was the vague notion of *participation* – that physical things *participated* in the ideas, and vice versa – which to Aristotle was at best a lovely metaphor and at worst no more than gibberish. It was not enough merely to spit out seductive and compelling propositions; the philosopher must *include and exhibit the ground also*, demonstrating how the idea worked step by painstaking step, moving from those things that we can sense to the concepts we form from them. In service of this, Aristotle elaborated a system for logical demonstration of astonishing power, promising to put all forms of discussion on the same indisputable footing as mathematical proofs. At the heart of this system was the syllogism, a way of structuring propositions that built chains of apparently unshakeable logic. *Socrates is a man*; *all men are mortal*; therefore, *Socrates is mortal*. Using these and similar tools to start from *what we can establish* and build a model of things from there, Aristotle was to compile an account of the world, from the laws of physics and the bodies of animals to accounts of dreams, theatre, ethics and politics, which was to remain at the centre of Eurasian thought in one form or another for almost two thousand years.[5]

While Aristotle's system was all very well for things that could be observed – the classification of animals, for instance, by their manner of reproduction, their shape and their habitat – matters became more complicated when attempting to deal with invisible things, as in his treatise *On the Soul* that Pico was reading in these years. In these instances, Aristotle proceeds in the same level-headed manner, showing no inclination to treat spiritual matters with any particular reverence. Living things can be observed to feed themselves, and, in order to do so, must be able to sense the location of their food and move towards it; the desire to move towards something that has been sensed in order to feed may be called appetite. So, living things, things with *anima*, or spirit, are those things that have sensation and appetite and that move and feed themselves. As well as sensing external things, living beings can also have knowledge about them: instead of sensing one particular, individual thing, we can consider that *type* of thing when it is not present. In doing so, we are moving from the sensation of individuals to the knowledge of universals, thinking not just about a particular tree but about the existence of many objects which can all be thought of as trees. A smaller class of living beings, by which Aristotle means man, can have knowledge not only of universal types or classes of things, but also an awareness of the rules by which this knowledge is structured. Aristotle's prime example here is grammar: it is one thing to say *I like to drink wine*, and another to know that *wine* is a noun, *I* is a pronoun, *like* is a verb, *to drink* is also a verb but in the infinitive, and that in English grammar we place the second verb in the infinitive. This quality, this ability to understand the abstract rules that govern knowledge and consciously put them into practice, defines for Aristotle the nature of man's soul.[6]

The extraordinary clarity and precision of Aristotle's system, even when applied to things as nebulous and hard to grasp as the human soul, was to make it immensely seductive to later thinkers. If this form of demonstration could be used to map and understand the workings of the human soul, it stood to reason that it might also be applied to the workings of those supernatural and divine things that seemed to lie just beyond man's grasp. Perhaps the feeling of elation, of elevation and ecstasy produced by certain kinds of rhythm and music could be understood in this way, the manner of provoking it reduced to a set of rules, a grammar; perhaps the world to which these feelings seemed to give access could also be understood, a world in which man rises above the constraints of his physical being. Legends were even to grow up that Aristotle himself had considered these things, that he had studied and charted this shadowy world in secret; some said that he had taught the methods he had discovered to his pupil Alexander the Great, and that in addition to his great body of works about everyday thought and objects Aristotle had also left another, hidden set of writings about this shadow world. We shall encounter these presently.

It is a great historical irony that Aristotle's methods were to be used in this occult way given that his thinking was motivated not just by a desire to be robust and rational but also by a fear, the same fear as that of Socrates, of the abyss that lay ahead if thinking went down the other path. His objection, for instance, to the belief of some philosophers that we must allow for the possibilities of other worlds beyond the one we can see, was not so much a reasoned argument as a drawing back in terror from the alternative: if we admit the possibility of one other world, we must logically admit the possibility of an infinite number of other worlds. This would mean that there were worlds only infinitesimally different from our own, making it very difficult to sustain any sense of what we do here as meaningful or valuable – a matter that has continued to plague philosophers to the present day. In a similar sense, his objection to the idea of Plato and Socrates' realm of ideas, where the transitory things of this world were given eternal and stable forms about which knowledge could be had, centred not so much on its intentions as on its potential consequences. In short, Aristotle sensed that Socrates remained too close to those who claimed that the difference between things was illusory, and that his system threatened to collapse back into the nightmarish world in which *all is one*. To prevent this happening in his own system, Aristotle proposed a series of categories, classes of things that could not be reduced to or translated into each other, and which ensured against the slippage back into oneness.[7]

Aristotle's description of the world had, however, left an even more fundamental loose thread, and it was one that was to be drawn out to immense effect. If it is true that humans can generate rules about the structures of knowledge, how is it that we generate the same rules, rather than each making our own, slightly different sets of rules that don't really make sense to anyone else? It must be that the rules are not simply subjective and arbitrary but that they in some sense really exist, that we are more discovering them than creating them. But *where* do they exist? In an uncharacteristically mystic passage of his book *On the Soul*, Aristotle proposes that while the knowledge we have when in our bodies comes from sensing things and reasoning about them, the fact that individual minds come to the same conclusions and so can share knowledge is down to the origin of each individual mind in a general, undifferentiated matter of mind, what later thinkers would call a *Universal Intellect*. This passage seems to be an attempt to paper over the cracks and save the whole edifice of

Aristotle's system of thought, and to put us back very close to Plato's notion of *participation*, but it was also a passage upon which many were to fixate, with explosive consequences.[8]

Pico spent three years after his arrival in Ferrara immersing himself in the thought of Aristotle, and beginning to astonish his elders by besting venerable authorities in public debate; one account recalls the adolescent Pico dressed in the toga that was the sign of his protonotarial office holding his own against an established and famous theologian. So great would his skills as a public speaker become that after his death many made it their proudest boast to have seen him once perform. Yet though Pico would later recall *the doctrines of philosophers over which he had sweated since boyhood*, all this work did not mean no play. Even academic affairs were conducted with the same combination of showmanship and raw aggression as carnival justice: in the year he arrived there was a bitterly contested election for rector of the University, with the followers of a professor from Bologna squaring off against supporters of a Cypriot scholar, a contest that turned into an armed brawl when the Bolognese professor lost. The loser had to be expelled from the city to keep the peace, but this did not prevent his side from dressing a donkey in academic robes and driving it through the streets yelling at it the name by which they had Christened it – *Cipro! Cipro!* – in mockery of the Cypriot Ass whose tenure they despised. This raucous incident may have been inspired by the newly completed translation by Pico's cousin, the Ferrara court poet Matteo Maria Boiardo, of the hilarious and bawdy classical Latin novel *The Golden Ass* by the North African writer Apuleius, which recounts the misadventures of a man turned into a donkey when he mistakenly uses the wrong magic spell. The metamorphosis is in part a literary device, which allows the donkey to be the unsuspected witness to and even subject of private lusts and vices, but it was also a window into a lost classical culture in which such magical feats seemed to be a matter of everyday life. The translation of these bestial frivolities into Italian would have put these stories into the hands of even less educated courtiers, including many ladies. As they would have read at the opening of Boiardo's translation, the world in which this miraculous transformation took place was one in which *rivers have by magic songs been turned back to their sources, and the seas frozen, the day broken and the night held still*. The novel may have centred on an uproarious and pornographic story, but it was also filled with matters of interest and worthy of serious study: the great humanist Filippo Beroaldo, with whom Pico may have overlapped at Bologna and with whom he was to become fast friends, was to publish a 600-page commentary on it, beginning with a preface that placed Apuleius within a long and august tradition of ancient magic, with roots in Egypt and in India and Persia but surprisingly connected also to the thought of Plato and even Aristotle.[9]

There was in fact little boundary between weighty matters of historical research and the treatment of the same subjects in forms intended to dazzle and delight a wider public, and everywhere in Ferrara were the signs of this fascination with foreign and ancient magical knowledges. Boiardo was even then beginning his masterwork, the epic poem *Orlando Innamorato* ('Orlando in Love') about a sorceress from the East who enchants the court of Charlemagne and sends the paladins of France into a frenzy of desire and distraction. This Angelica, who *seemed a thing not human, but more like an angel*, was daughter to a king who was *master of all incantations* and who ruled over Cathay, a hazily imagined place beyond Tartary and India. Eastern magicians are also given pride of place in the greatest work of Ferrarese Renaissance art, the resplendent frescoes of the Palazzo Schifanoia, which to echo Cavalcanti's words *make the air tremble with clarity*. The Sala dei Mesi gives a calendar of the courtly year, with scenes of jousting and hunting and procession above and below a midnight-blue ribbon of the zodiac; one fresco probably even portrays the wedding of Pico's brother to his Este bride. The images of the classical gods reigning over the constellations, however, are not the gods we might expect to see in Italy, resurrected in their Greco-Roman form: instead, they are flanked by turbaned scribes and surrounded by figures festooned with mysterious symbols, part of the mania for foreign knowledges that was sweeping Europe.[10]

It was with these gods and prophets that Pico was to become increasingly obsessed, and with whose images he was to decorate the walls of his family library back in Mirandola. Both the frescoes and the library they accompanied have since been lost, though we can reconstruct them in some manner, from descriptions of the paintings and from catalogues of the collection, which together provides a kind of scheme for Pico's memory palace. Library frescoes often served as picture-catalogues to the collection – illustrating on the walls above the shelves the spirits that were encased below them, and helping the reader to navigate the holdings of the library as if they were walking through the company of their authors, seeking out their books from where they hovered above – and Pico's seems to have been no exception. The frescoes were commissioned from Cosimo Tura, the same Ferrarese artist responsible for the eastern sages at the Palazzo Schifanoia and who may also have produced the earliest surviving portrait of Pico in this period, in profile in the Este style and not quite yet the delicate youth whose *beautiful body and face* (according to his nephew) *drove many women to distraction for love of him.* Tura's wall paintings at Mirandola seem to have been nothing less than an encyclopaedia of that global thought that Pico aspired to distil, with the great Greek writers being joined by turbaned thinkers in Persian and Medean costume. The catalogue of his collection, books on which Pico reportedly spent a fortune of 7,000 ducats, tells much the same story: in the three dozen cases that sat below Tura's paintings, Pico had gathered *books in Latin and Greek and barbarian languages*, one case bearing more Hebrew learning than in any other collection in Europe, and also a small but

Opposite: Image of the Orphic god Phanes, owned by Ercole d'Este, now in Galleria Estense, Modena

precious collection of books in Arabic and Aramaic. It is unclear how much of the collection stayed at Mirandola and how much went with Pico as he moved to Florence, though perhaps in a sense his library was with him everywhere: his nephew reported that *he read and mined with incredible speed entire libraries of Latin and Greek books*, committing their contents to his *most tenacious of memories*, such that when he spoke on any topic you would think he had the books in front of him. It is to be assumed that beneath the portrait of the Chaldean sage Zoroaster sat the books in the lost language that Pico was to unveil during his debate in Rome.[11]

Though there were a few first-hand reports of Asian cultures circulating from recent Italian travellers, interest was focused not so much on recent encounters – such as the Persian embassy that had recently visited nearby Urbino to propose an anti-Ottoman alliance – and more on an Eastern wisdom that it seemed had once been common in the peninsula but had long since been forgotten. Among the ancient sculptures unearthed and brought to the Estense palace in this period there is one that is perhaps the most intriguing, a marble tablet that shows a winged youth with a halo of fire who might almost be taken for one of the angels known to Pico's contemporaries from the walls and altars of every church. Any familiarity, however, would only serve to make more uncanny the realization that the winged figure is encircled by a snake whose head hovers over him, a snake that is not an enemy but seems to be part of the man; that emerging from the man's torso are the faces of a lion and a goat, and that like the Christian Devil the winged being had cloven hooves for feet. This confounding image, which suggested a shadowy and troubling history behind the angels and devils the people of Ferrara thought they knew, portrayed Mithras, god of creation in the stories told by the followers of the supernaturally powerful poet Orpheus, part of a cult once widespread in the Roman empire. Into this strange world, where gods and poets lost distinction, Pico was, despite his tender years, about to be plunged.[12]

V

Orpheo

I talian princes were becoming increasingly fond of theatrical spectacles, which allowed them to move energies of carnival inside the palace walls and call the tune, and undoubtedly the greatest production of the age was the staging of the *Orpheo* for the Cardinal of Mantua. The choice of subject followed the recent fashion for replacing *sacre rappresentazioni*, mystery plays on biblical themes, with theatre in the classical style, as at the staging of Plautus' *Menaechmi* (later the source for Shakespeare's *The Comedy of Errors*) at Ferrara, which drew 10,000 spectators into the *cortile* of the Este palazzo. Yet *Orpheo* made all else look like mere prentice-work, with music by Baccio Ugolini, the most celebrated *improvisatore* of the day, and a libretto by Angelo Ambrogini from Montepulciano, known to all as 'Poliziano'. A later production would have sets designed for it by none other than Leonardo da Vinci. Poliziano suggested that he had written the piece in a mere two days of continuous tumult, and that he himself would have preferred the thing to have been torn to shreds after the performance, sharing the tragic fate of Orpheus himself. Shrugging off the composition of the world's first opera as the throwaway effort of a pair of days was doubtless intended by the celebrated intellectual as a magnificent display of *sprezzatura*, the term for apparently effortless and unpremeditated brilliance so prized by the culture of the age as the surest sign of genius. *Wine worth the buying*, as Poliziano was fond of saying, *doesn't need to advertise*. It was around the time of this triumph that he met Pico, on whom he was to become *as dependent* (in his lovely phrase) *as Plato's rings are on the magnet*.[1]

In many respects Poliziano was a very different kind of man from Pico: rising from relatively humble origins, he had come to the notice of Lorenzo de' Medici after translating two books of the *Iliad* into Latin at the age of 16, and had been brought into the Medici household as tutor to Lorenzo's children – though during the period of *Orpheo* he was in exile from Florence after a furious and bitter row with Lorenzo's wife, apparently over who had the final say on the children's schooling. This fit of high dudgeon was entirely in keeping with Poliziano's refusal to bow to flattery or criticism. He was *no more raised or lowered by foolish or frivolous notes of praise or criticism*, he later wrote, than *by the very shadow of my own body: for just because it is longer and more distended in the morning and evening, but shorter and squatter at midday, I should not therefore seem to myself to be suddenly bigger and taller in the evening than I am at noon*. For all his tempestuous behaviour and his talents as a poet, Poliziano vested his own pride in work of a very different sort – philology, a kind of minute detective work upon ancient texts that aimed to restore the fragmentary remains of the classical world to pristine glory, to decode those passages now obscured from view by the passing of time, and to cast out later fabrications from among the company of great works. If this form of painstaking scholarship seems to some wincingly dry and pedantic, it helps to remember the immense stakes of the work: a trail in one direction could lead to the recovery of words and thoughts that had not been spoken for a thousand years, and in the other could demonstrate the most venerated texts to have been cheap forgeries. The philologist Lorenzo Valla had done just that to a text called the *Donation of Constantine*, and in doing so had shown that the Vatican's claim to worldly power was based not on the decree of that emperor but instead on a document trumped up centuries after the end of the fall of Rome.[2]

Poliziano's masterwork was with great and false humility named the *Miscellanea,* and consisted of a series of short notes in which he moved lightly across the knowledge of the ancient world in many tongues to solve in elegant fashion the knottiest enigmas presented by these ancient texts. In a typical entry he explained a reference to a certain 'crocodile puzzle' in the author Quintilian, unearthing the story in question: an Egyptian woman whose baby has been taken by a crocodile is given a challenge by the wily reptilian captor—if she can tell him *one thing unquestionably true* then it will return the baby. The mother responds to the crocodile with the statement that *you will not return the child,* so setting off a paradoxical chain so mesmerizing that the crocodile has to admit defeat and surrender its captive – if it had not, then her statement would be true and it would have to return the child (though as soon as it returned the child, her statement ceased to be true). In another chapter, Poliziano clarified an obscure passage referring to the famously luxuriant tribe called the Sybarites, bringing in a story from another text that recounted their decadent fashion for training their horses to dance to a certain tune on their rear hooves. This indulgence, Poliziano explains, gave way to disaster when one of their flautists betrayed them to their enemies and played the same tune to their advancing cavalry, causing all the horses to rear up and throw their riders. In yet another section Poliziano revealed that the word *panic* was derived from the uncontrollable fear caused by the frenzied cries of women during ritual orgies celebrating the god Pan. He even found a *knot worth the unravelling* in providing a detailed account of and guide to using the *Herculean Knot,* an unbreakable bind that was used to tie a pair of snakes to the *caduceus* – the wand of the god Hermes, or Mercury. To this magical knot he would also compare his attachment to Pico.[3]

We do not know exactly how or when the two met, but if not at the performance of *Orpheo* it was soon after, with Poliziano asking for a list of the Greek titles in Pico's library and Pico sending this and asking for a copy of Poliziano's in return. Within those circles dedicated to ancient learning known as the humanists there was no greater act of love than to lay open your library catalogue to another, mingling your collections and sharing your most sacred volumes. At an early stage in their relationship Pico also sent Poliziano a collection of erotic epigrams he had written, with a request from the late-adolescent prodigy for guidance from the man a decade older and wiser, initiating a correspondence shot through with raw-toned lust. Pico accompanied the manuscript of his poems with a note asking that he hoped Poliziano would chastise them and if necessary spank them, too, and that any errors he found in them would be punished with fingernail marks and spikes. Pico was later to write in one of his most audacious philosophical works about a man known to him whose extraordinary sexual appetite could only be satisfied when he was whipped with a vinegar-soaked rod until he bled. The story is told to illustrate the fact that even the most remarkable habits were not destined by the stars but were, rather, acquired through experience: this anonymous friend had grown up with other boys who gave him sexual favours and then hurt him, forever tying together the two things in his mind. It is unclear whether this unnamed masochist was Poliziano or perhaps even Pico himself, but their early letters were certainly heavy with gestures to this kind of exquisite pain: Poliziano responded to Pico's request by saying that he had *pricked* a few of the poems to mark them out for correction, though he felt like the god Pan thrown upon his back by love. Pico's reply was to ask *who wouldn't wish to die on the end of your sword?* and regretting only that Poliziano's chastisement had been rendered so gently.[4]

The relationship between the two young men was unusually intense but was also in keeping with the growing obsession with a new way of being in the world – namely, the bond that would come to be known as *friendship*. This kind of relationship has become so familiar that we assume it must always have been there, but in fact the habit of forming close ties with those to whom we are not linked by family or necessity or duty but, rather, only by shared tastes and thoughts is a somewhat unusual phenomenon that has not existed in all times and places. These new humanist relationships were modelled on classical ideas of friendship found in rediscovered texts, and while these same-sex relationships defined themselves against the basely transactional reproductive relationships between the sexes, this did not necessarily mean that they were chaste. The goal of bringing the friends closer together was more important than any consideration regarding the method pursued. Writing of his own experience of passionate intimacy, the French essayist Montaigne was to say that *in this friendship of which I speak, the souls of the two melt into each other so completely that the division between them is erased and entirely lost.* These feelings were for the followers of Plato a reminiscence of the underlying and original oneness of things, and indeed this attraction of one friend for another was held by the philosopher-magician Apollonius to be irresistible for the wise, and by the pre-Socratic thinker Empedocles to underly the chemical structure of the universe, causing simple materials to bond together into more complex structures through what would one day be called *elective affinity*. While the intention of Plato and his followers was that sexual desire should be harnessed to drive the lover towards ecstatic transcendence and thrown off once it had provided the required momentum, it is far from clear that these friends were always successful in directing their urges elsewhere. A legend even crept up after Poliziano's death that he was killed by a lethal combination of these two techniques of ecstasy, seizing his lyre while inflamed with desire for a certain youth and working himself into such a frenzy that, like a swan, he died in his song. For better or worse, a veil has been drawn over some of the intimate details of Pico's early relationship with Poliziano, as a subsequent letter reveals that Pico burned these youthful flirtations with erotic verse so that they would not become public. Poliziano joked that he had added fuel to the fire, augmenting the flames with his burning passion, and the illumination that came from burning books was to become a running joke among their circle, though it was later to take on a much darker edge.[5]

The plot of Poliziano's opera begins off to the side of the main Orpheus myth, among a group of shepherds, one of whom has fallen in love with Orpheus' wife Eurydice. The other shepherds attempt to describe the feelings provoked by the forlorn lover's laments using the humble vocabulary available to them: *No more pleasing is the murmur Of sweet and falling water Nor the breeze that makes The pines shiver and sound Than are your solacing verses.* The young man's undesired attentions, however, have given rise to tragedy, and news is brought that fleeing from him Eurydice has stepped upon a serpent, been bitten and died. A disconsolate Orpheus decides to descend into the underworld in an attempt to retrieve his wife using the only means at his disposal, his enchanting song, which was said once to have overpowered the Sirens themselves. Poliziano puts in the mouth of the infernal god Pluto an attempt to express the extraordinary power of the voice of Orpheus, which halts even the eternal punishments of the damned:

> Who is it that with such sweet music
> stirs the abyss, and whose resounding strings
> have stopped the wheel of Ixion in its place,
> brought Sisyphus to rest upon his stone,
> made the Danaïds' urn run dry
> and the water of Tantalus stand still?
> Even Cerberus is seen agape
> And the Furies silence their complaint.

The irresistible force of the Orphic song is too much even for death, and Pluto releases Eurydice on the condition that Orpheus not look at her until back in the land of the living. Not hearing her footsteps behind him on the ascent, however, he turns to check and in doing so casts her back into oblivion to return no more.[6]

Opposite: Leonardo da Vinci's designs for a production of Poliziano's *Orpheo*

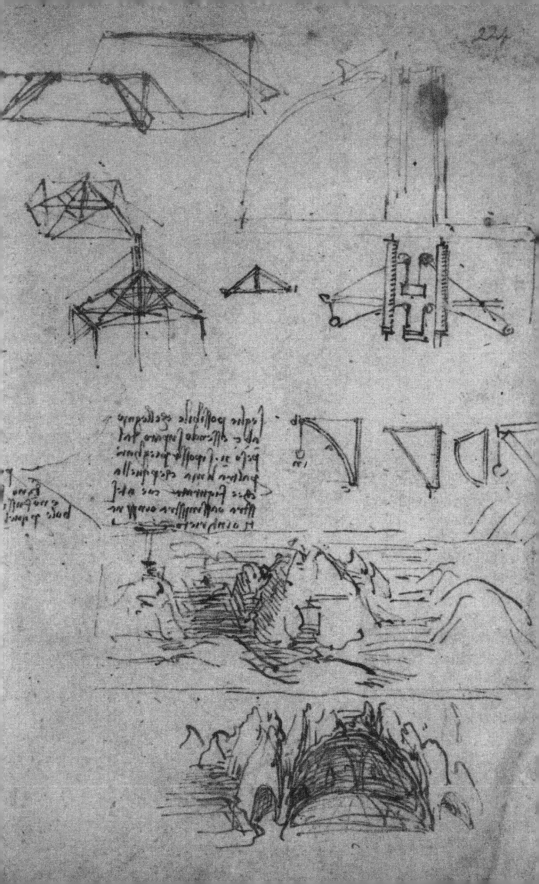

For all the suggestion that his *Orpheo* was a throwaway piece, a casual effort, there was nothing happenstance about Poliziano's choice of story. The figure of Orpheus was central to the intellectual scene in Florence, to which Pico would gravitate a few years later: Marsilio Ficino, the great translator of Plato who felt his life's work was tied to Pico, had prepared for this undertaking by translating certain poems that were believed to have been written by Orpheus himself. If this seems a strange choice for a scholar of philosophy, it is important to remember that Ficino and his contemporaries were guided in their understanding of Plato's works by those who followed in the philosopher's wake and interpreted his works. Most important among these were the group of thinkers who flourished in North Africa and the Levant in the third century of the Christian era, and who turned the reading of Plato into a veritable religion. For the 'Neoplatonists' Plotinus, Iamblichus and Proclus, Plato was not simply a great philosopher but the recipient of divinely revealed knowledge, and his works were to be studied and exalted but not questioned. As Socrates had feared, those encountering written texts rather than a person who could be interrupted and interrogated were quickly reduced to passive players in the making of thought. In one of the most significant turns in the history of philosophy, these thinkers fixated not on Plato's dialectic technique for arriving at knowledge nor his metaphysical framework for holding ideas in place, but rather on the mystical Oneness that Plato gestured to beyond the realm of ideas, and the ancient ecstatic rituals he had borrowed from in making his own version of transcendence. The attempt by Plato to turn the mystic, irrational and ecstatic impulses of Greek culture against themselves, using them as models of an eternal beyond which was better accessed by the rational mind, had the unintended consequence of passing on the very elements he was intending to supersede. By the time Ficino took up Plato's works to begin his translation, a belief had grown up that, rather than being an original thinker, Socrates was merely passing on a tradition that he himself had received from the poet-prophet of Dionysus – none other than Orpheus himself – as demonstrated by his use of dithyrambs to drive himself into a frenzy when speaking to Phaedrus.[7]

For this reason, the obsession with Plato in fifteenth-century Florence often wore the costume of the poet Orpheus. As well as translating poems attributed to Orpheus, Ficino had taken to imitating the legendary poet's style, reciting verse while accompanying himself on the lyre and achieving such astonishing effects that many contemporaries claimed Ficino was the spirit of Orpheus come again, with both Poliziano and Lorenzo de' Medici suggesting that the soul of the legendary poet had transmigrated into Ficino. The humanist Filippo Buonaccorsi, who had fled Rome to Poland in the 1460s after being accused of engaging in sodomy and paganism and insurrection, had even brought back from those regions a cape for Ficino made of bird's feathers as well as a horn-handled sword, a costume he said would make Ficino *a true Orpheus, since he had the song and lyre already*. It may be that this curious vestment was a souvenir from the Tatars who lived in eastern Poland and beyond, whose shamans wore bird-cloaks and (like Socrates himself) associated their out-of-body experiences with the flight and song of birds. Whether or not this was the case, the Italian humanists were not slow to see echoes of these ancient techniques of ecstasy in the ritual practices of the non-Christian world.[8]

At the centre of Ficino's investigation into the magical voice of Orpheus was the matter of harmonic resonance, which, along with magnetism, provided a second route for thinking about how one thing can have an effect upon others without touching them, as when the tone created by one guitar string or the rim of a crystal glass causes the same sound to be emitted by a counterpart elsewhere. This unsettling trick had long been used to dramatic effect: hollow vases placed at various points in a structure could be made to resound when noises of a particular pitch were made, a device known as an 'acoustical jar', which Europeans could see at

Strasbourg cathedral and which were in common use in Byzantine churches and mosques worldwide. At Gedi on the coast of East Africa architects were in this same period using Ming porcelain bowls to create this effect. As the philologists of Florence were discovering, this device may even have begun its life as a stage effect in exactly the kind of performance being revived by Poliziano: the ancient architectural writer Vitruvius noted the presence in Greek theatres of *echea*, or 'sounding jars', which could make the voices of the actors appear to be emerging from thin air at great distances from them. Many philosophers had speculated on the similarity between this extraordinary phenomenon and other kinds of action-at-a-distance: the Neoplatonist Plotinus had remarked upon the way that *the sounding of one string awakens what might pass for perception in another, the result of their being in harmony and tuned to one musical scale*, and had used this as a way to understand the power of prayers and incantations, which had an effect on things elsewhere as if they were tuned to the same key. The Neoplatonists were not the only ones to come to this conclusion: central to many strains of Chinese thought was the concept of *ganying*, which was the relationship between different things in the world imagined as a form of resonance, and which they similarly compared to magnetic force. Both Neoplatonists and Chinese thinkers speculated that there might exist a master note that resonated with *all things*, and man's route to perfection consisted of discovering this note in order to attune himself with the universe entire, so experiencing what was known in Chinese Taoism as the *Great Merging*. Ficino had concluded in the earliest summaries of Plato's philosophy that it was precisely these kinds of harmony that provoked his poetic frenzies and allowed his spirit to reach transcendence.[9]

Poliziano's treatment of the Orpheus story did not end with the return of the poet from the underworld, nor was the effect of Orpheus' song upon the dead the only kind of incantation in the opera. In the final Act the bereaved Orpheus retires to the wilderness

60

and foreswears the love of womankind, provoking the animosity of a troupe of bacchantes, women who rove the mountainsides naked, engaging in orgies of bloodsport and lust in ecstatic worship of their god Bacchus. They work themselves into a rage, calling upon each other to give Orpheus the death he deserves, and, arming themselves with rocks and fire and branches and the Thyrsus-reed staff sacred to their god, pronounce a sentence of death upon the apostate, to be inflicted by tearing the beating heart from his chest. Their frenzy climaxes in a chorus of dithyrambs, that rhythmic chant of whose power Socrates made use, famous throughout the ancient world; it was said that the dithyrambs included by the playwright Euripides in his play *The Bacchae* were of such force that enslaved Greeks had used them to win power over their captors. The ritual associated with these verses is described in a dithyramb by Pindar, where *the whirling of tambourines lead off,* followed by *the blazing torch beneath the yellow pine trees,* before *the loud-sounding groans* and *ecstatic cries are aroused in the agitation of tossing necks.* In Poliziano's opera the evisceration of Orpheus happens offstage, but the women return to declare that their victim *has been scattered through the forest, that every branch drips with his blood, that limb has been torn from limb and the pieces of him tossed about,* sacrificing the dismembered poet-prophet to their god. Drunk on bloodlust and drunk as well on the wine that is sacred to Dionysus, they descend into a whirling dance and a fevered song, the bodies and voices of each becoming difficult to distinguish from the others.

> Ognun segua Baccho te
> Baccho Baccho eu hoe
> Chi uuol beuere chi uuol beuere
> Vegna a beuere uegna a beuere . . .
> Ognun gridi Baccho Baccho
> Et pur cacci del uin giu
> Poi con suoni faren fiaccho

Beui tu et tu et tu
I non posso ballar piu
Ognun gridi heu hoe
Ognun segue Baccho te
Baccho Baccho hue hoe

The parts of the chant that can be translated consist of a raucous drinking song, a provocation to become inebriated for the glory of the god. But parts of the song cannot be translated, because they are nonsense, consisting only of the ecstatic and orgiastic cry that is both the sign that someone has become lost in the frenzy of the god and also the very thing that makes it happen – *EU HOE!*[10]

The story of Orpheus is a parable of the force of poetry in both its power to create and destroy, to bring eternal motions to a halt and resurrect the dead, to make of many people a single, many-headed multitude, and to provoke this thing to engage in acts unspeakable to most, outrageously blending the desires for sex and food and violence. In choosing to put these matters on stage, Poliziano was not merely providing entertainment for the gathered crowds, but was also pursuing answers to the questions that lay at the heart of Florentine thought, questions that time and again returned to Orpheus. Poliziano was to open his Florentine series of public lectures on Virgil with a meditation on the Orphic lyrics; in a learned poem he wrote for the King of Hungary he declared that these poetic songs are precisely that charioteer described by Socrates, capable of transporting the soul beyond its bodily cage, and also that it was this sweet eloquence that first tamed the barbarous soul of man and brought him to the subjection of law. Working himself to a fevered pitch, Poliziano praised the *fervour that takes the one who cries 'eu hoe!' as his mind is enraptured by a surge of fury*, for this man is inhabited by a god, taking up residence in his evacuated breast and possessing him completely, filling his human heart with the chant. Not everyone shared Poliziano's enthusiasm for the ecstatic powers of song. For all that he modelled himself after Orpheus, Ficino himself cautioned that this kind of voice was so forceful that it tended to be infectious, causing those who start as mere passive participants, only reciting the song or listening along to it, to become possessed by its rhythms and to begin themselves to play out the motions and the acts that the song suggests.

Poliziano's opera was suggestive of possibilities both transcendent and troubling. The widespread attestations to the power of song suggested both a tool of immense power for use in this world and perhaps a portal to some elsewhere. But it was unclear whether these enchanting rhythms could only be used to raise the listener to divine thoughts and acts, or if the same powers could be used to more sinister ends as well. And what could it mean that the ecstasy of the bacchantes was provoked by a bloodcurdling and senseless cry, a sound without meaning – how could the imperative for man to act rationally be understood when the most powerful things were irrational, meaningless and closed to understanding? The bacchantes' cry was not alone in suggesting the power of the nonsensical: many of the ancient magical amulets or *intaglios* that were the prize possession of Renaissance collectors similarly featured nonsensical formulas. One such amulet made of serpentine portrays a lion-headed deity and is inscribed with the words *chuch bachuch bakachuch bazakachuch bakaxichuch bainchooooch*; another dedicated to Harpocrates, god of silence, is engraved with the palindromic phrase *ablanathanalba*, a lisp away from *abracadabra*. These are groups of sounds that linger on the edge of meaning but in fact mean nothing at all. What was this ancient knowledge, in which certain syllables repeated forwards and backwards were thought to have some power over people, and perhaps over the supernatural world as well? The Greeks were far from alone in holding this belief: shamans of the Araweté people in what is now Brazil used the *music of the gods, Maï marakã*, to wield immense power, a form of humming and droning that also used meaningless phrases, understood to be a divine language left

63

behind to men when the gods departed from this earth. And the amulets familiar to Pico and his contemporaries would have been known to them by the name of *talisman*, itself a nonsensical sound believed to be produced by saying an Arabic word backwards. The word in question is *musallat*, which means *to give power or mastery over something.*[11]

VI

The Studious Artizan

The fame had spread across Europe of a youth who, when not a boy but not quite yet a man, was capable of performing extraordinary feats of mind and memory: having mastered the scriptures by the age of 10, he went on to study mathematics, philosophy and jurisprudence, as well as astronomy, natural sciences and metaphysics. His appetite for knowledge was gargantuan. *I did not sleep a single night through in that time*, the prodigy recalled, *nor did I think of any other task. I would return at night to my home and place a lamp near at hand and press on with my reading and writing. Whenever sleep began to take me or I felt weak I would take a glass of wine to gather strength.* Everything came within the sweep of his understanding. *Medicine is not one of the difficult sciences*, he said, *and I mastered it in a short time*, to the point where famous doctors came to learn at his feet. He came to the attention of the powerful when he cured the local potentate of a mysterious disease, and as a reward he asked only to be given access to his wondrous library of rarities so that he could continue his studies. *In this way when I reached my eighteenth year I was finished with all these sciences*, he declared, and *afterwards there was nothing else to discover.*[1]

Though the similarities to Pico's legend are uncanny, these memories are not his but those of the eleventh-century Persian intellectual giant Ibn Sina, whose name was corrupted to 'Avicenna' as it moved through languages and across the Mediterranean. During the course of his extraordinary life, Avicenna would use the books he encountered in the Samanid library in Bukhara, now part of Uzbekistan, to lead the movement that swept the Arabic-speaking world: the study of *falasafa*, or philosophy, undertaken by philosophers, or *falasifa*. *I entered a house with many rooms*, he said when recalling the Samanid library, *and in each room there were chests with books one on top of the other, one room of Arabic books and poetry, another of law, and so in each room another science. I looked in the index of the earliest books and was given whichever I requested. And I saw among them books whose names few had heard, which I had not seen before nor was ever to see again.* Avicenna's encounter with a closely guarded library and its mouthwatering catalogue of forgotten books was to set the pattern for an age in which untold wonders were woken from where in hidden cases they had for many centuries lain dormant. The volumes most prized by the *falasifa* were those of the master Aristotle: it was through their hands that The Philosopher's works were to conquer Christian Europe in the centuries before Pico's birth, and it was to understand their revelations arising from the thought of Aristotle that Pico moved from Ferrara to the freethinking safe house of Italy at the University of Padua, seeking (as his nephew put it) *many things that for centuries were lost to our people.*[2]

The bracing legacy of the *falasafa* movement lay in large part in its willingness to revisit the vertiginous and radical implications of ancient thought, as in the famous debate between Avicenna and his friend al-Biruni regarding a certain device known as the *clepsydra*, or *water-thief*. Once again we are in the terrain of invisible forces, this time the mysterious power that can make water flow upwards or prevent it from falling down through a hole. While these tricks were usually used to demonstrate that nature abhors a vacuum, the idea that the vacuum does not exist is equally problematic: if the vacuum is not allowed to exist, that suggests that what lies beyond the boundaries of our universe must be another world – and beyond that another – reopening the road to the infinitely many worlds against which Aristotle recoiled in horror. This was a route Avicenna was also unwilling to take: he argued that worlds beyond our realm of understanding nevertheless implied others who *could* understand them, condemning man to live in a universe of whose knowledge he could only ever possess an infinitesimal fraction. His companion al-Biruni – a polymath who among other things authored a chronology of the world, a tract on yoga and a comprehensive treatise on the nature of shadows – was much more open to these explosive ideas, encouraged perhaps by the thought of the neighbouring Indian lands to which he had dedicated much of his life, and which he saw as a living repository of the lost elements of Greek thought. Though he began his study of Indian culture by reassuring his readers that Indians were people who believed in one God and in a world made up of multiple different objects – the bare minimum required for a culture to be given a hearing – he quickly admitted that in fact the truth was more complicated. Among both Greeks and Hindus, he noted, there were those *who thought that all things are one*, and *that man only has this prerogative before a stone and the inanimate world, that he is by one degree nearer the First Cause. But for this he would not be any better than they.* Troublingly, these neighbours to the east seemed perfectly comfortable with a vision of the world in which there was no essential difference between various material objects. More than this, the Indians had, like some Greeks, concluded that true wisdom consisted in this recognition of the arbitrariness of distinctions, a wisdom enshrined in their holy books, the Vedas. These texts, al-Biruni reported, were of unimaginable antiquity, and they had in fact been lost and rediscovered many times, once in the belly of a fish that had brought them up from their resting place in the deep waters, and another on the tusks of a wild boar which had dug them up where they lay buried. He was puzzled to record that even in his day Indian priests recited these Vedas without actually knowing the meaning of what they were chanting, though this would not prevent the mantras from being adopted by the Buddhists and spreading from India to China and beyond, where the knowledge of them fetched a high price.[3]

The several Gods worship'd by the Gentiles in the East Indies.

If Avicenna would not allow for the possibility of multiple worlds, he was at least convinced by the line of argument that Aristotle's theory of knowledge required the existence of a single Universal Intellect shared by all mankind – which Avicenna called by the name of 'Angel' – and set out to demonstrate that this was reconcilable with Platonic thought. Whether or not Aristotle's argument could be squared with Plato, the problems for Islamic theologians proved insuperable: Aristotle's theory suggested that when individuals died and ceased acting individually, their minds returned to the common reservoir of the Universal Intellect, and all distinction was lost, an idea impossible to reconcile with the individual rewards and punishments of the afterlife. Indeed, the very idea that such fundamental questions on the nature of existence could be rooted out by rational analysis, not requiring the revelations of the scriptures or even faith in God, provoked a backlash against the thought of the early *falasifa*. The leading voice of this counter-attack, al-Ghazali, argued in texts such as *The Incoherence of the Philosophers* and *The Revival of the Religious Sciences* that God's unbridled power to determine things not according to laws or logic but, rather, simply however he pleased meant that the world could never be entirely understood by rational analysis, and that in some matters the submission of faith was required. In a move so predictable that it begins to feel like an inevitability, al-Ghazali was to bring forth as a key example of divine and unfathomable things the effect that rhythm has upon the human soul: *And I say that to God Most High belongs a secret consisting in the relationship of measured airs to the souls of men, so that the airs work upon them with a wonderful working.* The power of poetry and song upon those listening to it could not be understood by analysing the words of the poems and songs themselves, as is evident (al-Ghazali argues) from the fact that these songs also work upon those who mishear or

Opposite: Vishnu's avatar Matsya recovering the Vedas from the deep and returning them to Brahma

misunderstand them, even upon uncomprehending children in their cradles, and what is more upon camels, whose drivers had been known to lead them even to death by exhaustion using the sweetness of their droving songs. The reasons for this mystery were for al-Ghazali at the heart of divine revelation and at the core of the Sufi mysticism on which his writing drew and to which they became central: *The knowledge of the cause why souls receive impressions through sounds belongs to the most subtle of the sciences of the Revelations which Sufis are granted.* Not everyone was convinced: the captive Muslim historian Leo Africanus described how among the Sufis *at times some of them driven by the verses being sung tear at their clothing and it is believed that these men's brains are deranged, being at that time enflamed with the fire of divine love,* though Leo went on wryly to say that *I think instead they are enflamed with too much food, as each one stuffs himself with enough for three.*[4]

Pico was drawn to Padua less by the thought of Avicenna than by his twelfth-century successor Averroes, the philosopher from Muslim Spain through whom the work of the *falasifa* was transmitted to Christian Europe. Averroes also accepted the argument that the mind must be detachable from matter, and in being so must be eternal, not subject to that decay that is a property of matter; and, in order to explain the fact that minds independently arrived at conclusions that were universally true, they must derive from a common, unique substance. The problem remained that these ideas where wholly incompatible with the dictates of the Abrahamic faiths. On the one hand, the idea that God's powers were constrained by a set of rigid laws governed by and discoverable through logic seemed an insult to divine dignity. On the other, the idea that there was a single Universal Intellect, from which all individual minds were derived and to which they returned when no longer constrained by their bodies, wholly undid the ideas of sin and the afterlife; if after death our individual consciousness was absorbed into an undifferentiated mass, could a person truly be said to have an afterlife – and how could their virtue or vice in this life make any difference in the next when we are all blended and indistinguishable one from another? As Pico's mentor Ficino had said, *whenever we consider the unity of mind, we find it repugnant and turn to plurality, if only for the desire to survive.* The idea that human minds and souls were not at all times single independent entities was simply too appalling for most even to consider. This did not, however, hold true for Pico, whose legend would have him recant the idea on his deathbed, suggesting that he was known to have believed in it until that point.[5]

In response to the apparently unresolvable deadlock between logic and faith, Averroes produced an ingenious fix in twelfth-century Al-Andalus, a wondrous piece of sophistry designed to prevent the entire system from breaking down and the course of philosophical enquiry being blocked by religious fundamentalists. This was the notion of *double truth*, which argued that when reason demonstrated the absolute necessity of one thing, and that the demands of faith required the exact opposite, both things must be true *in their own sense.* Averroes had in effect created a bubble within which radical philosophical thought could continue by detaching its conclusions from how people lived in the world: the wise could know certain things to be the case, but the common mass of people could and should continue to behave as if the exact opposite was true, as the consequences of them not doing so were felt to be catastrophic.[6]

The doctrine of double truth, which later entered Christian thought through the philosophers of Paris, was also what allowed Padua to thrive as a cosmopolitan hotbed of radical thought. The same logic that allowed Averroes to argue that the idea of a Universal Intellect was not heretical, being true only in a limited sense, could be and was applied more widely, allowing very different ways of thinking to live at the heart of certain European institutions, alternate visions of the universe that were tolerated as long as they made no claim to being the sole and uncontested truth. One of the main things that drew Pico to Padua seems to have been the presence there of Elia del Medigo, a Jewish scholar from the Venetian colony of Candia in Crete, who was a leading authority on the thought of Averroes and who taught at the Hebrew College of the university. The older man was soon drawn within Pico's orbit, and was sharing with Pico those parts of Averroes that were not yet available in languages that Pico could read, which del Medigo drew out of Hebrew into Latin for his young disciple. Del Medigo was evidently taken with his illustrious follower, though his letters to Pico, written in a macaronic blend of Italian and Latin with a sprinkling of terms in Hebrew and Greek, attest to the two men's very different ideas of what they were about, and the professor's exasperation at his young charge's desire to forge ahead at a breakneck pace. *Your lordship knows very well*, del Medigo wrote, *that the said Aristotle and Averroes are of such a sort that hardly a single syllable of theirs is without an idea that needs to be studied.* While del Medigo was sure that Pico would one day be an admirable Aristotelian, time would be needed for them to sit together and work through each of the lines of thought in turn.[7]

Such a painstaking and methodical approach was not, however, in Pico's nature, and it seems that soon, as well as asking del Medigo to translate and expound the works of Averroes for him, Pico was also having the scholar teach him the rudiments of Hebrew. Though part of Pico's eagerness to learn the language may have come from his desire to throw off the shackles of his master's caution and have direct access to Jewish translations of the *falasifa*, he also seems to have conceived a fascination with Hebrew in its own right. Hebrew had long held a mystique for Europeans as the language of the Old Testament and the tongue in which it was believed that God spoke to Adam. Dante even proposed that while all of the other languages of the world descended from one of the groups of craftsmen at the Tower of Babel, only those who had abstained from the blasphemous project had been allowed to continue speaking the original language of God – Hebrew. Yet knowledge of Hebrew among European scholars remained extremely limited, and Pico's study of the language was in many respects pioneering. The mystery and intrigue that surrounded this strange semitic tongue for Pico and his contemporaries, and the attraction some among them felt to the unfamiliar and iconic shapes of Hebrew writing, were intensified by the belief that Hebrew preserved in its very syllables and letter forms traces of the voice of God. As Pico was to discover under Elia del Medigo's tutelage, this belief in the divine properties of the Hebrew tongue was not confined to those for whom it was an exotic mystery: rather, a long-standing and central tradition of Jewish thought held that God had imbued the first language with super-natural properties, encoding its sounds and even its letter shapes with hidden meanings that, properly used, could reveal the secrets of the universe. Although Pico appears to have first encountered this art or science of kabbalah through Elia del Medigo, the teacher seems to have regretted his student's strong attraction to the subject, and to have been unable or unwilling to communicate to him any more than the bare rudiments of the tradition. While for Pico the kabbalah seemed to hold out a potential solution to the mysterious connection between language and the deeper structures of being, a connection that was felt viscerally when hearing strange tongues and seeing the unfamiliar characters of a foreign script, del Medigo probably feared that dabbling in these occult matters would be a bridge too far for the tolerance he enjoyed in Padua, shaking the tottering edifice that allowed foreigners and their thought to live in relative peace in parts of the Christian West.[8]

An exchange of letters between Pico and another of his professors at Padua gives us some sense of the direction in which his thought was tending. With all the impetuosity and wilfulness of youth, Pico had responded to a letter of advice from the older man by calling him out on some of the sacred truisms of the age, which the letter had rehashed – namely, that the works of the *falasifa* and those who had brought them to the attention of the West should be consigned to the rubbish heap of history, their almost unreadable works being expressed in painful jargon, and displaying no know-ledge of the Greek originals or attention to proper Latin style. Following the new humanist fashion, the professor pronounced that *however valuable the contents of a work, only the elegance of its style can assure survival*. Pico's daring response to this was to suggest that in matters relating to the deepest nature of existence the question of eloquence was wholly irrelevant: philosophical works were produced not to seduce and impress the multitude but to wield the tools of language, blunt as they may be but lacking any other means, to prise open the fundamental truths of being. Indeed, it could not be otherwise that when discussing things of true importance one should give little thought to how they sounded to others, and should seek truths that are equally valid in all languages and not just those that could be made to sound pleasant. This position was so contrary to the thought of all the fashionable intellectuals of the day that many took Pico's widely circulated letter to be a joke: expressed as it was in such exquisite and learned Latin, they assumed that he must be performing a trick, showing his mastery of eloquence by attacking eloquence in the most persuasive manner possible. The course that his life took suggests, however, that he was entirely in earnest. Despite or perhaps because of being lauded as a prodigy from his earliest age, Pico showed little sign of interest in the approval of others: he was instead determined to use such mental powers as he had to do something real, not to settle for the cheap rewards of fame gained through the bandying of fancy words, but, rather, to surge beyond the boundary that held thought back from transforming the world. It was one thing to speak beautifully and lead others by the ears, but quite another to understand how it was that this could happen, to see the deeper structures of our being that allowed these hidden powers to work upon people, to resonate across distance. Pico seems to have felt more keenly than most the frustration that arises from the feeling that thought, no matter how keen and forceful and exalting, seems for ever to remain bounded within the circle of its own conceiving, never making the slightest change to the set laws that govern the world outside.[9]

This turning point in Pico's life, where he began to venture beyond what were considered the acceptable boundaries of thought, was to become the stuff of folklore in the decades after his death. A story first written down in the sixteenth century in the German lands to the north told of a young man of prodigious abilities who quickly tires of what is offered to him by traditional areas of study and becomes obsessed with the promise of supernatural and occult knowledges, eventually entering into a pact with the Devil himself to gain immense powers in exchange for giving over his soul to the bonds of hell. Although these myths became attached to the figure of 'Doctor Faustus' and may have been based in part on a real historical figure named Johann Georg Faust, the stories recorded in the *Faustbuch* draw upon a wider fascination with those who ventured beyond the prescribed bounds of knowledge despite the peril of eternal damnation, and many parts of the myth seem to derive ultimately from the story of Pico's life. The opening of the English stage version of the Faustus myth, penned by Shakespeare's rival Christopher Marlowe, sees the young prodigy move swiftly to dispense with the traditional disciplines that he feels he has already surpassed: *having commenc'd*, like Pico, to *be a divine in show*, he then decides to *live and die in Aristotle's workes*, before concluding that even The Philosopher's logic can do no more than convince other lowly mortals; like Avicenna, Faustus dismisses medicine as too easy, and like Pico he disdains the Law – *this study fits a mercenary drudge, who aims at nothing but external trash: too servile and illiberal for me.* Even the study of theology cannot actually alter God's providential plan for the world and man, and so offers no power over the inevitable course of things.[10]

Despairing of the feeble inability of these studies to effect any real change in the world, the *Faustbuch* tells how the young man surrounds himself with those *that had the Chaldean, Persian, Hebrew, Arabian and Greeke tongues, using figures, characters, conjurations, incantations, with many other ceremonies belonging to these infernal artes, as Necromancie, Charmes, Sooth-saying, Witchcraft, Inchantment, being delighted with their bookes, words and names so well, that he studied day and night therein.* Though distorted through the storyteller's lens and the requirements of a morality tale, the shape of Pico's life from Padua onwards is plainly visible in the sequence of events here described, from the list of languages in whose study Pico was to immerse himself to his incipient obsession with characters and incantations, with peculiar books and words and names, and the accusations of diabolic practices that arose unstoppably from these preoccupations. In the climactic words of Marlowe's opening scene, Pico, like Faustus, seems to have concluded that

> Lines, circles, schemes, letters and characters:
> Aye, these are those that Faustus most desires.
> O what a world of profit and delight,
> Of power, of honour, of omnipotence
> Is promised to the studious Artizan?
> All things that move between the quiet poles
> Shall be at my command. Emperors and Kings,
> Are but obey'd in their several provinces:
> Nor can they raise the wind, or rend the clouds:
> But his dominion that exceeds in this,
> Stretcheth as far as doth the mind of man.
> A sound Magician is a mighty god.

Pico was increasingly obsessed with finding a kind of knowledge that rose above the petty goal of persuading and impressing his fellow men, a knowledge that was not confined to one region or tradition of thought but, rather, gathered together from the knowledges of the world those hidden universal truths that tied everything together, the mastery of which promised a power to work upon the world in ways that it could not resist. In pursuit of this knowledge, Pico felt himself inexorably drawn towards Florence and the circles around Poliziano and Ficino, who seemed to share the same ambition but whose achievements in this domain Pico was confident he would soon surpass.[11]

VII

Poppysma

Pico seems to have first arrived in Florence on more than one occasion. According to a later report he had visited the city early in his relationship with Poliziano and had made rather a poor showing, seeming aloof and arrogant and not terribly impressed with the bourgeois culture of the city. It is possible that the adolescent Pico had not by that point understood that if Florence was less courtly and aristocratic than Ferrara, this was because the chief citizens of Florence and their leading merchant-princes, the Medici, were playing an entirely different game from that of the petty lords of other Italian states. In look and feel and civic architecture Florence was not aiming for the stolid subjugation of feudal lords but, rather, at reviving the glories of the ancient republics: the city was dominated not by a ducal castle but by the Palazzo della Signoria where the ruling council met, and all other houses were conspicuously level, no one raising itself too far above the others. Cosimo de' Medici and his grandson Lorenzo had set a pattern by building immense private wealth from banking and trade and leading their city to a dominant position among the warring Italian states, all the while professing this was no more than their humble service to the republic and offering to step back from public life whenever it was no longer required. On the one hand they demonstrated their magnificence by their patronage of architecture and of the most famous artists and thinkers of the day, and on the other their humility by the construction of rustic villas on the outskirts of the city where (following the Roman model) they could retire from the distasteful bustle of commerce to lives of peaceful and bucolic contemplation. The Florentines paid Pico the compliment of remembering his first arrival in the city in a manner more fitting to the part he was destined to play: not only did the leader of the Florentine academy Ficino later write that Pico presented himself in Florence on the day and even at the very hour when the great translation of Plato was finally complete, but moreover that the time of his coming had been determined by the spirit of Cosimo de' Medici himself. Ficino's rather grandiloquent piece of myth-making seems to have been a reaction to the extraordinary behaviour of the 21-year-old Pico who, through self-possession or somehow otherwise possessed, congratulated Ficino only briefly on his great work before going on to suggest what he should do next.[1]

The Medici household that was to become the centre of Pico's orbit in the coming years was a paradise for the inquisitive, a loose association of the talented drawn together by the freedom Lorenzo gave them to wander among his treasures and to make new ones. While Ficino continued his translations and held annual banquets on the anniversary of Plato's death at the Medici villa of Careggi, with prophetic songs provided by the *Orpheo* star Baccio Ugolini, a young Michelangelo Buonarotti was soon to begin his studies under Lorenzo's patronage, putting him in a company of artists that already included Botticelli and Ghirlandaio. Michelangelo began his sculpting career with a subject suggested by Poliziano, and by some accounts Botticelli's famous *Birth of Venus* – completed a few years before Pico's arrival – was similarly guided in its details by Poliziano's close readings of ancient texts. Pico wrote that he was drawn to Florence by the promise of its libraries, and among these the Medici library was unsurpassed, a humanist's dream-archive of ancient texts hunted down by agents from across the Greek archipelago and beyond. Lorenzo was later to say, with his characteristic elegance and generosity, that he would have happily bankrupted himself to build a library fit for Pico and Poliziano's use, and then to have sold his furniture as well to help complete the task.

With Pico increasingly by his side, Poliziano spent his days in the library working on his lectures and his *Miscellanea*, solving puzzles in the long-unopened texts by following the thread of his memory to places where similar terms were used in other books. In a passage of Suetonius' biography of the emperor Claudius describing how in his unsatiable bloodlust Claudius would make even the craftsmen at gladiatorial shows fight each other if he found their work wanting, Poliziano noted that most texts mistakenly had the phrase *aut ornatum* ('anything decorated') to describe the handywork, whereas a twelfth-century copy belonging to the Medici showed that this should instead be *automaton*. *It appears,* he writes, *that this word automaton was used to describe those things which were constructed by the mechanics so as to seem to do things spontaneously, as if without any visible cause.* Just such an automatic wonder had in the same period kept Poliziano transfixed for many days: a new astrological clock made for the Medici by the watchmaker Lorenzo della Volpaia, which Poliziano described minutely in a letter to a friend. Atop a marble obelisk the artisan had set a series of rotating bronze discs which modelled the movements of the planets and predicted the timings of full moons, sunrise and sunset, the positions of the zodiacal signs, and even the occurrence of eclipses. This was for Poliziano not merely a tool or a toy but a window into the past, as it convinced him that a device described by the ancient inventor Archimedes must have been of a similar nature. If an art could be found to reproduce the movement of the heavens with such exquisite precision, what other hidden motions could be made subject to human ingenuity?[2]

Some of the secrets uncovered in the library suggested that the knowledge of the ancients had not so much been lost or buried but had, rather, passed on into folk traditions, living on unobserved under the noses of the learned. Another of Poliziano's notes deals with a passage in the Roman cosmographer Pliny the Elder, whose *Natural History* undertook an encyclopaedic description of the known world. In a chapter of the book dealing with the question of *whether there is force in words*, Poliziano restored a term that was missing in most copies but which was to be found there in several manuscripts held by the Medici library. The corrupted text found in most versions simply mentioned that *it is a custom of the common folk to venerate lightning*, which made little sense as having nothing to do with the matter of word power. In a thirteenth-century Medici copy, however, it became clear that scribes at some point in the past had simply chosen to omit a word that seemed to them to make no sense, and that the passage should in fact read *it is a custom of the common folk to venerate lightning with poppysma*. Poliziano then drew evidence from the ancient playwright Aristophanes and elsewhere to show that this *poppysma* was an onomatopoeic word – a word that imitates a sound – and was nothing other than the Greek term to describe smacking one's lips, which was indeed the way in which it was customary to respond to lightning in the ancient world. Poliziano noted, moreover, that this sound was also used in the ancient world and also in his own day to calm the nerves of untamed horses, suggesting that folk practice could perhaps hold its own library of ancient knowledge. Poliziano was not alone in this dawning realization: at Taranto in southern Italy, the site of the ancient cult of Bacchus, there existed even in Pico's day a local cult centred on the astonishing powers of rhythmic sound, used as a cure for a local epidemic of frenzied and delirious dances, supposedly caused by the bite of a spider named *tarantula* for the district. This spider was the subject of a number of strange stories: Leonardo da Vinci recorded in one of his notebooks the commonly held belief that the bite of the tarantula fixed unshakeably in the victim's mind the thought that they were having at the moment of puncture. The mostly female participants of the dance, or *tarantella*, were driven to acts of lasciviousness that shocked fifteenth-century observers, and local tradition held that they could only be returned to their senses by the playing of particular tunes, which worked upon the infected persons and restored them to themselves. The belief that horses and lightning were calmed by *poppysma*, spiders by the *tarantella* and al-Ghazali's camels by their drovers' songs, all pointed to a half-forgotten knowledge about sound and its power.[3]

Pico quickly settled into the Medici household and before long was writing to Lorenzo to give his verdict on the older man's poetry: more stylish than Dante, he suggests, and more substantial than Petrarch, and so in some ways better than both. Lorenzo was indeed an accomplished poet and one who had recently moved from writing lighter pieces on love and carnival to more mature and reflective works, so Pico's letter is not merely hollow flattery; but it was perhaps also a chance to think through the relationship between sound and meaning that he had begun to think about in Padua – Pico was after all, as he said to Poliziano, a philosopher among the poets and a poet among the philosophers. Petrarch's ability to *make the common uncommon by his way of speaking* is here a source of anxiety, one that Pico, following classical models, condemns as an *Asiatic* vice, *that is, stuffing in words just to fill the cracks, summoning full and consonant noises not just to beautify but to make the whole thing stand up*. The insistence that substance is more important than style had been around since at least the time of Plato and was often directed at the worryingly seductive 'Asiatic' rituals coming from the unknown places to the east. It has become such a familiar and conventional belief that we often forget what is at stake, and why belief in it needs constantly to be reaffirmed: namely, the worrying possibility that we are moved more by the sounds of the words than by what they're actually saying, which threatens to turn man from a rational judge of what he is being told into a powerless instrument at the mercy of the patterns of sound.[4]

During his periodic stays in Florence in the 1480s Pico seems to have been all but inseparable from Poliziano, the pair dividing their time between study and affectionate games. A touching story later told by Poliziano recounts how, when working away at one of the Medici villas in the country, Pico had once come to him in disguise, pretending to be a stranger to the area and asking Poliziano what he thought of this man Pico della Mirandola, waiting to hear how his soulmate spoke of him before throwing off his disguise and revealing his true identity. One imagines that Poliziano affectionately played along with what could only have been a most unconvincing attempt by the striking youth to conceal his appearance: as Poliziano was himself to put it, Pico *resembles no-one so completely as himself*. They can be glimpsed together as bystanders in at least one of the miraculous Florentine paintings of the period, the glorious frescoes in the Cappella del Miracolo at Sant'Ambrogio by Cosimo Rosselli. Here a small group loiters in the foreground, picked out by an aura that surrounds the seraphic and androgynous Pico, with the darker-haired, square-jawed figure of Poliziano hovering at his side, and Ficino on his other flank, so that the two clasp Pico between them. They stand apart from the group of women in the background, who look on at the miraculous transformation of wine into blood that had occurred there two and a half centuries before. Rosselli's portrait of Pico, says the celebrated biographer of artists Giorgio Vasari, is painted *so excellently that he seems not drawn but rather alive*. Some have also suggested that Pico is there, this time with Lorenzo de' Medici, in Botticelli's *Adoration of the Magi*, gesturing towards the submission of the Wise Men in token of what he himself expected to achieve.[5]

Many of these same figures are also in what must be the greatest ensemble piece of the age, Domenico Ghirlandaio's sequence for the Tornabuoni Chapel in Santa Maria Novella, where the prominent citizens of Florence huddle in threes and fours in shimmering red silks at the sides of an immense fresco of a miraculous occurrence. The painting is its own minor miracle, stretching back into the wall by use of shadow and perspective in such a way that the viewer feels as if they may be falling through the levels of its foreground towards the altar in the middle of the scene. There was a school of medieval Islamic thought which held that pictures of Christ were made without shadows so that they could not be mistaken for idols: one feels the haunting depth and verisimilitude of Ghirlandiao's painting could make an idolator of most. There in the bottom-left corner are Poliziano and other chief scholars of the day, including Cristoforo Landino, whose triumphant edition of Dante with illustrations by Botticelli was felt to have finally given the great Florentine poet just recompense for his life of exile from the city. The biblical narrative at the centre of the fresco is one that will be unfamiliar to most, depicting the moment in which a curse is spoken by an angel upon Zacharias in the time before the birth of his son John, one day to be The Baptist. The gospel story goes that when the angel Gabriel appeared to the priest Zacharias in his old age to tell him that he and his wife Elizabeth would have a child called John who would prepare the way for the Messiah, Zacharias had not believed the angel, and in punishment for his doubt the angel had pronounced upon him a curse of voicelessness until such time as the child was born. Pico has not been identified in this scene, though there is one impossibly angelic figure among the crowd who bears a striking resemblance to the depiction of Pico by Ghirlandaio's friend Rosselli. Above the head of this figure is a frieze depicting someone holding forth to a crowd in the *adlocutio* stance, a symbol of the power of words to yoke the listener to their will, as on the ancient Roman *sestertii* which show emperors upon a raised platform, or *suggestum*, addressing a body of troops who have been made a single, many-headed thing by the emperor's oration. The scene depicted by Ghirlandaio is a parable of the powers of angel speech, the way that Gabriel merely by pronouncing something makes it to be the case, here stopping the mistrustful and blaspheming mouth of Zacharias with a curse, making his words into flesh in a glorious reversal of the Incarnation that was to come. One philosopher of the period even coined a verb to describe the power wielded by Gabriel: *angelizare*, 'to angelize', meaning to speak in such a manner as to work wonders upon those who heard, collapsing the distinction between speaker and listener and making them act as one.

Angels are everywhere in art of the period, perching at the top of paintings, an aviary of beings that ranges from the rainbow-winged archangels, beautiful and androgynous adolescents indistinguishable from people other than the vast plumed spans that they tuck behind them, up to the fluttering seraphim, often differing from birds only in having human faces. Thinkers of the period were fascinated by angels, and one question that troubled many was the total number of the angelic host: the vision of the Last Judgment in Revelation 5: 11 speaks of *ten thousand times ten thousand, and thousands of thousands* gathered around the heavenly throne, but there were those who felt that a more precise census of angels was desirable. The foremost authority on the subject, a man named Dionysius the Areopagite, who was believed to be a disciple of St Paul – and in whose works Ficino was immersed – pronounced there to be an almost infinite number of angels, even if he suggested that man could only access the lowest class of these, and not the archangels, principalities, authorities, powers, dominions, thrones, cherubim and seraphim above them. In Dante's *Paradiso* the poet estimated the angelic host to be *more than the thousands of moves at chess*, which would be a number with more than a hundred places in it. Wanting an even more exact figure, a Jesuit scholar later calculated the total of them to be at least 58494093197555440108325890601385984000000000000000 0000000000000000000000000, even if the real total (he surmised) was likely to be a figure 1,062 numbers long – 999 more than the count of sand grains Archimedes reckoned it would take to fill the universe. It was pointed out that the process of giving that many angels each their own name would in itself require an inordinate number of sounds, confirming the testimony of the Bible, where an angel reveals only that his name is *wonderful* (Judges 13: 18). One of Pico's contemporaries went further, saying that the number of syllables required to name all the angels would produce *unknown, stupendous words, signifying nothing according to the normal use of language*, though producing in us an irresistible desire to stoop before the angels in worship. For Dionysius the Areopagite, this faltering of language on the ascent towards the divine was the sign of approach to the final and immense silence in which the One was to be found.[6]

As the statue of Mithra at the court in Ferrara suggested, the Abrahamic faiths were far from having a monopoly on angels: the word itself, from the Greek *angelos*, or 'messenger', appears already in the Homeric poems as a title for wing-footed Hermes, who both bore instructions from the gods to men and guided men to their destined place in his role as *psychopompos*, or leader-of-souls, while Hesiod spoke of as many as 30,000 such go-betweens, tasked with mediating between the human and the divine. By the time of Plato these *daemones* had again multiplied, and each individual was believed to have their own guardian spirit, an entity whom the Romans would call a person's *genius*, a word suggestively close to the Arabic term for these beings, *jinn*, which was eventually retranslated into French as 'genie'. The early Greek arrangement, in which demons stood between man and heaven and angels were go-betweens from the underworld, was later inverted when blended with Jewish and Persian beliefs, with *angels* becoming associated with the *mal'ak* of the Bible and *demons* with Lucifer and his followers. The scattered mentions of angels in the Bible were drawn together and mixed with other traditions during efforts to chart the systems of the heavens: while not all angels in the Bible were winged – requiring instead ladders to ascend to heaven – increasingly this became their distinguishing feature, and the suggestion that their central role was the production of heavenly music was fused with Greek ideas about the harmony of the spheres, increasingly associated with choirs of angels whose speech took on that irresistible quality described by Plato. *So enamoured was I of it*, Dante writes of his encounter with angelic song in the *Paradiso, that at last there was nothing else which bound me with such sweet chains.* This led perhaps inevitably to questions about the language used by angels: Dante suggested that their intellects were so powerful that they did not need words to communicate, and indeed made themselves *entirely known to each other* by their thoughts alone, raising further questions about whether those that shared their thoughts so completely could really be considered separate beings; Pico himself was to speculate that there was in a sense only one of each kind of angel, defined by the kind of thought they shared. So intermingled had the various traditions of ethereal beings become that it was hard to resist the conclusion that they all drew upon some shared truth, witnesses to a universal intuition – as, in a sense, they did.[7]

The challenge that Pico had set for Ficino, following on from his translation of the entire works of Plato, was also to render into Latin the writings of Plotinus, the follower of Plato who was felt to provide the best explanation of the secrets hidden in Plato's writings. Plato had spoken only in riddling fables about the relationship between the One first thing that unifies existence and the many things that emanate from it, and his followers were eager to have clearer and fuller answers about the structure of this universe. As is the case with any successful idea, those who followed in Plato's wake elaborated from his philosophy a variety of systems of bewildering complexity, turning his philosophy into a mystery cult accessible only to the studious initiate. In the third to fifth centuries of the Christian era this group of philosophers, mostly from the Eastern Mediterranean and North Africa, traversed the known world in search of clarification: Plotinus was said by his student and biographer Porphyry to have travelled east from Alexandria driven by a desire to learn Persian and Indian philosophy, while Porphyry's student Iamblichus (whom Ficino was later to translate) delved into the mysteries of Egyptian religion. In doing so they were following teasing hints in Plato's own works that suggested his wisdom was not so much of his own making as an ancient knowledge that he was simply passing on; one of Plato's works records the belief that the Greeks were mere children compared to the Egyptians, condemned repeatedly to forget the great truths that they discovered, whereas the Egyptians kept them safe by writing them in secret letters or *hieroglyphs*, which they carved upon the stone of their temples. By the time of the Roman empire this had developed into a firm conviction that Plato had himself studied under the priests in Egypt.[8]

It made sense, then, to look for the missing pieces of the puzzle elsewhere, and there was ample confirmation that they were right, that there was indeed a way of understanding that had been scattered across the world, though it remained nowhere complete and the fragments were often puzzling. In Persia the Zoroastrians worshipped fire as the primal element, and a central Zoroastrian ritual involves the priest covering his face while he chants himself into an ecstatic state, just as Socrates had during his conversation with Phaedrus. In India there was a fire ritual also, and a belief that at the heart of being was *Bráhman*, a kind of divine speech, which was captured in the Vedic poems and chants that were kept and recited by the Brahmin. Like the knowledge of the Greeks, the meaning of these Vedas had been many times lost and rediscovered, and in fact was often intentionally obscured by the adding of nonsense syllables to the words of the ancient hymns to make them fit into various rhythmic patterns, exhibiting precisely that kind of troubling Asiatic use of sound Pico had been considering. Those who mastered these apparently meaningless formulas, or *shastras*, had at their disposal a weapon of immense power, such as the shastra known as 'Brahma's Head' which the hero Arjuna is given in the epic poem the *Mahabharata*: it is said to *spew forth thousands of tridents, deadly clubs, venomous snake-like missiles, capable of killing evil spirits, powerful demons*; to be, indeed, the *weapon that will atomize the world at the end of time.*[9]

From their findings the followers of Plato filled out the gaps in the master's account, a system in which the soul remembers its belonging to a primal oneness through experiences like that of beauty. In the words of Plotinus, beauty is *something that is perceived at the first glance, something which the Soul names as from an ancient knowledge and, recognizing, welcomes it, enters into unison with it*, and which brings about *wonderment and a delicious trouble, longing and love and a trembling that is all delight*, a *Dionysiac exultation that thrills through your being, this straining upwards of all your soul, this longing to break away from the body and live sunken within the veritable self*. Indeed, not just man but all of existence can be seen to be in love with itself in this way: *We cannot think of the universe as a soulless habitation*, Plotinus says, *however vast and varied, a thing of materials easily told off, kind by kind – wood and stone and whatever else there be, all blending into a cosmos: it must be alert throughout, every member living by its own life*, with all parts endlessly drawn to each other by desire. This was what explained the constant copulation of one thing with another, their joining together to create infinite new forms. These followers of Plato believed it possible to influence this attentive world through the use of magical talismans and perhaps most powerfully through the use of incantation and music, to make some things of the world enamoured with other things and draw the two together; the word used for this union of things was the ancient Greek term to express the joining of things together like the links in a chain – *synapse*. While the true form of this magic worked in concert with the primal unity, evil men could turn it from its rightful use and employ it for other means, acting directly upon the things of this world. Some believed that these rhythms and harmonies worked directly on the things themselves, while others that they worked instead upon the attendant spirits linked to their essences, which meant that there were as many of these spirits as there were things in the world. The Neoplatonist philosopher Iamblichus records the number of books that had already by his time been written trying to record the partitions of the divine beings: 6,525 books by one Egyptian priest, while another wrote a hundred books each on the kinds of spirits called *etherials* and *empyreans*, and another thousand on *celestials*. A later theory suggested that the gods prayed to by the Greeks and Romans were just one part of this greater pantheon. The use of mysterious and barbaric tongues was better for communicating with these gods because these languages were older, and also because they were more firmly connected to the things they describe, like the onomat-opoeic words 'bark', 'laugh', *poppysma* – which do not just use an agreed term but, rather, reproduce the sounds they refer to. Moreover, there were many things in these languages that could not be expressed in other tongues, the power that they wielded being lost in the act of translation.[10]

The similarities between the theory of angels developed by Dionysius the Areopagite and the universe of spirits or godlings developed by Plato's followers was hard to avoid. Some were beginning to suspect that Dionysius could not have lived as early as he did, could not indeed have been a companion of St Paul, but for others this was simply evidence that the same truth was rais-ing its head at different times and in different places. Following this logic, it was perfectly sensible to believe that while the Christian scriptures may have been the highest form of revelation, they did not have a monopoly on the truths about the universe, and those things left confused and obscure in Christian writings could be supplemented by these other witnesses to an ancient truth, even if few dared suggest that pagan writings could be given more than a supporting role. Certainly, Ficino needed no convin-cing of the importance of this tradition nor of the worth of translating Plotinus as Pico suggested: he had in fact already translated a text called the *Pimander*, believed to have been writ-ten by a shadowy figure called Hermes Trismegistus, which was thought to be among the oldest texts recording this system of beliefs held by the Egyptians and passed down to other cultures.

Mosaic inlay portraying Hermes Trismegistus, from the floor of Siena Cathedral

Others believed that the Egyptians were not the only source of this wisdom. A major proponent of this theory was Gemistos Plethon, a Byzantine Greek who had come to Italy in the early fifteenth century, who claimed to have synthesized the thought of the Brahmins and the Persians and the Greeks, and who planned a radical programme to revive the cult of ancient Greek gods in the present day, along the lines laid down by Plato's followers. Plethon pronounced that the same revelation about the world had been given to the ancient Persians through the figure of Zoroaster,

whose teachings he first encountered among a sect of Jewish poly-
theists in Crete, and who was believed to have lived 5,000 years
before the Siege of Troy. Writing to a friend in Hungary, Ficino
laid out the various branches of this complex genealogy through
which the deepest mysteries of existence were supposed to have
been transmitted over the millennia: *through the wish of divine
providence to attract to itself in wondrous fashion all men in accordance with their intellectual ability, it came about that a religious
philosophy arose long ago among the Persians thanks to Zoroaster
and among the Egyptians thanks to Hermes, without any discrep-
ancy between the two. The doctrine was then sustained among the
Thracians under Orpheus*, Ficino continues, *but it was finally
consummated at Athens by the Divine Plato.*[11]

In this heady atmosphere of discovery and revelation, there
inevitably arose people who claimed to have mastered this
ancient tradition and to be the bearers of its powers in the present. One such figure was the popular prophet Giovanni da
Correggio, who called himself 'Mercurio', and who in 1484 made
a memorable appearance in Rome. He was accompanied by two
attendants carrying a book and a sword and dressed in sky-blue
liveries bearing a curious insignia, of mountains surmounted by
thunderclouds and sending out lightning bolts. Mercurio himself
rode upon an ass dressed in a white shirt upon which was represented a bloody head. In his hand he carried a slender reed as a
staff, and from his saddle hung a basket containing a skull and
two boxes, which read *full for the Full, empty for the Empty*. On
his head he wore a crown of thorns, and above that a silver cres-
cent upon which was written: *This is my servant Pimander, whom
I have chosen. This Pimander is my supreme and waxing child, in
whom I am well pleased.* After passing through the Vatican, he
entered the city through the Caelimontine gate and preached a
sermon outside of San Giovanni Laterano, which ended by him
removing the skull from its basket and striking it three times

with his reed staff. Copies of the sermon were distributed bearing the following title:

> I, Giovanni Mercurio of Correggio, the Angel of Wisdom and Pimander, with a loud voice in the greatest and sublime ecstasy of Christ, preach this water of the kingdom for the few.

According to one of Mercurio's disciples, a man called Lazzarelli who took the name of the prophet Enoch, the crescendo of this astounding performance came with Mercurio depositing his costume upon the altar of St Peter's church, the most holy site in Western Christendom.[12]

Mercurio was later to claim that his authority came from having *mastered all the ancient knowledge of the Hebrews, Greeks and Latins*, though he said he had surpassed them all, *being conversant in all the knowledge of this world, understanding all mysteries and secrets of nature*. In him we see a version of Pico's aspirations to a universal philosophy, though as if reflected in a circus mirror: it is clear that Mercurio's act relied heavily upon creating a messianic aura through gesturing to arcane symbols and texts, taking advantage of people's impulsive need to decode what they do not understand, and to treat the solution to these puzzles as a revelation that marked them out as one of the elect. Yet for all the differences in substance between the projects of Mercurio and Pico, they shared a fascination with some of the core ideas inherited from the ancient world. According to Mercurio's disciple Enoch, the Master obtained his powers and indeed could transfer them to others through an *operation* in which certain words were sung in a peculiar manner, transforming the listener by the infusion of a spirit into them, much like the breathing of God during the act of Creation. This strange operation was later to form part of Pico's thinking about the relationship between language and the deeper textures of existence.[13]

Though in the excitement of discovery this current of thought tended to race ahead of itself and make hasty assumptions about the history of these texts and figures, it was perhaps understandable in the circumstances. The world of the Italian humanists was being flooded with newly available materials from across much of the known world and stretching back to the beginnings of writing, and it was clear that many of the same intuitions and beliefs had been recorded in widely separated times and places. Many of these beliefs related centrally to the experience of sound and rhythm, and cultures as widely separated as India and Egypt had drawn strikingly similar conclusions from the nature of these experiences. Indeed, as the geographic horizons of Europe expanded, it would become clear that these experiences and these conclusions were not confined to the world known to the ancients, but were instead to be found in lands of which the classical world had no knowledge or conception. To be living in the time when all things become clear is a heady feeling, and the race to find the key that had tied all these things together was understandably heated. Pico, however, never seems to have considered that there were others in the race: like the leader of the pack, he saw and thought only of the finishing line.

VIII

Panurge in Paris

The belief that ancient Greek philosophy had been gathered from the wise men of Egypt and India developed over time into a profound conviction that the love of learning was inseparable from a rootless and restless desire to journey in search of thoughts foreign to the thinker. In the words of St Jerome, translator of the Bible into Latin, we *read in old histories of those who traversed whole provinces, sought out new peoples, and crossed oceans to see the faces of those only known from books.* The letter in which these words appear had recently been used as a preface to the first book printed in Europe, which meant that those who read Gutenberg's Bible in Jerome's Vulgate translation would begin with the story of how Plato had forsaken Athens to become *a pilgrim and a pupil,* seeking to learn from others rather than keeping his own counsel, *pursuing knowledge across the whole world almost, captured by pirates and finally sold to a cruel tyrant, a captive, a bondsman, and a slave.* The legends of Plato's adventures in quest of ideas were only surpassed for Jerome by the travels of the late-antique philosopher Apollonius of Tyana, who travelled through Albania, the Caucasus and Persia, eventually reaching India, where he found the Indian sage Hyarcas sitting on a throne, drinking from a magical cup and discoursing with the Brahmin on the secrets of nature. As Pico would have learned from his copy of Philostratus' *Life of Apollonius*, the philosopher's return to

Alexandria went by way of the Elamites, the Babylonians, the Chaldeans, the Medes, the Assyrians, Parthians, the Syrians, the Phoenicians, the Arabs and the Palestinians, until he eventually reached Ethiopia, land of the *gymnosophists*, masters of meditation and bodily control. Jerome exhorted the Christian faithful to follow the example of these philosopher-explorers, and Pico – who was to be compared to these two great itinerant seekers in his nephew's biography – was soon on the move again, this time towards Paris.[1]

To many of Pico's humanist friends his desire to visit Paris may have seemed a move backwards, away from the light of the ancient world towards the obscurantist thicket of scholastic thought to which the fashion now stood so vociferously opposed. The great humanist Erasmus, who was a student at the University of Paris a decade after Pico, was to describe it bitterly as a barren place, where those who *spend their lives in sheer hair-splitting and sophistical quibbling . . . exhaust the intelligence by a kind of sterile and thorny subtlety*, and, *worst of all, by their stammering, foul, and squalid style of writing*, wrapping in darkness even the greatest mysteries of divinity. Erasmus was to joke that he was *trying with might and main to say nothing in good Latin, or elegantly, or wittily*, for by following this path he believed there was *some hope that, eventually, they will acknowledge me*. In a darker humour, Erasmus was also to suggest that the doctors of the Sorbonne kept among them as a sainted relic the skin of Epimenides, the famous Cretan who paradoxically pronounced that *all Cretans are liars*. The skin of this supreme and wrangling charlatan, who *wove such cat's cradles of syllogisms that even he himself could never untie them*, had (Erasmus facetiously wrote) been found after his death marked with mysterious lettering, and this macabre textual corpse was revered as an oracle by the professors of the Sorbonne.[2]

For all his acerbic and dismissive remarks, Erasmus was drawn to Paris for the same reason as Pico, for it was here that the flood of Arabic learning that had entered Western Christendom a few

centuries previously had catalysed the most audacious experiments made by European thought in almost a millennium. It was
at the University in Paris that the great battle had been waged over
whether the precision of Aristotle could be applied to understanding the mysteries of God's universe, and where Thomas Aquinas
and his followers, guided by the thought of Avicenna and Averroes,
sought to burrow down into the atoms of existence and understand the basis of Creation. Erasmus' jokes about hair-splitting
were pointed, as questions about such matters as the *minima
naturalia* – the smallest possible fragments into which the matter
of the world could be divided – were precisely the kind of thing
that interested the scholastics. Returning to the head-spinning
paradoxes that so troubled Plato, there were those who argued that
change would not be able to make its way across an infinitely divisible universe – being faced with an infinite number of steps
through which to travel – though setting a limit on division also
seemed to be one of those natural laws which threatened to limit
the omnipotence of God. In Paris as in Persia, the assertion that the
universe could be probed to its depths by reason quickly prompted
a backlash from those who saw this as an offence to the dignity
of the Divine, and who argued (as al-Ghazali had) that God's
absolute power to create things according to his will meant that the
complete submission of reason to faith was the only possible
response. At the centre of the controversy once again was the
idea that the boundary between human minds was artificial and
temporary, and much as Aquinas tried to distance himself from
the Universal Intellect of the *falasifa* it was no good: in 1277
more than 200 ideas by *the cursed Averroes* were condemned as
heretical, and with them the entire body of thought by Aquinas
and Aristotle became a subject of scandal and danger.[3]

The temptation to search for a single, unifying code – to which
all things could be reduced and which allowed all things to be
converted into one another – proved, however, time and again irresistible in the centuries that followed Aristotle and in which his

influence often reigned unchallenged. There was even a popular boardgame that survived to Pico's time from late antiquity called the *Rhythmomachia*, supposedly handed down by a disciple of Pythagoras, in which players practised converting arithmetical, geometrical and harmonic proportions, learning how numbers and shapes and sounds were all essentially the same. Driven by similar impulses, Pico also travelled in these early years to the University of Pavia in part to learn more about the *calculatores*, a group of Aristotelian thinkers who believed that all aspects of nature could be converted to number and described mathematically. In a move that foreshadowed the quantitative fetish of modern science, this early-fourteenth-century movement added to the various physical measurements a new way of plotting the change in a quality over time, with Nicholas of Oresme producing what might be considered the first graphs, so reducing even abstract phenomena to digitization. Pico apparently reserved a particular disdain for this group of early data scientists, suggesting that their attempts to reduce the mysteries of the universe to mere statistics served only to *smear their side in infamy*. This dismissal anticipated the criticism of the new experimental science that was repeatedly voiced in the seventeenth century, only largely to be silenced: while ever more exact observation could produce an infinitude of knowledge about a thing, it rarely took us any closer to what we really wanted to know, a sense of its essence, leaving us no more satisfied.[4]

For all Pico's dismissal of the *calculatores*, his fascination with the idea of a unifying code remained undiminished, and he gravitated towards Paris where the systematic thought of Aristotle, Averroes and Aquinas was once again precariously enshrined at the centre of the curriculum. The craze for these theories was driven at least in part by the bitterness and anger of those teaching the undergraduate arts courses in Paris, who rankled against the assumption that what they were teaching the students was merely an ornament and a foundation to the more serious study of theology and the Church careers to which that opened the door.

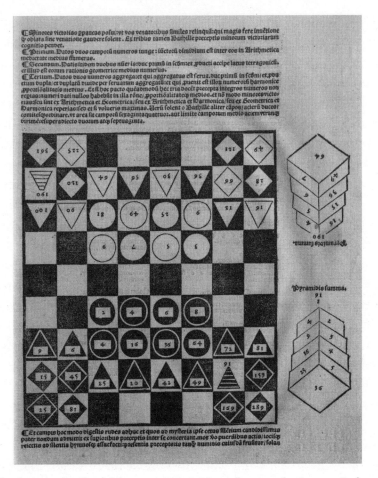

Rhythmomachia board from a 1496 giuide to the game by Jacques Lefevre d'Etaples

Never grow old in the arts was the mocking phrase recited around the Latin Quarter, warning the young that an obsession with such things foreshadowed a lifetime of penury and unemployment. The professors of arts responded by pointedly teaching their students precisely those parts of philosophy that shone light on the hollow places of the Christian faith, breeding generations of students with a polished disdain for the humdrum nature of Church orthodoxy and the dull business of priesthood.[5]

The Aristotelian craze also opened the floodgates to a vast body of writings attributed to The Philosopher, books in which the master was supposed to have pronounced upon all those things that remained unresolved in the near-encyclopaedic canon of his works. Everywhere these works spoke to the desire to harness the scalpel-sharp precision of Aristotelian thought to prise open the edges of the known world, texts of astrology and alchemy that hoped to make an instrument of the immense cosmos in which man's existence was set, and test how far the stability of matter could be pushed. One of the most famous of these was the *Problems of Aristotle*, a text that may have had a genuine origin among the writings of the philosopher but which had developed among his later followers into a vast compendium of questions dealing with the mysteries of existence – a number that rounded off at 900, precisely the number of theses that Pico was soon to propose for argument in Rome. Among the problems encountered in the text we find: *Why do the one who is having sex and the one who is dying cast their eyes up, whereas the one who is sleeping casts them down? Why does one sneeze twice in most cases, and neither once nor many times?* A great many of these problems dealt with the matter of action-at-a-distance, questions to do with how things affect one another when there is no perceptible connection between them. So: *Why, in response to people yawning, do other people yawn in return?* At the centre of this conundrum was the matter of sound, of resonance and the ability of noise to produce peculiar effects. One of the questions asks, *why do some things painful to hear make us shudder – for instance, sharpening a saw, cutting a pumice stone, and grinding a stone*, also causing the roots of our hair to ring and the hairs of themselves to stand on end? Later it becomes clear that it is not only painful sounds that can have this involuntary effect upon us: in the section of the *Problems* on harmony, the questions repeatedly probe at the mystery of music. *Why does what is heard, alone of perceptible objects, possess ethical character?* The text continues by pointing out that this is not because words can persuade us either to good or evil, as *even if a melody is without words, it nonetheless possesses ethical character; but neither colour nor smell nor flavour possesses it.* The answers provided in the text are vague and unsatisfying, suggesting that music is ethical because sound alone possesses movement, and these problems would continue to puzzle those who asked them. One of the great literary critics of recent times noted that this question was still unresolved, that we still cannot produce rules for great poetry or music or predict what will work upon us and what will not, but the presence of the real thing is often confirmed by a physical response – *the shudder*, accompanied by hair-raising and gooseflesh.[6]

It was into this raucous arena that Pico entered in 1485, at a time when tensions were further heightened by the recent accession to the French throne of the boy-king Charles VIII and the fierce battle to control the regency during his youth. The details of Pico's stay are hazy at best, though he evidently made a name for himself in Paris as he had everywhere else, as it was here that he would flee for sanctuary after the tumultuous Roman debate. Pico was later to express some disappointment at the conservatism of the Sorbonne, complaining that the opponents of Aquinas and Aristotle still had too much of a stranglehold, though he evidently took from Paris certain points of style. He would have attended the *disputations sorbonniques*, marathon debates in which the proposer was expected to stand his ground against all comers from dawn till dusk, and as well as borrowing this atmosphere of performance Pico was provocatively to announce that his *900 Theses* were framed *not ascending in the Roman style, but in imitation of the most celebrated Parisian debaters.*

Once again, the liveliest picture of Pico's stay in France comes from the folklore and legend into which it passed: decades later the unparalleled French satirist Rabelais was to create a character for his comic epic *Pantagruel* who presents an outlandish and carnivalesque imitation of Pico. The character Panurge (whose name means 'universal force') makes his entrance by introducing himself in thirteen languages, among which a number are nonsense or at least still to be decoded. Among these is a tongue called 'Lanternese' and a language from the 'Antipodes', redolent of the semitic and Slavic tongues on the fringes of the European world:

> Al barildim gotfano dech min brin alabo dordin falbroth ringuam alarbas. Nin porth zadilkin almucathim milko prin al elmin enthoth dal heben ensouim: kuth im al dim alkatim nim broth dechoth porth min michas im endoth, pruch dal maisoulum hol moth dansririm lupaldas im voldemoth. Nin hur diavloth mnar-bothim dal gousch pal frapin duch im scoth pruch galeth dal chinon, min foulthrich al conin butathen doth dal prim.

The trickster Panurge proceeds to take centre stage in Rabelais's circus-like caricature of the Europe of his day, agreeing to face all comers in a debate over 9,764 theses which are posted up at every crossroads in Paris. The climax comes when an English scholar travels to France to take up the challenge, and furthermore proposes *not to argue the pros and cons, as the foolish sophists of this town do,* nor *to dispute by declamation in the manner of the humanists, nor yet by numbers, as Pythagoras did and as Pico Mirandola planned to do in Rome.* Instead, the Englishman proposes only to argue by *signs,* gestures not subject to the same confusion as spoken words. In preparation for the contest, Panurge stays awake all night studying a stack of volumes which, while non-existent and entirely the product of Rabelais's imagination, read like a shelf of Pico's library:

> Bede, *On Numbers and Signs*
> Plotinus, *On the Indescribable*
> Proclus, *On Magic*
> Artemidorus, *On the Interpretation of Dreams*
> Anaxagoras, *On Symbols*

Ynarius, *On the Nameless*
The works of Philistion
Hipponax, *On the Unspeakable*

Needless to say, Panurge goes on to wipe the floor with his
English opponent, constructing an argument out of apparently
grotesque signs (such as thumbing his nose and poking his fore-
finger in and out of a ring), which his opponent nevertheless
accepts as incontestable evidence of genius. Rabelais's affectionate mockery of his predecessor Pico, with its sense that the
deepest of mysteries are being treated in a language entirely
incomprehensible to the audience, captures some of the atmosphere of the time—the sense that man was on the verge of getting
responses to some of the most fundamental problems of existence, though it was an open question whether he would
understand the answers he received.

Though Aquinas had publicly and vociferously distanced
himself from some of these fundamental problems contained in
Arabic thought, such as the idea of the Universal Intellect and its
worrying implications, Pico was to trace the path of others entirely
willing to plunge into the depths of these matters. In his writings
Pico followed a line of thought back through the thirteenth-
century English scholar Roger Bacon to the work of the earliest
failasūf al-Kindi and a model of the universe in which all things
are related to each other by the 'rays' or beams of energy that
emanated from them. At the heart of this vision sat the experience
of speech, which if used correctly was capable of focusing these
rays and directing them to specific ends. *Certain people*, the work
De Radiis ('On Rays') explains, by *studying the secrets of both the
higher and lower nature . . . have found the forms of the utterances
and names that are efficacious for producing motion in things.* Once
again, the argument returns to the same observations made by
many others: that often these utterances *signify nothing*, many are

combined *without the laws of grammar*, do not seem to be complete sentences, can often be uttered backwards as well as forwards, and often work when sung or chanted but not otherwise. Most troublingly, al-Kindi writes that *the will of a person is changed through speaking certain words, so that he desires something which if his will ran its natural course he would not want. Thus the favour of rulers is acquired through speaking certain words, and women are roused to love people, and in general, by words pronounced with due ceremony, every kind of power in every kind of living creature can be transformed.*[7]

While al-Kindi's treatment of these subjects remained on a theoretical level, there were others prepared to go further, providing collections of these utterances or spells that work upon the listener. The most famous of these works in Pico's day was the *Picatrix*, a translation of the Arabic work *Ghāyat al-hakīm*, or 'The Goal of the Wise', which records secret ways of achieving 2,325 desirable outcomes through a variety of potions and spells to be uttered at specific moments of astrological alignment. The author of the work was then unknown and is still disputed, though Rabelais jokingly suggested that it was written by the Reverend Father-in-the-Devil Picatris, head of the Diabological Faculty at Toledo. Although the *Picatrix* declares in grandiose terms that its science of magic is *too deep and powerful for the intellect*, the ends towards which its powers are directed are often touchingly modest, cures for lovesickness and ways of gaining the favour of the powerful, painting a revealing portrait of the lives of those who sought its help. One section describing how to make a young woman fall for a young man involves the crafting of metal figurines of the pair and *in the hour of Mercury* to *join them in an embrace, and wrap the hands of each around the sides of the other*, promising that once this charm is made and buried the two will fall in love *and have high-quality sex*. Many of the spells involving sounds and symbols show the immense power wielded by the shapes and patterns of language: the incantation for a scorpion sting must be written

Arabic talisman to protect against scorpion bites, 10th century, Louvre

precisely in seven lines and have the six-pointed star, symbol of
Solomon, at the end:

> zaare zaare raam zaare zaare
> fegem bohorim borayn nesfis albune
> fedraza affetihe taututa tanyn zabahat
> aylatricyn haurane rahannie ayn latumine
> queue acatyery nimieri quibari yehuyha
> nuyym latrityn hamtauery vueryn
> catuhe cahuene cenhe beyne ✡

Strikingly, the practice of writing segments of verse on different
lines here appears as a kind of magic: the shape of the lines on the
page reflects the experience of hearing it, breaking language up

105

THE GRAMMAR OF ANGELS

into shards that reflect upon each other like a kaleidoscope. In other places the spellbook prescribes the writing of symbols in an unspeakable language, as in the inscription *So that a person you desire comes running to you or to a specific place*:

The most powerful of these rituals involve bringing together those things at the heart of people's intimacy, in hopes of directing the aura generated by the sacred and the private elsewhere. One such passage instructs the reader how to summon a storm by making a mirror of blood and anointing it with semen as well as the smoke from a burning lock of a woman's hair, before writing upon it *the names of the seven stars, their seven figures, the seven angels and the seven winds*. The collections of magic words are often merely parallel lists of names for things in different languages, as if by putting back together the fragments of language scattered across the tongues of the world the essence of the thing itself could be recovered. *If you gaze into that mirror and guard it well, know that through it you will bring together men, winds, spirits, demons, the living, and the dead. All shall be obedient to you and heed your command.* While many would simply dismiss these books as so much foolish superstition, they provide a poignant witness to the raw experience of language, of how in its sounds and symbols and its arrangement upon a writing surface it shocks us into feelings that lie outside the normal bounds of everyday life.[8]

Many including Pico protested their disdain for this debased magic, which aimed at petty victories in the here and now; for Pico's part, he also objected to the magical theory that considered these talismans and spells to be ways of focusing and directing the powers of the stars, and he was to become a leading critic of astrology in his later years. Yet even Pico could not resist an interest in these common spells, and among the books of his library was a *Book of Secrets* which claimed to be written by Albertus Magnus, and which (among many other things), contained directions for understanding the speech of birds. If a raven's eggs (it says) are cooked and returned to its nest, it will fly to a certain island in the sea and return with a stone; this stone will not only uncook the eggs, but will also spring a chained man from captivity by its mere touch and, if placed under the tongue, will make the voices of birds comprehensible to the listener. As with the other virtues of this stone, there is a strong sense that when sucked it reverses the normal order of things, returning the user to an earlier, more primal and perhaps more powerful stage of speech.[9]

There were plenty of learned people who took seriously the implications of such powers circulating among the peoples of the world. While Roger Bacon reassured his readers that such magical words could not compromise the free will of those to whom they were spoken, his interest in the rays of al-Kindi and other parts of natural magic was driven by a fear that ignoring them would mean losing an arms race with Muslims and heretics. In his plea to the Church to make these things weapons for good he was able to point to several instances within the memory of his contemporaries in which crowds of people had been drawn unstoppably to their deaths by those who wielded over them an irresistible power. Describing the thirteenth-century mass delusions during the Children's Crusade and Shepherd's Crusade, Bacon writes:

> Perhaps you saw or heard for a certainty that the children of the kingdom of France once followed in countless numbers after an evil man, so that they could not be restrained by fathers, mothers, friends, and were placed on board of ships and sold to Saracens. This event happened less than sixty-four years ago. Likewise in our times the Shepherd leader stirred up all Germany and France,

107

and drew to him a multitude of men, and had favour in the sight of the whole body of the laity in contempt of the clergy and to the confusion of the Church. [. . .] The wise should not doubt that they were emissaries of the Tartars and Saracens, and that they had some means by which they fascinated the people.

Closer to Pico's time reports had circulated of a handsome and well-dressed man of 30 who had appeared upon the feast of St John and St Paul in the German town of Hameln (later 'Hamelin') and by playing on a certain *strangely shaped silver pipe* drew after him 130 children from the town out of the Eastern Gate to the place called Calvary *and they disappeared and no-one knew where they had gone to.* The powerlessness of priests and even mothers to restrain those who fell under the influence of these forces speaks to the terrifying strength that could be wielded over people by these means.[10]

Though a great many works were made available to European readers during the centuries-long obsession with the occult knowledge of the Arabs, the finding of one text in particular is perhaps without parallel in the history of book-hunting stories, a narrative rabbit hole of successively astounding encounters. This was the discovery of the *Kitāb sirr al-khalīqa,* which Hugo of Santalla found in the library of the Banū Hūd dynasty at their fortress of Rueda Jalón, to which they had been chased west from Saragossa by the puritanical Almoravid dynasty, who were advancing across Muslim Spain in the eleventh century. The cosmopolitan Banū Hūd gave access to their well-stocked library to the Christian kingdoms to the north, and there among the most secret parts of the library Hugo found a book claiming to be by none other than that Apollonius of Tyana who had traversed the known world and stood for Jerome as the model of the restless mind. Hugo would translate the book for his patron Michael, Bishop of Tarazona, as the *Book of the Secrets of Nature.* The book relates how Apollonius had uncovered a secret vault beneath a statue of Hermes in his native Tyana, and descending into it he had come upon an ancient corpse sitting on a golden throne and holding in his hands a tablet made of a single gemstone. This engraved jewel came to be known as the *Tabula Smaragdina* from the Arabic word for emerald (*zumurrud*), certain enormous specimens of which were rumoured to have existed in the ancient world, and the *Tabula* purported to bear the inscription of nothing less than the words of the Egyptian priest-god Hermes Trismegistus, whose cadaver had held the slab through countless generations.[11]

Some, though, connected the text with an even more astonishing origin and antiquity. Stories dating back to the first century told of two pillars erected by the grandchildren of Adam upon which they carved the secret knowledge of the first man to preserve it against destruction by time and tide. One pillar made of brick had been swept away in the Great Flood, but the other was made of stone to stand against these onslaughts and was reputed still to be standing somewhere in the Syrian desert. Others believed that these carvings were made not by Adam's grandchildren but, rather, by the Egyptian king Sesostris, and associated the pillars with the hieroglyph-covered obelisks that could still be seen in Pico's day, scattered around Rome. Hugo promised that whoever studied the words of the Emerald Tablet would *obtain the leadership in philosophy over all his contemporaries*. The *intricate web of words* spun by Hermes said that

> Just as all things came from one thing
> So the working of wonders is from one
> By the carrying out of the plan . . .
> This operation has its existence
> By the fabric of the heavens.
> This is what Hermes the Philosopher calls
> The Triple Wisdom or the Triple Science.

Overleaf: A depiction of the discovery of the *Tabula Smaragdina*, 1602

These words as they appeared to their European readers from the twelfth century on were the product of an odyssey of wonders: a text written on an immense jewel, found by a great ancient philosopher-magician in the hands of a dead god buried in a hidden chamber, and preserved within the secret library of a doomed Arabic dynasty. The fabulous nature of its provenance, however, was in some senses only a way of expressing the explosive nature of the message that it contained, the same message that had reared its head time and again despite the best efforts of a great many to put an end to it – that in their origins *all things are one*, that this primal state can be called forth by those who know the correct method, and that to the one who did so was promised unthinkable power over the world.[12]

The later emergence of more such texts in equally astounding circumstances makes it begin to feel as if there is a fateful link between certain writings and the strange manner of their discovery. Some time later in Egypt, a little way north of the Valley of the Kings at a place called Nag Hammadi, as a farmer dug for rich soil at the foot of a cliff, a jar was revealed, which he held back from opening for fear that it might contain a *djinn* – which, in a sense, it did. The jar had been sealed in accordance with the instructions given to the biblical prophet Jeremiah to take indispensable documents and *put them in an earthen vessel, that they may continue many days*. The Nag Hammadi jar contained a library of twelve books and fragments of a thirteenth, containing within them fifty-two works, which had been buried as the Tenth Legion of the Roman army advanced on Upper Egypt. The legion had recently been converted, with the rest of the empire, to the new imperial cult of Christianity, and it was reasonable to fear that these books would not escape destruction at their arrival. Among the writings in this sealed library was another text that claimed to be transcribed from the Steles of Seth, containing the wisdom inherited from Seth's grandfather Adam, and which recorded the hymns or prayers that could transport the singer on an ecstatic voyage through the heavens. There were also in the jar sequences of meaningless vowels and magical words, and an account of what was said by a certain female entity called *Thunder, Perfect Mind*:

> I am the honoured one and the scorned one,
> I am the whore and the holy one,
> I am the wife and the virgin . . .
> I am the silence that is incomprehensible
> and the idea whose remembrance is frequent.
> I am the voice whose sound is manifold
> And the word whose appearance is multiple.
> I am the utterance of my name . . .
> Why then have you hated me, you Greeks?
> Because I am a barbarian among the barbarians?
> For I am the wisdom of the Greek
> and the knowledge of the barbarians. . . .
> Hear me, you hearers
> and learn my words, you who know me.
> I am the hearing that is attainable to everything;
> I am the speech that cannot be grasped.
> I am the name of the sound
> and the sound of the name.

The library that was found at the foot of the cliff in Nag Hammadi contained an immense reservoir of a culture that had been almost entirely lost and had even been thought by some to have been a fiction: the Gnostic cult that flourished in Egypt in late antiquity, and which attempted (as Pico would) to weave together the many subtle knowings of their world. But Pico would be long dead before this treasury was uncovered; the discoveries at Nag Hammadi followed shortly on from the withdrawal of German troops from El Alamein and from the North African theatre of the Second World War.[13]

Pico arrived back in Florence from his year in Paris during the early months of 1486. By the end of the year he would be in Rome and his *Theses* would be pinned across the city and flowing inland, ideas which Pico expected would make him (in the words of the poet Pindar) *glorious in the mouths of men*. Before that could happen, though, a great many things lay in store.[14]

IX

The Death of the Kiss

P ico arrived back from Paris with an appetite for secret knowledges from the peripheries of Europe and beyond, and in
service of this he formed a connection with a man calling himself
Flavius Mithridates, the same who had preached in tongues at
Rome in 1481 and then been chased out under circumstances hard
to establish. Mithridates had set himself up as a sort of black
marketeer of the intellectual world, peddling ideas and texts that
were only spoken about in hushed tones and behind closed doors,
which made him the perfect partner for Pico's undertaking to set
aside all the polite boundaries of thought and gaze into the beyond.
Mithridates picked up where Pico's former tutor Elia del Medigo
had discreetly withdrawn, supplying the texts and techniques that
were considered by others disreputable or worse. Among the
translations Mithridates was working on at this time was a tract,
On the Resurrection of the Dead, by the Jewish philosopher
Maimonides, in which he pronounces that the idea that people will
someday return and look and live as they had before was merely a
fable, a promise to lure simple folk into following the commandments. It was obvious, Maimonides said, that in the eternal
hereafter there can be no eating or drinking or sexual intercourse,
all aspects of a transitory and changing mortal world, and that
therefore the resurrected beings could not have mouths or stom-
achs or livers or genitals, as these would be without purpose. The

truth of the afterlife, Maimonides cautioned, was only to be discussed among the learned, as most people are fixated on these questions of whether in eternity they will be naked or clothed, and cannot begin to contemplate the unbounded manner in which those ever after must exist.[1]

Pico's tutor Mithridates had come by this traffic in forbidden thought as his birthright, hailing as he did from one of the last cosmopolitan outposts in a Europe increasingly intolerant of outsiders and their ways of thinking. He had been born Samuel ben Sabbetai al-Faraj in Sicily, part of the large Jewish community who lived unghettoized among the Arab aristocrats, Coptic Christians and Greeks who populated the island, which had once been integrated into the Islamic Maghreb. Many of the Sicilian Jews still used Arabic as their lingua franca, and served as translators between Italian-speaking Christians and Arabic-speaking Muslims from Tripoli and Djerba, writing things down when they had to in Hebrew letters to avoid drawing unwanted attention to themselves by the use of the Arabic script. Here as elsewhere in Europe the position of the Jews was increasingly fraught, in part because preachers of the mendicant orders had recognized the ease with which popular anger could be directed at the Jewish populations in their midst. Samuel ben Sabbetai converted and was christened Guglielmo Raimondo Moncada after the local noble who served as his godfather, and moved to Naples to study for the priesthood. He seems, however, at an early stage to have realized that as well as being a source of danger his status as a cultural mongrel was a saleable commodity, and before long he had moved to Rome, attached himself to the circle of a prominent cardinal, and renamed himself Flavius Mithridates, though he also variously went by Flavius Siculeus, Flavius Romanus and Flavius Chaldaeus. The name Mithridates seems to have been chosen as a reference to an ancient King of Pontus who, according to the classical encyclopaedist Pliny, had spoken a staggering twenty-two languages. The encyclopaedist and polymath Conrad Gessner later chose *Mithridates* as the title of his work that attempted to document all known languages. The name also linked Flavius to the guardians of secret knowledge passed down among poets and philosophers, meaning as it does 'Given by Mithras', the pagan god for whom Orpheus was thought to have served as priest.[2]

During his early time in Pico's employ Mithridates greatly impressed the Florentine intelligentsia. Ficino recorded an episode in which Mithridates was set in debate at Pico's house against two Jewish doctors, Elia and Abraam, who asserted that the Old Testament prophets did not at all predict the coming of Jesus Christ, but, rather, themselves made clear that they meant something entirely different. For a tense moment it seemed as if the Hebrew argument would win out, until Mithridates swooped in to snatch victory from the jaws of defeat. He pointed out that knowledge of the future could not lie in the mind of the prophet, but only in the mind of God, who uses the prophet's tongue and his imagination as His tools – were this not the case we would have to concede that even certain donkeys and birds that had predicted future events were not simply instruments of the Divine Will but, rather, visionaries themselves. This being so, the events predicted in prophecies were known only to God, hidden even from the prophets themselves until such time as He pleased to make them clear. The Prophets themselves, then, had no authority to interpret their own prophecies. *At this point the Hebrew cavillers fell silent,* Ficino writes, *Jewish sophistry was vanquished and Christian truth prevailed.*[3]

Pico set about studying languages under Mithridates, immersing himself in the Hebrew and Arabic tongues, while on the side Mithridates began to undertake an immense project of translation at Pico's behest, churning out Latin versions of Hebrew texts at such an astonishing rate that 5,000 pages seem to have been produced in the middle months of 1486. This flood of material brought to European readers for the first time the most important texts of the Jewish tradition of kabbalah, that hunt for secrets hidden within the Hebrew language, which was given by God to Adam and alone survived the confusion of tongues when the Tower of Babel fell. Pico made his way through Mithridates' translations, marking key passages as he went with a distinctive sign, a trace that can be followed through the pages of his reading: two dots side by side, with a long tail beneath like the trail of some double asteroid in the margins of the book. His excitement at the promise of kabbalah is palpable. *It is the firm opinion of all the ancients*, Pico later wrote, *unanimously asserted and beyond doubt, that the five books of the Mosaic law contain the entire knowledge of all arts and wisdom both divine and human. This knowledge is hidden and concealed, however, in the very letters of which the phrases of the law are composed.* He would find in the Hebrew writings provided by Mithridates strong echoes of the Universal Intellect of Avicenna and Averroes, which Abulafia said was also called by the name Metatron and Enoch, as well as the promise of a ladder to ascend into this realm. Pico was clearly determined to have access to these mysteries for himself and he wrote excitedly to Ficino later that year of how, after a month of ceaseless study day and night, he was able to write a letter in Hebrew, *if not quite with honour then at least without error*, and that he hoped shortly also to be able to do the same in Arabic, agreeing to return Ficino's Latin translation of the Qur'an but not just yet, as he *soon hoped to hear Mohammed speaking in his own language.*[4]

Brilliant a linguist as he may have been, Pico could not have hoped to understand the dense kabbalistic texts without the guidance of Mithridates, and the margins of the translations produced for Pico are also filled with pleas to the younger man to slow down and accept that such things could not be done at a gallop. *O Pico*, Mithridates writes alongside one passage, *great are these matters but they will be impossible for you to understand without their proper Hebrew letters and words.* In some senses, though, Pico was perfectly primed to understand the message of kabbalah, which drew upon the wonder felt by the reader at the ability of language and writing to be transmitted across vast ages and distances and then to be unlocked and once again release their ancient power. One part of the kabbalah deals for instance with *gematria*, the hidden meanings held to be contained within the very iconic shapes of the Hebrew letters, with their alluring combination of curling lines set within squared-off blocks. Pico seems to have been almost equally entranced by Arabic writing, which can seem in its fluid continuum to be a seismograph of the human soul. Anyone who has learned a new script in adulthood will know the curious sensation of feeling meaningless symbols begin to stutter into life and speak in a strange voice, and Pico was very much under the spell of foreign tongues in these months.[5]

Yet Hebrew and Arabic were not even the most prized commodities among what Mithridates was offering to Pico. As well as these distant but living tongues Pico also wrote to Ficino of how Mithridates had opened for him the gates to the ancient and forgotten tongue of the Chaldeans, the language in which the Persian prophet Zoroaster was supposed to have written down his own revelations, which paralleled those of the Egyptian Hermes. It may be that his study of these tongues inspired in this period the lost frescoes in his library at Mirandola, which featured figures in Persian and Medean dress. Pico wrote excitedly to Ficino of how *certain books in these languages have come into my hands, not randomly or by chance, but by God's counsel and the divine power favouring my studies*, listing among the Chaldean tomes a short volume on *The Doctrines of Chaldean Theology* and another in which the religion of *The Persians, Greeks, and Chaldeans* was fully explained. There were also the oracles of Ezra, Zoroaster and that Wise Man Melchior who had knelt before Christ in Bethlehem. Pico boasted that these gave him access to full and trustworthy versions of Chaldean texts, which were until then only known in mutilated Greek translations. He ended his letter to Ficino with an exclamation capturing his feelings at having acquired this trove of all but unheard-of material. *O Gracious God, God of the secret Pythagorean teaching as well as the open teaching of the ancient philosophers, a powerful prayer has suddenly invaded my breast, to be able to read and make a thorough study of these books by myself, without any intermediary. And this I am now doing: I am tirelessly and continuously turning this stone.*[6]

The concern of Pico's friends that he was venturing into forbidden territory, searching for new truths beyond the bounds of Christian orthodoxy, was unlikely to be assuaged by the air of secrecy with which Mithridates shrouded their joint study of Chaldean. Mithridates had reportedly sworn his young apprentice to silence on this subject, so that even when writing to friends of his kabbalistic studies Pico mentioned his pursuit of Chaldean only in the most vague and guarded terms. In another incident, Mithridates had flown into a rage when Pico's close friend Girolamo Benivieni had stumbled in upon their lessons in Chaldean, chasing Benivieni away in his determination that the circle on this matter should remain very small indeed. The reasons for this obsessive secrecy can be guessed at but are somewhat unclear, and are inevitably coloured by a later revelation that was not known at least to Pico at the time: that the script that Mithridates was teaching him was not in fact some ancient Levantine script, but, rather, Ge'ez, the holy and liturgical language of Ethiopia.[7]

Later tradition has written Flavius Mithridates off as a charlatan and dismissed the use of this ancient African tongue as no more than a ruse by the shifty Sicilian to win the admiration and confidence of his wealthy patron. Indeed, a similar Chaldean gambit had been used before by Sicilian Jews, with one of them a few decades before convincing a Sicilian priest that the Kufic Arabic writing above the Porta Patitelli in Palermo was Chaldean, and telling him that it recorded the foundation of Palermo by Esau, grandson of the biblical patriarch Abraham. The focus on Mithridates' motives, however, risks distracting our attention from the extraordinary fact that he had any familiarity with the Ethiopic

Opposite: A page from Flavius Mithridates' *Sermo de Passione*

& angustijs: vijs ne tu hec pati. sin minus puniã
eos. respondit messias letor: & volo hec patiẽ
caritate, ut omnes aīe mortue a protho pla(
sto per me sint salue: statuit deus. Extemplo
subijt velle pati omnes cruciatus ex amore Ex
Esaie sentencia: oblatus est quia ipse voluit.
hec ille. (Antiquissimum hyonetis oraculū
in lingua chaldea id idem affirmat ⵣⵇⵯⵕⵟⵝ

ⵀⵚⵯ: ⵇⵯⵎⵅ: +ⵌⵯⵚⵣⵔ ⵉⵔⵟⵝ · humiliabit
homo & debilitabit deus omnipotens. Vbi Rabi
Salomon · וישח אדם וישפל איש זה והק בה הם
נרמולו להראות בעבורם כאיש עדהם וכן הוא אומר
צור ילדך תשי ותשכח אל מחלליך
hoc est
humiliabit homo & debilitabit deus optim9
maximus: & pro homine efficiet velut vir
pauidus. ex secunde legis sentencia: deum
qui te genuit debilitabis & oblinisceris dm p te vul
neratum: (CAP · VIII ·

Cvm autem ad discipulos orto cum illis
tribus redijsset: ecce obstinatus animus:
spiritus inquietus: impaciens feritas: quẽ nisi

Rabi salomon

secunda lex

tongue at all, and to the clues it provides to his mysterious flight from Rome a few years earlier, when he seemed to be at the height of his fame following his virtuoso sermon in many languages. Mithridates may have first encountered the Ethiopian language through the pilgrims from that region who congregated at the church of Santo Stefano degli Abissini near the Vatican, and he was certainly studying it by 1481 when his sermon included a snippet written in Geʿez characters. Yet interest in Ethiopian culture rose to new levels later that year when an unusual embassy from the Negus of Ethiopia arrived at the papal court. The small group led by the priest *Ɨntonəs*, called by the Italians Antonius, were in fact only a tiny contingent of a delegation of thousands who set off from the Ethiopian highlands and travelled up the Nile to Cairo, charged with obtaining a representative or metropolitan from the Patriarch of Alexandria to crown their new boy king *Ɨskəndər*, or Alexander. After visiting Egypt the spectacular procession had set off for the Holy Land, but at Jerusalem the Guardian of Mount Zion (as the ranking Franciscan was grandiosely titled) persuaded the leading Ethiopians that other Christians were merely heretics, and that an envoy from Rome was needed to confer true legitimacy on the coronation. A small party accordingly set off for Rome, guided by an Arabic-speaking Italian through whom they were able to converse, and arrived before Advent 1481.[8]

Although the Ethiopians made an immense impression on Roman society with their native garb, which was captured in not one but two frescoes that were then being painted on the walls of the Sistine Chapel, the mission was not without complications. They were received by Pope Sixtus, who publicly conducted Mass with them in a show of favour, and the Ethiopians in turn requested that men learned in the Catholic rites be sent back with them, in return for which they offered to launch a crusade against the Mamluks in Cairo and use a dam to *disrupt the flooding of the Nile, which the Moors fear greatly.* However, despite the Pope's best efforts and stern commands, he was unable to find anyone willing to return to Ethiopia with the emissaries. Given Mithridates' public displays of his Arabic learning, and the fact that he was already studying the Ethiopic script before the embassy arrived, it is hard to believe that he was not among those the Pope had in mind for this mission. If this was the case, his reluctance was understandable: as he might have learned from Ǝntonǝs or from other rumours circulating through the Sicilian ports, those Europeans who arrived in Ethiopia were seldom allowed to leave and remained in comfortable captivity to monarchs who wanted to retain their exotic skills and knowledge. Although a dozen clerics were eventually rounded up for the purpose and were sent to Venice in mid-1482 to await transport to Alexandria, the delegation fell out when a certain man showed up claiming to be head of the mission, which caused the others to resign, *not without arousing the indignation of the pope.* The whole affair ended in disaster, with the Ethiopian delegation never making it further towards home than Jerusalem, where one of their number converted to Islam and Ǝntonǝs was rumoured to have pawned the Pope's presents to the Ethiopian king and to have squandered the profits in dissipated living. While there is no concrete evidence that Mithridates was involved in the affair, the debacle in Venice smacks of his trademark blend of high learning and low imposture, and his spectacular fall from favour in this period might be explained by a refusal to go to Ethiopia or an attempt to hijack the mission – or, perhaps more in keeping with Mithridates' unpredictability, both.[9]

Whatever the case, Mithridates' decision to learn the Geʽez script used by the Ethiopian church should not be dismissed as an attempt to deceive. There was in fact widespread confusion and uncertainty about the identity of the ancient Chaldeans, and, given the associations between the Chaldean Hymns and the biblical Magi or Wise Men, it made sense to associate the language with the African kingdoms from which the magus Balthasar was held to have come. Other accounts of the 1481 embassy referred to it as Chaldean, and there is a copy of the psalms in Geʽez in the Vatican

እርሱ፡ ፋኩሬ፡ ዘዴይቀኜ፡ ወንዋዋእ፡
በዋዐ፡ በእሒ፡ ዘእሐሬ፡ በዎ፡
ወእቆሎ፡ ወዕት፡ ፋኘ፡ ዋኘእ፡
ወእ፡ ነከሬ፡ ወስት፡ ከበ፡ መስተስን፡
ዘዴእወ፡ ሐን፡ እግዘእብሔር፡ ከዎኑ፡
ወሐን፡ ደነ፡ በከ፡ ማዐልት፡ ወለት፡
ወደከው፡ ከመ፡ ዕወ፡ እንተ፡ ተከለት፡
ኗበወ፡ንዘ፡ ማይ፡
እንተ፡ ተሁ፡ ፋሬ ሃ፡ በበዘዜሃ፡
ዐቲ ሕለፊ፡ እደትነገራ፡
ወከኡሱ፡ ዘገብሬ፡ ሃደ፡ ደዐ፡
እስ፡ ከወዘ፡ ዋእነ፡ ከ፡ እ ወዘ

Library – perhaps the very one from which Mithridates learned the script – which is labelled *A Psalter in the Chaldean or Ethiopic Language*. There was also an ecstatic cult in Ethiopia called the *Zar*, and the suggestive similarity between this and the name of the prophet Zarathustra (otherwise Zoroaster) may have further increased the conviction that the Ethiopia of their day was the resting place of ancient Chaldean culture. Mithridates does not seem to have made much progress with the language, and both his and Pico's use of it was restricted to writing out snatches of Hebrew and Aramaic using the Ethiopian script, but there is no reason to doubt that when they were doing so they believed they were recreating the Chaldean forms of some of the most ancient knowledge in man's possession.[10]

The frenzied summer months of 1486 not only saw Pico sleeplessly studying languages under Mithridates and receiving reams of kabbalistic translations from his guide, but also beginning a slow progress towards his Roman debate and embarking on an encyclopaedic commentary on a sonnet sequence by his friend Girolamo Benivieni – the very one chased away by Mithridates from their secret lessons in 'Chaldean'. Though a commentary on some poems by a friend might seem a rather lightweight undertaking for an emerging virtuoso, the immense and learned treatise that Pico was producing for this purpose was wholly in keeping with a tradition of drawing from the most apparently insignificant bits of text whole expositions of being and time. Indeed, it was generally the case that the greater the disparity between the text considered and the meanings derived from it the better. Pico's commentary is no exception to this, dwarfing as it does the rather unremarkable poems of Benivieni with a voluminous treatment of the entire universe as Pico was coming to understand it. The sensational grandeur of this vision also formed the backdrop to another

Opposite: Vat Eti 20, a psalter in the language of Ge'ez, possibly used by Mithridates to teach Pico

incident that occurred that summer, a scandal in the town of Arezzo which almost put a stop to Pico's triumphal plans for his Roman debate, and which involved the wife of the local Medici governor attempting to flee her much older husband to be at Pico's side during his moment of glory.

If Margherita Mariotto de' Medici had access to Pico's commentary, which was one of his few works in Italian rather than Latin and so legible to laypeople, she would have read that we live, as the poet Pindar says, *in a world of shadows*, but that we can by following our urges have access to a higher world of the angels in that *union of the spirit* so lauded by the followers of Plato. To understand how this worked it was important to know that God himself was not beautiful, as beauty involves the harmonious balance between separate parts, and as there are no parts to God this cannot apply to him; *but after him begins beauty, as after him there is opposition, and without that no thing can be created*, the definition of beauty being nothing other than the *union of contraries and the concord of discord*, in which delicate balance all things continue and which was present in the harmony of creation, *like the tempering of the most perfect voices into a harmony*. It is for this reason that when we contemplate beautiful things we feel (in the words of Zoroaster) *very near, very near to paradise*, a reminiscence of the first experience of beauty in the mind of the angel as it contemplated the Ideas of things that emanated from God: the first angel *having in himself the beauty of the idea, but imperfectly, and from the opacity of its tenebrous substance, must needs have arisen the desire to possess it more perfectly*. It is in the same manner that we feel desire for beauty, *like one who in a nocturne has seen a beautiful body, and desires to see it in the clearer light to more fully partake of its beauty*, and so it was with the prophet Tiresias who saw the Goddess of Love in her nakedness and was blinded by the vision but also gained the gift of second sight. Pico noted that *in love there must always be reciprocity, as Plato says in many places, which is when one loves the other in the same way and for the same reason he is loved*; also how *desire has a certain goal, in such manner as it is capable of happiness, and is drawn towards it as all things fall towards the centre*; and, further, how the lover already in some senses half possesses the object of desire, as he knows it, and knowing is a form of having. And when we see beauty in a body we desire to copulate with it, *which is nothing more than to join with it in the most intimate manner*, just as we wish to become one with the very concept of beauty and *be entwined with her in an indissoluble knot, and with a kiss the spirit of the one transfusing with the other, not so much changing them, as being so perfectly united, that each of the two souls could be called a single soul.* And it was important to remember that *the most perfect and intimate union that the lover can have with the celestial beloved is the union of the kiss*, and that according to kabbalah we know that herein lies the secret, just as Solomon began the Song of Songs with the line *Kiss me with the kisses of your mouth*, so the most blessed take leave of this life in a moment called *binsica, which means in our language the death of the kiss.*[11]

One can certainly understand how coming into contact with Pico, his reputation preceding him as an ethereal beauty, the glow of destiny upon him and speaking words like these with their heady blend of eroticism and transcendence and climactic fulfilment, might have turned the head of the bored and lonely wife of a provincial governor from a minor branch of the Medici family. In the aftermath of the scandal Ficino was to give a poetic and mythic account of the event to shield his young protégé, writing in code about how the abduction of *a nymph of surpassing beauty* by the demigod 'Rÿco' was nothing but an act of justice, nymphs being rightly the brides of gods and not of men; however, *Mars, the destroyer of laws and happiness, envying such a lawful and blessed union, immediately spurred his daemons into action.* The details of the event are obscured by this later mythmaking and attempts to defend Pico and smooth things over, but it seems that, having fallen for Pico and knowing him to be leaving Arezzo that day,

Margherita failed to appear at Mass, instead having taken only her young pageboy and made for the Siena gate whence she knew he would be bound to depart. It is said that arriving at the gate she leapt up on the crupper of the saddle of the young count and so departed with him.[12]

There being at that time no difference between a wife absconding and a wife being abducted, her husband the Captain of Arezzo immediately raised a posse of 200 men to pursue the pair, catching up with them around the towns of Marciano and Lucignano, a dozen miles to the southwest, where the pair were separated and Pico was cast into prison. Dramatic though this sequence of events was, the entire affair seems not to have lasted very long, and Pico soon escaped from captivity apparently having bribed his jailer with 100 florins, taking advantage of the patchwork jurisdictions of the peninsula to move beyond the clutches of the jealous husband and continue his progress towards Rome. For all that he was no longer under arrest, Pico had committed a serious blunder by getting involved with the wife of a Medici relative, who immediately wrote to Lorenzo demanding redress for this humiliating slight. Though Lorenzo did not seem inclined to come to the rescue of his incensed cousin, a vast machinery of Pico's friends mobilized to try to save him from the consequences of his indiscretion. Mithridates even went so far as to compare Pico to the biblical King David, likening Margherita's ardent desire to follow Pico to Rome to the way that women were drawn to the Old Testament figure. For all the suggestions that the desire was entirely on Margherita's side, it seems clear that Pico was not some innocent angel caught up in the snares of someone else's lust: even the sanctimonious and whitewashing biography written by his nephew, probably referring to this affair and perhaps others, admits that *because of his beautiful body and handsome face many women were driven to distraction for love of him, whom he not disdaining for a time fell from the straight and narrow and wallowed in lustfulness.* Pico himself chose a middle path between mythmaking, excuses and honesty: writing to a friend later that year, in a passage some chose to later omit, Pico pointed out that even David and Solomon, even Aristotle and Jerome, had been tempted aside by the lure of female attractions, saying that he made no excuses other than that he was unaccustomed to temptation and so did not recognize it when it came for him. Whether or not we are to believe this claim from Pico, who had lived a single and untrammelled life among the bon viveurs of Ferrara and of Paris, is unclear: but he makes no attempt to deny that he as well as Margherita succumbed to temptation.[13]

However full his writings were of erotic language and whatever the truth of his physical intimacies at this time, it was at least Pico's intention in his *Commentary* to gesture to sexual desire only as a stirring that gave us an inkling of our profound desires for union with beautiful things, and one which should be moved past quickly on the way to more disembodied modes of transcendence. It was for this reason that Zoroaster commanded us to *extend our eyes and direct them above*, towards where through the *sublimity of the intellect* we are *purged by the fires of love* and take on our full angelic forms. This kind of transcendence is a form of disembodiment, only accessible to those who have left their physical selves behind, *so that they can say with Paul that they do not know if they are in their bodies or out of them, which state whenever it comes to man only stays briefly, as with those who are called ecstatics*. Later in the treatise he gives a sense of how to achieve this state: *when someone whose imagination is fixed on something profoundly, their senses are reduced, and he does not understand what is spoken to him, or what is put in front of his eyes*; when this person is focused on the transcendent, *he loses the workings of his reason and all lower cognitive function*. This man, Pico says, can no longer be said to live in the human world, *but rather in the world of the angels*, appearing senseless and astonished to us but really transformed into an angelic mode of being, as Enoch in the Bible was said to be transformed into the angel Metatron. It was out of the desire to understand these foundations of the world, Pico said, that he was dedicating himself to the study of the Hebrew and Chaldean languages, as these secrets were veiled in ancient works, in the same way that Jesus had hidden truths in parables and the ancient Egyptians in hieroglyphs. Rightly read, however, Plato and others had shown the way to see the Oneness in the manifold world and to reduce that many-ness back to One, *and who knows how to do this should be followed as a god, an earthly angel, able to ascend and descend Jacob's ladder at will.* Pico had even begun to go by one of the hereditary titles of his family, which seemed as if by destiny to signal his intention to wield the power of universal harmony: he was, in one way and another, Prince of Concord.[14]

It was in the course of these flights of enthusiasm that Pico resumed his journey to Rome, throwing caution to the wind and shrugging off the advice of friends to be prudent and turn his attentions to more practical matters. There was good reason to fear unorthodox public spectacle: shortly before Pico had left Florence the huckster-prophet Giovanni Mercurio da Correggio had been arrested there at the order of Lorenzo de' Medici, his occult standard-bearers strappadoed and Mercurio himself shackled to a post in a public square, exposed to public ridicule as he rent his own flesh in despair. Pico nevertheless made his way from Arezzo to Perugia and on, not apparently hurrying and continuing along the way to devour new materials and to write compendiously, but in any case inexorably set on his path towards the Eternal City and the desire to make public his systematic treatment of the universe and the extraordinary powers to which it could give rise, promising to reveal *secret links* between many areas previously thought unconnected or incompatible. The philosopher Voltaire was later to joke that Pico meant in his Roman debate not only to treat *all knowable things* but also *a few more besides*, and as with all the best jokes there was in this more than a smattering of truth.[15]

X

The Language of Birds

Along with the Ethiopian pilgrims and Arabic-speaking Jews who were flooding Rome in the last decades of the fifteenth century, there also came from the Rhineland a breed of German artisans peddling a curious magic. These men were mostly former goldsmiths and silversmiths, who produced vast collections of miniature metal dice each intricately carved on one side with a single character, letters and symbols of great variety with an unexpected shared trait: every one was backwards. These talismans would be arranged in rows by assistants trained in the bizarre skill of reading things in reverse, before being tightly framed and set into a machine whose screws and levers amplified the forces of nature to manufacture an artefact both extraordinary and new: a thing without an identity of its own, indistinguishable from others of its type, able to be everywhere at once and yet always the same. With their upper and lower cases of movable type, compositors and proofreaders, and oleaginous ink, these printing outfits manufactured words on industrial scales. Not everyone, however, was so impressed with this new development. In a magisterial dismissal of the printing press, Poliziano lamented in his *Miscellanies* that *by means of a new device, turning even the stupidest opinions into a thousand books is the work of a mere moment.*[1]

Pico was in Rome by November, possibly staying with his brother Antonmaria in the Campo Marzio, and whatever the feelings of his friends had engaged the services of one such printer, a German from Würzburg called Eucharius Frank or 'Silber' from his trade as a silversmith. Silber had set up shop in the Campo di Fiore almost a decade before and had a line in producing texts quickly and for wide distribution, including Bulls pronouncing the Pope's verdict on key questions but also newssheets and almanacs predicting events in the year to come and maybe trying to influence them as well. One such prognostication Silber had printed for 1483, written by a Russian scholar in Bologna named Georg Drohovicz, noted the dominance of Mercury over the longitude in which lay Constantinople, Caffa in the Crimea, Vilna and Moscow and predicted that the Saracens would not escape the plague that year. The almanac for this Year of our Lord 1486 predicted that the illustrious Florentines would continue in their accustomed tumultuous fashion, with the overthrow and murder of some citizens and the exile of others, though with penitence and reformation to follow shortly after. Penitence, however, would have to wait: for now Pico was furiously revising his *Theses* and the oration that was to be spoken before the commencement of the debate, and continuing to read the texts sent from Mithridates, marking the most important passages with his distinctive and peculiar mark, the double asteroid that traces a path through his reading. He wrote to his friend Benivieni that while the initial list of 700 theses had grown to 900 and might have grown further, he had chosen to halt there, because 900 was a symbolically important number as it was *a symbol of the soul flowing back into itself through the frenzy of the muses*. He does appear to have removed some theses likely to prove particularly controversial and to have written into his preliminary oration a humble caveat regarding his limitations, admitting that *no-one has ever been nor ever will be after us to whom it has been given to comprehend the entirety of truth*, for *it is of greater immensity than human capacities can equal*. Pico also appears to have gone back before the final draft and crossed out these same lines. By 7 December the *Theses* were printed and on their way across the peninsula and soon beyond, where they would be reproduced in Ingolstadt on the Danube before long. Although Pico was later to claim that he was not intending *to spread these things at the common crossroads*, it is hard to see how he was doing anything but precisely that.[2]

After all the fanfare and the hullaballoo, the cryptic promises and secret studies, what then was this revelation that Pico intended to share with the world? The *Theses* took the form of 900 statements, the first 400 of which were taken from other philosophers and the remaining 500 were Pico's own personal opinions. The opening voyage through the history of human thought as it was known to Pico's age worked backwards from the ideas of those in Western Christendom in recent centuries, to the *falasifa* of the Islamic world, through the followers of Aristotle and Plato in the late classical Mediterranean, and on to the Greeks themselves and then their presumed forerunners, the Chaldeans, the Egyptians and the Hebrew sages, following the genealogy of those through whom Pico believed a series of ideas had been passed. This extraordinarily cosmopolitan history of philosophy is vast in its range and often deeply cryptic, in part because it isn't clear that Pico was in agreement with each of these 400 key points from other philosophers, rather than simply marking them out as areas that he had mastered and in which he would best any challengers. Indeed, many of the theses appeared to be in direct contradiction to one another, and so could not possibly be beliefs held simultaneously by one person. The presence of these contradictions, however, was precisely the point, and gestures towards the heart of the system Pico was outlining: namely, that many of these apparently contradicting ideas were in fact true *according to their own manner*, and what was more that this layering of different truths reflected the way in which the universe unfolded. In essence, Pico's first feat was to offer a vision of existence that was populated not, as in previous and worrying iterations, by an infinitude of alternate universes, which threatened to devalue our existence here as being merely one of a countless many, but, rather, by a series of superimposed levels of reality emanating from the first things on down, enriching the universe in which we live with a near limitless depth, like a palimpsest on which each of these ways of being have been painted one on top of the other, and which the adept soul could navigate as steps on a ladder. The apparently indissoluble categories of Aristotelian logic, the Universal Intellect in which was lodged the power to know about the things of the world, the Platonic realm of ideas, the hierarchies of angels, and the first and everlasting One were all parts of this synthesis of belief.

At the heart of this way of thinking was the question that had vexed a great many cultures known to Pico and his contemporaries and a great many others beside, namely the question of how it is possible to say that a particular thing is a single individual entity rather than simply part of a larger structure or, contrariwise, a collection of other single individual entities. How can we say that a person is an individual – *that-which-is-undivided* – rather than just a collection of organs working together, or else just part of a crowd of people working together? The intuitive feeling that things *must* exist is easy to undermine, as one might be able to point to a wave and count the number of them crashing upon the beach before recognizing that the wave has no existence separate from the wider ocean. These are not Pico's examples, but they mirror many of those that are in his theses, which consider how immaterial souls can be in a particular place when 'being in a place' is a property of matter, and how without a place the immaterial soul can be distinguished from all others, and similarly how there can be many angels when there is nothing to separate them. Pico uses this apparent riddle as the central strand in his new philosophy, arguing that as one ascends through the levels of reality these apparent contradictions are reconciled, as indeed they must be when we reach the original and central Oneness of existence, from which all multiplicity emerged and within which all apparently incompatible things must co-exist. In an act that must have staggered

134

his contemporaries by its arrogance, Pico began by sweeping away the central tool of Aristotelian logic, the 'principle of non-contradiction', that idea that I cannot be both one thing and its opposite at the same time – because, as Pico argues, there must have been a time when in the first and undifferentiated being both things co-existed. This is why, he argues, we find paradoxes (like Poliziano's crocodile) so enchanting: because they remind us of an earlier state of being, in which contradictions were reconciled and did not in any true sense exist.[3]

Pico was, of course, aware of the pitfalls of such arguments and the controversies they had created in the past and were likely to create again, and he took pains to reassure his audience that there was no incompatibility between the idea of a shared, universal intellect and the idea that *my soul, particularly my own and not shared with anyone else, remains intact after death*. This was, however, only a technical and temporary concession, as we else-where find that for Pico the *self* is only and most truly itself when it recognizes that within itself it holds the traces of all other things, with which it was once mixed in the initial Oneness of being. Or, to put it another way: I may have life after death, but only as a more true version of myself, revealed to be so made up of the infin-ite parts of all other things as to be indistinguishable from them. According to this way of thinking, the individual only continued to exist in the afterlife in a state of ecstatic self-dissolution, coming into a true state in which the artificiality of the boundaries between itself and everything else is recognized. Pico's theory here is based on a central paradox in the thought of the ancient Greek philoso-pher Anaxagoras, who held that the state of being totally pure and totally mixed were in fact the same – in both cases, we find uniformity across the whole. This was an insight that emerged again and again across different cultures, which used the idea of being totally mixed to demonstrate how two initially separate things could become one new coherent thing – as when a mixture of water and wine was used to demonstrate how Christ's divine

and human natures were so intermingled as to become inseparable, or how the commentaries on the Indian Vedas in the
Upanishads use the dissolution of salt in water as a metaphor to
explain how the mysterious principle of *animan* (which means 'a
certain minuteness') suffuses the whole of existence. In like
manner, for Pico, the disembodied soul becomes one with the rest
of existence, so entering a truer state of selfhood.[4]

Much of the logic of this argument comes from a series of
thought experiments regarding how Being developed from the
first thing to exist into the multifarious world in which we now
find ourselves, and considering what is retained of that original
kinship as things separate, in terms of shared properties or residual
links. But the compelling nature of these arguments, the reason
why they arose again and again in cultures far distant from one
another, also has to do with the widespread observation that our
most powerful experiences are often ones that involve a loss of
boundaries, feelings of transport, transcendence and disembodiment or ecstasy, and these experiences are often prompted by
sounds and rhythms and voices whose messages we do not understand. This was also at the heart and the climax of Pico's system, as
forceful evidence that buried within us we all have deep urges to
convert back to the undifferentiated forms of existence from which
we derive, to coalesce towards the Oneness at the centre and beginning of it all. *Voices and words have a magical effect*, Pico states,
because in that first magic worked by nature the voice was God's.
Every voice has magical power in that the voice was formed by God.
His series of statements on the power of voice crescendos with the
same strange conclusion reached by many before him: *Voices that*
mean nothing have more magical power than those that mean some-
thing.[5]

Pico avoids setting down his thinking on why this may be the
case, vaguely asserting that the reason for this will be obvious to
the profound, and from that point his theses descend into cryptic
and largely incomprehensible statements regarding the wisdom to

be gained from the Chaldean Hymns and from kabbalah. Yet in reaching this point he had come to that cliff's edge of thought that only a select few had reached before in the history of philosophy. Everywhere incomprehensible tongues had been found to be central to ecstatic experience, from the medieval mystic Hildegard von Bingen, who channelled her visions in a *lingua ignota*, or unknown language, complete with its own alphabet, to the Guarani people of Brazil and the reciters of the Vedas in India, who intentionally added nonsense syllables to ancient poems to enhance the effect. In almost all cases the assumption was that these languages were not nonsensical, but merely incomprehensible *to us*, being remnants of some divine or angelic language that we have forgotten or never knew, but which still has power to work its effects upon us. Few had dared to take this thought experiment to its natural conclusion, to consider what it would mean if it really was gibberish that was holding sway upon this. One of the few who did follow this through was the Indian grammarian Kautsa, whose ideas are preserved only in the accounts of those who were attempting determinedly to refute them. Writing in the fourth or fifth century, Kautsa pointed out that the sacred Vedic mantras were full of contradictions, but that, crucially, this did not seem to matter; furthermore that, despite the fact that it would not change the meaning, it was not possible to change the word order of the mantras, or to substitute any synonyms or phrases even if they meant exactly the same as the original. The conclusion, he argued, was obvious and inevitable: that these phrases were *anarthaka mantrah*, meaningless formulas, and that it was only the pattern of sounds that had any effect – hence the strict injunction never to alter the precise wording of the formulas. This even made sense of the legends in which the meanings of the Vedas were lost and found and lost again: this didn't affect their continuing importance during the periods of ignorance because the meaning of the mantras was, quite simply, irrelevant.[6]

While few were willing to make statements like this openly and explicitly, and to open the door to the idea that humans at their most spiritually intense moments are under the sway not of divine wisdom but rather more simply of particular patterns of sound, evidence that others had intuited the same thing was everywhere to be found. Immense projects had been undertaken to record and preserve the various rhythmic devices found around the world, and we often find that among the first things written down about a culture were the rhythms of its poetry and song. During the tens of thousands of years in which there was speech but not yet writing, these tools of sound had reigned supreme, and when writing eventually came they were clearly felt to be among the foremost things to be recorded. Aristotle dedicated lengthy sections of his *Poetics* and *Rhetoric* to discussing the various forms of rhythm, and Avicenna's friend al-Biruni had dedicated extensive parts of his *History of India* to recording the poetic metres of the *Rig Veda* as taken from its Brahmin custodians. The great thirteenth-century Icelandic intellectual Snorri Sturluson had gone to extraordinary lengths to gather the metres of the Nordic skalds or bards in his *Háttatal*, anxious lest these oral traditions should be lost with the coming of writing. According to an early biography of Plato recently recovered from scrolls charred by Vesuvius, he used his final words to complain about a flute girl's failure to keep proper rhythm. The desire to collect these beats often appeared a kind of madness even to contemporaries: the story is told of how al-Khalil, the first to study Arabic rhythm, was declared insane when he was found muttering to himself nonsensically

> Fuchulun mefechilun fuchulun mefechilun
> Fuchulun mefechilun fuchulun mefechilun.

It was only when al-Khalil was at the point of being carted away that he revealed to the lamenting onlookers that these meaningless syllables were a system for recording the metres of Arabic poetry. A similar system of nonsense words was used by the Aztecs to encode the cadences of their songs – *tico tico toco toto, tiquiti titito titi*. These lists of metres are often omitted from modern editions of the texts in which they occur, being considered too dull and dry and technical, but the labour dedicated to the painstaking collection of these rhythms makes more sense when we remember that these were tools, fragments of a technology that allowed the adept to wield power over the souls of others. In a remarkable manuscript in Copenhagen, Snorri's treatise on skaldic rhythms is followed by a poem called the *Rigsthula*, which tells the story of how a god called Rig – suggestively similar to the Vedic word *Rġ*, meaning 'poetry' – made the first king (*Konungur*) through the gift of verse to the youngest and weakest created being. After mastering this skill, Konungur *knew runes, life-runes and fate-runes, and he knew how to help in childbirth, deaden sword blades, quiet the ocean. He understood birds' speech, and quenched fires, pacified and quietened men, made sorrows disappear, had the strength and vigour of eight men.* Having mastered the skill of poetry, this silver-tongued man even came to equal the gods themselves.[7]

Here as in many other places the possession of this hypnotic talent for poetic speech is associated with the language of birds: the fact that Konungur *understood birds' speech* may be a half-memory of the story that among the wisdom given to Solomon by God was the ability to understand the language of birds, which is preserved in Sura 27 of the Qur'an. Another ancient story told of how a traveller named Iambulus was swept seaward to an Indian Ocean island where the inhabitants had forked tongues, could pronounce many things simultaneously and spoke the language of birds; a similar idea is found in India, where the yogic master Patanjali said that those who had mastered the divine speech *Bráhman* could be said to *know the language of birds*. Similarly, the story that the Norse hero Sigurd gained a knowledge of avian speech when he tasted the blood of the dragon Fáfnir may have descended in some way from the classical myth of Melampus, whose ears were licked by dragons and opened to the meanings of birdsong. According to one tradition, the legendary Sirens themselves were not seductive women but, rather, an actual species of bird that lived in India, capable of captivating any who heard its song. Whether or not these traditions were linked, it seems unlikely that they would have travelled so widely or survived so long if those who repeated them did not sense some kernel of truth, some compelling intuition that at its most powerful human speech reaches towards the immediate and compelling nature of birdsong, which seems to pass unadulterated from generation to generation and to allow whole flocks to act in unison, in undulating and coherent murmurations of which human groups can scarcely dream. Perhaps the greatest expression of this idea, the *Mantikh al-Tayr*, or *The Conference of the Birds*, of the Persian poet Farah ud-Din Attar, relates the quest of a flock of birds from many species to find a legendary and magical beast called the Simurgh, only to realize in the end that they, collectively, *are* the Simurgh – that what the speech of birds allows is the dissolution of boundaries between individuals and the creation of new, unified entities: super-organisms. This association between bird speech and magical, unifying power was even there in the figure of the *Iynges*, the wryneck woodpecker, or *pico tocciolo*, with which Pico was playfully associated: these birds were held by the Greeks and Chaldeans to be messengers from the gods, bearers of *voces mysticae*, or secret words, which allowed the possessor to spellbind the world. The revelation given to the initiate was that the secret formula was in fact nothing other than the bird's own name, a name they chanted incessantly, and which allowed the magician (in Pico's phrase) to *marry the world*, as when (in the child's game) two people speak the same thing at the same time and appear to become one person: *JINX!*[8]

The most powerful expression of this idea for Pico and those around him was the figure of the angel, those bird-men whose voices can work upon the world by annunciation, and who in their choirs merge from many beings into a single unified entity, their halos making clear the aura that surrounded these enchanting beings. The difference was that for Pico these beings were not merely an object for admiration but a state to which man could aspire. The angels were, in a sense, the links that held together the various levels of existence that stretched between man's isolated and mundane experience and the limitless being of the One, and using particular rituals the adept could move up and down this Great Chain of Being like a ladder – for a chain is, after all, also a ladder when looked at a different way. And, as the oration that Pico was preparing to open the debate suggests, he was not merely proposing in Rome to outline the techniques for using this poetic frenzy to scale the ladder and fuse together things previously held separate, but, rather, to work himself into this very pitch of poetic furore, sparking a blaze that would send forth on that Epiphany rays into the world which would act as proof positive that he had broken through to another level of existence. *If we want to be the companions of angels, speaking our way up and down Jacob's Ladder,* Pico wrote in the climactic section of his speech, virtue alone will not be enough, *unless we had been instructed in how to move from level to level as the rites demand, never leaving the ladder.* Once we have been initiated into this *speaking or reasoning art,* we will be *infused by a Cherubic spirit,* and, through our mental exercise, move along the ladder of being, *passing through all things from centre to centre, now tearing the one into many, as happened to Osiris, and then, as with the limbs of Osiris, fusing the many back into One.*[9]

Pico's plan for a very dramatic transformation into angelic form was not, however, to be: he had set himself further apart from society than society could well abide, and the retribution was swift and ruthless. Although he continued to prepare right up to and beyond the chosen day, borrowing volumes of Aquinas and Roger Bacon from the Vatican Library perhaps in hopes that the interdict against his long-planned debate was only temporary and would lift in time, something else awaited him. *Owing to the obstruction of his enemies, which like fire always seeks what is highest up, he could not obtain a day for his debate,* his nephew writes darkly in his biography. *For this reason he remained in Rome a year, during which time the nay-sayers never dared to meet him in open contest, but rather tried to lure him into snares and traps, corrupted by insidious envy.* His nephew's version of events rather downplayed the dangers into which Pico was about to fall, a confrontation that was to lead to an unprecedentedly violent reaction from the Vatican, with consequences that would reverberate for centuries to come.[10]

XI

Illumination

W hen on 20 February 1487 the Pope finally broke his silence about Pico's debate, the wording of the official document had the cold and balanced precision of a foregone conclusion. *As the pastoral care of all of Christianity falls to us, and we must look diligently to those things especially which concern the strength of the universal church,* Innocent writes, *it has come to our attention from many sources that Giovanni Pico, Count of Concord, did publish various theses with the intention of debating them publicly. Some part of these seem by virtue of their words to have deviated from the true and orthodox faith, while others are so suspect and dangerous, wrapped in unheard-of terms and shrouded in obscurity, that they require urgently to be explained.* A papal commission of sixteen was convoked to consider the *Theses* and pronounce upon their orthodoxy, meeting at the Vatican in the apartments of the lead deputy, Jean Monissart, Bishop of Tournai. Less than two weeks later Pico was summoned to attend a hearing in which he would be given the chance to speak further about seven of the theses whose contents were under suspicion. Pico was afterwards to write that while most of those who had informed against him to the Pope were merely peeved that he should presume at so young an age to treat of the great mysteries of religion in public, rather than deferring to older and wiser heads, there did not lack those who declared that he was *not merely audacious, impudent, and arrogant, but impious, a magician and a new ringleader of heretics inside the Church.*[1]

It may have been as much of a surprise to Pico as it is to us that the scheduled theses were not drawn from the more outlandish propositions put forward among the 900. In part this may have been because some of those ideas were (as the Pope's letter put it) so *wrapped in unheard-of terms* that the commissioners struggled to get a handle on them, but in reality such witch-hunts often followed the path of least resistance, ferreting out matters on which there was precedent for convictions of heresy, a tactic that avoided getting bogged down in uncharted territory. The first condemned thesis, then, regarded the thorny question of whether Christ had actually, physically descended into Hell during the three days between the Crucifixion and the Resurrection, during that 'Harrowing of Hell' which, according to a popular (but largely apocryphal) tradition, saw Christ fight the Devil and secure life everlasting for the faithful. The contention at Pico's trial was not in fact over whether or not this event had happened, but, rather, *how* it had happened. As had long ago been pointed out, the fact that Christ's body had remained in the tomb during those three days meant that only his soul could have descended into Hell. This, however, created its own problem, as given the soul is an immaterial thing, it is not clear how it can really be said to *be* anywhere – having a location being a quality of material things, which have dimensions and can be said to stand in spatial relation to other things. This may seem like an immense triviality to us, but it was a matter of great importance to late medieval thought: not only does this dilemma suggest that some of the most sacred texts of the Church were saying something that didn't make sense, it also opened the floodgates to that enormous and fundamental problem regarding souls more generally – namely, that if they aren't material, how in the afterlife are they kept separate? How is it that they do not simply overlap and merge into one indistinguishable mass, one unified soul – that

One which was the magnet attracting and repelling so many previous chains of thought?[2]

A fix had been concocted for this problem, and in this instance Pico was guilty of little more than subscribing to this workaround: in essence, the proposal was that immaterial things could be said to have locations *when they acted upon things*, as those acts gave them a presence in a particular place. So Christ did indeed descend into Hell, and his presence there should be understood not as material presence but, rather, the kind of presence that is associated with an act. For many, however, even this clever patch-up job was too much of a concession to those who could not leave off poking around in the mysteries of existence. To a certain way of thinking the whole point of faith was to believe in things you didn't or even couldn't understand, and to insist that everything was comprehensible was to set limits on God's power to make things however he bloody well pleased. To some fervent believers, this line of argument could be extended ad infinitum: as we can never know which things God may have chosen to create in a manner inaccessible to reason, the only possible way forward was simply to accept everything, or at least everything said in the established canon of orthodox writings, as a matter of faith.

One of the other theses under scrutiny addressed this contention more openly, and whether intentionally or not this thesis contained one of the most radically subversive ideas yet formulated. This seemingly innocuous sentence states that *it is not within the free power of man to believe things to be true just because it pleases him to do so, and to believe other things to be false just because it pleases him to do so.* What this means is that people cannot simply force themselves to believe something when their understanding tells them it is not true; for Pico a statement of belief that is not underpinned by understanding is simply false. Many readers may find themselves agreeing with this, but in fact accepting this idea undermines a core principle that kept Pico's world afloat. For Pico's contemporaries to accept this would be to accept that the onus was upon the Church to make people understand and so believe in the teachings of religion: if anyone did not believe in them, it would be the fault of the Church for not explaining matters clearly or persuasively enough. Worse than this, the line of thinking suggested that two equally problematic paths lay open to the Church: either to accept a world in which people were free to behave however their understanding suggested was correct, or to allow that some or possibly most people must be obliged to live their lives in ways that they quietly and secretly understood and believed to be wrong or even absurd. The ultimate consequences of this line of thought are in fact even more devastating, because in a sense, structures of authority *cannot* be built on things understood and believed to be true – we don't need an authority to impose upon us things that we understand to be objective facts – so authority must necessarily consist in getting people to affirm things that they actually believe to be untrue.

It would have been a challenge for the coolest of heads and the wiliest of diplomats to navigate the pitfalls that presented themselves at this hearing, and Pico was neither of those things. While many members of the body may already have been set against him when the hearings began on Friday, 2 March, seeing him as an upstart and an agent provocateur, Pico made no attempt to hide the fact that he considered these august deputies beneath him in myriad ways. Early on in the proceedings Pico clashed with one of the commissioners in a scene that was to set the tone for what was to come. The disagreement centred on whether the early Christian writer Origen was a heretic, and by extension if Pico was a heretic for taking an interest in Origen's rather free-wheeling blend of Christianity and paganism. Pico sought to defend himself by rather condescendingly pointing the interrogating commissioner to a particular Greek text that he felt would exonerate him. When the commissioner responded – as Pico doubtless knew he would – that he had no Greek and that his trusty Latin textbook suggested otherwise, Pico shot back that not only was the textbook a bundle of shit, trusted by no one, which could go straight to Hell, but also that the commissioner would find that even this textbook didn't really back him up. When the commissioner proceeded to read from the relevant passage and found Pico's memory even of a book he disdained to be correct, he went white as a new tooth and scrambled to change his position. Another commissioner sought to turn the tables on Pico by saying that *he had a pair of texts which couldn't be gainsaid* and Pico replied, *if you've got a pair let's see them,* and the commissioner said, *oh yes, I've got a big pair,* but when he found out what the commissioner was holding he said it was nothing, and NOTHING? said the commissioner, YES, NOTHING! said Pico and so the commissioner starts to read and after every word shouts at Pico, IS THIS NOTHING? and IS THIS NOTHING? and IS THIS NOTHING? and Pico (in his own account cool as a cellar) says yes it is nothing and a whole lot of nothing at that.[3]

By the Monday the commissioners were ready to begin ruling upon the matter and they declared that four of the seven theses brought before them were *false, erroneous, heretical and against the truth of the Holy Scripture,* and that the other three were *scandalous, offensive to the ears of the pious and against the customs of the Holy Church, and savouring of heresy.* They further added that Pico's defences in no way mitigated his guilt but, rather, in many instances deepened it. As these declarations continued, Pico decided either from disdain or a dawning sense of the trap into which he was falling to absent himself from the proceedings, and from the Tuesday sent only written arguments in his own defence. This did nothing to improve matters and by the Thursday the Pope had ruled that Pico was now forbidden from attending the hearings and that the matter would continue without his presence. On Saturday a further six theses were singled out for inspection, and on the following Monday and Tuesday the commission proceeded to declare these also false, erroneous and not in accordance with the teachings of the Church as Pico had claimed.

At this point a more cautious spirit, or even one with any sense of self-preservation, would have gone to ground, would have back-tracked and sought the intercession of his many powerful friends to have the whole affair put down to inexperience and youthful intemperance. That was not Pico. Instead, in a period of furious activity over twenty days and sleepless nights, he wrote an *Apology* that was anything but an admission of guilt; instead, over the course of a hundred pages he laid out his response to the condem-nations and, drawing heavily on the overweening speech he had written to open the planned debate, launched a wholesale defence of the *Theses*. The text seems to have been circulated in manuscript form at first but soon after Pico took the extraordinary step of having his version of events printed, and the fact that he had it printed not in Rome but in Naples, beyond the Pope's jurisdiction, strongly suggests he knew how provocative an act it was. What was more, the *Apology* was not merely a refutation of the accusations against his theses, but also an attack on the body that had been set up to pass judgement upon them, a satire dripping with contempt for what Pico saw as the incompetent, ignorant dullards who had presumed to interrupt the course of his triumph. Interweaved between the dense arguments regarding theological and philo-sophical matters were caustic anecdotes relating how during the short time of his presence at the hearing Pico had embarrassed and exposed the commissioners by revealing the shallowness of these clerics' understanding on the most basic underpinnings of Church doctrine.

The Roman Curia clearly decided that the time for careful consideration of the matter had ended, and the fury of their response was palpable. Shortly after the publication of the *Apology* the Pope summoned a tribunal of the Inquisition, and even went so far as to have the brief on Pico sent to Spain for Torquemada, the mastermind of inquisitorial entrapment who was beginning to launch his campaign to cleanse the Spanish realms of Muslims and Jews. The language of the warrant to the Inquisitors gives them *full authority in the present matter to charge, capture, imprison and keep imprisoned, to examine and according to the canonical sentence to punish, and to do all and any things that Inquisitors are allowed to do in such cases by right or by custom.* However well connected Pico was, it was not clear that all the diplomacy in the world could save him from the ominous threats that lay beneath the language of this warrant, and during many tense weeks it must have appeared possible that the angelic prodigy in this great age of light would in his twenty-fourth year be plucked into darkness and remain, if he survived, a broken and bloody thing.

It is not clear what came between Pico and this fate, but when the judgement of the Inquisition came the hammer of the law fell not on Pico but on his writings. In addition to forcing Pico to subscribe to a statement signed off on personally by the Pope abjuring all those beliefs that were condemned by the commission, a Papal Bull was issued by Pico's own printer, Eucharius Silber, denouncing them as execrable in such ferocious terms as had not previously been seen. While the signed confession of guilt privately conceded that most of the theses were not problematic, it nevertheless remarked that those which were condemned meant that the whole project needed to be eradicated: *one bit of ferment*, it said, *sours the whole dough.* The Bull, which was to be read in every parish in Christendom, noted less leniently that the *Theses* were *contrary to the faith, erroneous, scandalous and discordant, suspected of being of unsound doctrine and so likely also to outrage the minds of many faithful people*, and furthermore that they *dredged up the errors of pagan philosophers long since abolished and made obsolete, and also those lies cherished by the Jews and not a few which under the colour of Natural Philosophy have pretended to honesty but which arts are inimical to the Catholic Faith and to the human race and which propositions have been sharply damned by the sacred canons and the learned Catholic doctors.* The Bull declines to publish the condemned theses or the arguments against them, seeking to prevent their further spread, but says that the Pope declared them damned and reprobate in the presence of the cardinals, and charged all Christians under the pain of excommunication never again henceforth to *read, write about, or print, or cause to be read, written about, or printed, or to presume to hear anyone else read in any manner whatsoever* the said *Theses*, and furthermore commanded that such copies as were already printed be burned within three days of the publication of the Bull.[4]

We should not allow the proliferation of such orders that lay in the future to distract us from the significance of this event: more than half a century before the first Index of Prohibited Books was issued by the Catholic Church, Pico's *Theses* was the first printed book to be subjected to such a total ban by the Curia. The attempt by Pico to use the distributive powers of the printing press to put his thoughts and his arguments beyond recall had prompted an equally dramatic response from the Vatican; later that year, the Church was to issue its first general edict against the printing of heretical books and provisions for burning those that were found. The fact that five copies of the original printing of the *Theses* exist, and nine of the German edition from the next year, as well as dozens of copies of the *Apology*, suggests that Rome was right to be anxious about their ability to put the products of the printing press back in the box. One of the commissioners went so far as to have the arguments of the commission against Pico's ideas published a few years later, in an expensive edition printed on parchment and richly illuminated by hand; but to attempt to enshrine the official view in this fashion was no more than to bring a sword to a gunfight. The Bull similarly sought to use every means at its disposal, both ancient and modern, to eradicate the threat of Pico's thought: as well as being printed, the Bull was authorized for distribution in notarized manuscript copies, so that it should reach every single village and parish, and was directed to be read out after Mass, meaning that everyone in their obligation to attend Sunday services should also be required to hear this condemnation

Paul Delaroche, 'The Childhood of Pico della Mirandola', 1842, Musée des Beaux Arts, Nantes

Opposite: 'April' from the frescoes at the Palazzo Schifanoia, Ferrara

Above: Cosimo Rosselli, detail from the 'Miracle of the Sacrament', showing Pico clasped by two figures traditionally associated with Poliziano and Ficino, Sant'Ambrogio, Florence

Below: Golden lip plug in the form of an eagle head (teocuitcuauhtentetl), before 1521, Saint Louis Art Museum

Domenico Ghirlandaio, 'The Annunciation of the Angel to 'Zacharias',
Tornabuoni Chapel, Santa Maria Novella, Florence

Above: Detail from Raphael's 'School of Athens', showing an unidentified figure looking out of the picture, associated by some with Pico

Opposite: Botticelli, detail from 'The Trials of Moses', Sistine Chapel, Vatican, portraying the Ethiopian ambassadors from the 1481–82 embassy

Portrait of Girolamo Savonarola, 'Il Frate',
by Fra Bartolomeo della Porta, from the Museo di San Marco

HIERONYMI·FERRARIENSIS·ADEO
·MISSI·PROPHETÆ·EFFIGIES

and could not plead ignorance as an excuse. It is notable that only three copies of the Bull survive, far fewer than the document it was meant to suppress.[5]

The injunction that all copies of the *Theses* should be burned was also highly significant: this was an act of sacrifice by substitution, a ritual in which the work stood for the author who created it, perhaps even a warning shot that signalled the auto-da-fé that awaited Pico if he persisted. In a sense, readers across the Continent were being invited to participate in a communal burning of Pico. There was, however, a sense in which these acts of violent destruction could be turned into symbols of transcendence. Pico's friend and mentor Marsilio Ficino was later to console an acquaintance whose library had been lost in a fire by saying that *as he had been seeking illumination in his books, so they had been transformed into light*, and this was more than just an insensitive joke. As Pico had suggested in his manic pronouncements about what he had hoped to achieve in Rome, when he would put on a display of *tearing the one into many* and *turning the many back into one*, a particular tradition held that all sacrificial acts of dismemberment were re-enactments of that original act of dividing the One into the multiplicity that came after, and by immolation returning the fallen material of this world into that light which was the insubstantial substance of true being. Such thoughts would at any rate have been some consolation to Pico for the total collapse of his grand ambitions and his great hopes for what the Roman debate would achieve.[6]

The extreme nature of the Church's response to the *Theses* is an indication of how Pico's ideas struck at the very heart of the worldview that had become enshrined in the Church of Rome. In resurrecting a fascination with ecstatic rituals, along with the entire notion of being that could be extrapolated from it – a vision of being in which the existence of the individual was temporary and illusory, and should be sloughed off as soon as possible in favour of dissolution in various ascending forms of unity – was incompatible with the Christian belief in individual free will, and the doctrines of sin and salvation that went with it, in which people were always responsible for their own actions and would be punished and rewarded as individuals in the eternal hereafter for what they had done. The fear that this entire system was under threat from the mere mention of an alternate way of conceiving things, and that such a mention might spread like wildfire throughout the Christian dominions, gives some sense of the part these ideas played in holding it all together, and of the awareness that people might all too easily be persuaded to see things differently. This also lay behind the violent rejection of the idea that it was possible – indeed necessary – to look into all things with a view to understanding them: whereas Pico asserted that people could not truly believe what they did not understand, it was clear to others that the entire edifice of Christian doctrine rested on certain mysteries that were beyond human understanding, and any attempt to subject them to reason risked total collapse. The determination of the Bull to cast these ways of seeing things as dangerous, foreign ideas – the long-forgotten and suppressed thoughts of pagan philosophers, Jews and Muslims – also began to draw battle lines between Christian Europe and the rest of the world, a world of light and shadows in which beyond the borders of the familiar lay ways of thinking which were backwards, irrational and dangerous. The young philosopher's grand project to synthesize the thought of the known world, showing it all to be different versions of some underlying shared truth, was buried so deeply under interdictions and execrations that nothing like it was to be attempted for centuries.

It is possible that a tribute to Pico's daring was left by one of the greatest artists of the age in what might be his crowning work, namely the *School of Athens* fresco, which is part of a series by Raphael in the Stanza della Segnatura of the Vatican. These frescoes, which probably formed a picture-catalogue for the private library of Pope Julius II, create tableaux of the greatest legal, theological, poetic and philosophical minds known to Europe, arranging them in significant and dramatic postures according to their characters and relations to each other. In the left foreground of the *School of Athens*, showing the thinkers descended from Plato who oppose the Aristotelian figures on the right, stand a group of those who had sought to mine from the riddling paradoxes of thought the secrets of existence: the forerunners of Socrates, Heraclitus and Zeno, the mathematician and cult leader Pythagoras, and a beturbaned Averroes, leaning forward to read from a book held by Parmenides. Of all the dozens of figures in the scene, only one looks out at the viewer, as if having leapt in thought into a dimension unseen by the rest of the figures. This impossibly angelic figure is so androgynous that some have seen it as the mathematrix Hypatia, though given the way that this figure brings together the entirety of philosophy, and given its strong resemblance to the portrait of Pico by Rosselli, others have identified this as a portrait of Pico.[7]

Pico's friends and supporters must have hoped that the papal judgement had drawn a line under the whole affair, but it seems that Pico could not leave well enough alone. While the papal condemnation of the *Theses* was drawn up in August, it appears that the publication of it was postponed, perhaps on the condition of Pico reforming his conduct; in December of the same year, however, that stay was lifted and the Bull was sent across Europe, and at the same time a warrant was issued for Pico's arrest. It is not clear what made the smouldering embers of this controversy flare back into life: there is speculation that while Pico had circulated his unapologetic *Apology* in manuscript during the summer of 1487, he had not gone so far as to have the *Apology* printed until later in the year, and that it was this which ignited the Pope's anger. Though Pico later explicitly denied this to Lorenzo, his defence that he was not obliged to obey the injunctions of the Bull until it was published is a tacit admission that his behaviour between August and December was what caused the trouble. Whatever it was, Pico clearly sensed that he had exhausted all clemency and he fled from Rome, headed for France, where he had reason to believe that he might be safe from the authority of the Pope. The warrant for his arrest was dispatched to two papal commissioners headed to Paris on a diplomatic mission, who caught up with him close to Lyons, where he was arrested by the Comte de Bresse and for the second time that year imprisoned, awaiting an uncertain future whose shape would be determined at the highest levels of power.[8]

In the event, and not for the first time, Pico was to benefit from the patchwork jurisdictions and petty antagonisms that character-ized the concert of power in fifteenth-century Europe. While the papal emissaries lobbied Charles VIII to send Pico back with them to Rome, in order that *through a single man scandal should not erupt in his kingdom*, the French king was not to be rushed in his decision-making. Pico also seems to have received an offer of amnesty from Ferdinand of Aragon, though it is unclear whether this was merely an attempt to acquire a valuable bargaining piece to use in international affairs. In the meantime a squabble erupted among the members of the French clergy to whom the matter of Pico's heresy had been referred: a certain Bishop of Meaux had worn his cardinal's robes, complete with a lengthy cape and a bearer to carry it, to a ceremonial event at the Parisian episcopal palace in an attempt to assert a precedence to which he was not by protocol entitled, and a heated exchange of words had ended with the entourage of the Bishop of Paris cutting said cape in half as the offending wearer stormed off. A series of tense negotiations followed to defuse the situation, which resulted in the summoning of the Bishop of Meaux to Rome, depriving the papal commission-ers of a key ally in putting their case against Pico to the University, who had the final say on matters of orthodoxy in France. In the meantime, Pico was moved from Lyons to the king's palace of Vincennes just outside Paris, and it seems that even the papal commissioners during the many long delays had been charmed by Pico. When in the spring of 1488, a few months after Pico's flight from Rome, he absconded from France as well, the papal commissioners attempted to save face by suggesting that he had been chased from the French realms in disgrace, while at the same time assuring the Pope that Pico was deeply penitent and suggesting that he should be treated with leniency.[9]

There is little evidence that Pico was either ejected from France ignominiously or that he was particularly penitent: rather, he seems to have left France in order to fulfil a long-standing wish to visit the great library of the philosopher Nicolas of Cusa in the Rhineland. Pico's desire to riffle through the pages of Cusa's books makes sense, given that the philosopher-mystic had anticipated many of Pico's interests in angel-language and in the *coincidence of opposites*, though it was also useful that this library lay in a part of Germany where the Pope's jurisdiction was even weaker, and which offered him a passage through Savoy back to the friendly territories of northern Italy. By May, Ficino, who during the entire Roman fiasco had been ensuring that Lorenzo de' Medici remembered his love for the young prodigy and paid no attention to the various slanders being spoken of him across the Continent, was writing to Pico in Turin and summoning him back to Florence. Ficino related a conversation in which he and Lorenzo had agreed that Pico was like a modern Moses: both men had paths to greatness that were beset by immense dangers, and this (Ficino argued) was only to be expected – *a configuration or harmony of the heavenly bodies which portends a safe and easy life is so different from one which promises glory and pre-eminence in virtue that very rarely can they coincide, if ever.* To suggest that the explosive consequences of Pico's reckless and impetuous acts were themselves proof of his great destiny was a masterful piece of spin by the old philosopher. Doubtless Ficino hoped that the tempestuous course of Pico's young existence would now settle into a more stable and a safer pattern. And it did, in a sense, and for a while.[10]

XII

The Isolate Song

During Pico's absence from Florence, Lorenzo had received a curious visitor from Egypt, a giraffe sent from the Mamluk Sultan Qaitbay in token of friendship, which Poliziano was able to compare to a text written a thousand years earlier: he noted that the painted and rolling eyes, the strange gait unlike any creature on land or sea, and the docility that allowed the captor to control it with only a slender lead rather than a chain, were exactly as described in Heliodorus' Greek novel *Aethiopica*. The giraffe, which the Florentines still called a *camelopard*, arrived in Florence in November of 1487 and was soon appearing in paintings by Piero di Cosimo and Gentile Bellini, as well as earning itself an entry in Poliziano's *Miscellanies*. Poliziano complained of how busy he was in these years, at everyone's beck and call for whatever trivial piece of Latin or Greek they wanted to keep up with the fashion: *if anyone wants a motto fit to be read on the hilt of a sword or the signet of a ring, if anyone wants a line of verse for a bed or a bedroom, if anyone wants something distinctive (not for silver, mind you, but for pottery plain and simple!), then straightaway he dashes over to Poliziano. And already you can see that every wall has been smeared by me (as if by a snail) with diverse themes and inscriptions.* His annoyance is partly to be understood as jealousy of his time and reluctance for anything that took him away from Pico, and the private idyll that the two shared during these years, moving from

157

one Medici property to another, from the inexhaustible riches of the library to the villa at Fiesole.[1]

The giraffe was not the only one arriving in Florence from Egypt in those years. At around the same time Poliziano was succeeded as Greek tutor to the young Medici by a man named Urbano Bolzanio della Fosse, recently returned from a voyage that had taken him to Egypt through Thrace and Syria, and who was to play a central role in the Egyptomania that unfolded in Europe over the next century, feeding to his nephew Pierio Valeriano a fascination with hieroglyphs that would produce the most important study of them before the breakthroughs of the Napoleonic period. The roots of Renaissance interest in hieroglyphs can be found even earlier, with the return from the Aegean in 1419 of the traveller and encyclopaedist of islands Cristoforo de Buondelmonti, who in his scouring of the Eastern Mediterranean had come across a book that contained, in addition to a life of the philosopher-magician Apollonius of Tyana, a treatise on Egyptian picture-writing attributed to a priest named Horapollo, one of the few copies of which made its way to Pico's library. This *Hieroglyphica* seemed to confirm what many ancient authors had intimated: namely, that the Egyptian carvings represented an undecaying picture-language, designed to survive the vicissitudes of time by representing ideas not by conventional sound-symbols, the meanings of which over time became garbled and eventually lost, but, rather, images of the things of nature, whose significance was immediate and eternal. So in Horapollo's telling a hieroglyph of a lion represented spiritedness, and three great water jars are the overflowing of the Nile, though the images quickly become composite, rebuses that require some decoding by the intelligent observer. A figure with an ass's head represents a man who has never travelled abroad, *because he does not listen to any story, nor know what is happening in foreign lands*, whereas a distant voice is represented by air, meaning thunder, *than which nothing speaks more loudly or more forcefully*. A drawing of a hawk is said to represent the human soul, as the hawk alone among birds does not bother with flying aslant but instead proceeds straight upwards, tending the same way as the yearning human soul. The sense that the secret knowledge of the world was waiting to be discovered through study of enigmatic Egyptian artefacts led to a new interest in those broken obelisks which lay strewn around Rome, erected by Roman emperors but long since collapsed, as well as encouraging a daring few to visit Egypt itself. The early fifteenth-century travel writer and antiquary Cyriac of Ancona studied Horapollo before travelling to Cairo, where as well as seeing the *huge and unsearchable hero-shrine and wondrous work* that was the Great Pyramid, he visited the remains of the Lighthouse at Alexandria and claimed to have decoded the writing on an obelisk that lay outside that city's Pepper Gate. Pico was in the years following his arrest also to embark on a quest to decode these and other symbols, continuing in his retirement his search for the most elusive of truths.[2]

The Fiesolan villa to which Pico and Poliziano removed themselves sat beside a ruined Roman amphitheatre at the end of a steep track up a hill above the city, and it gave the pair a view of Florence's beauty without the importance and noise of being there, with cooling breezes to replace the heat and smell of the streets. As for the house itself, it was surprisingly modest, not much more than a seat on a hillside, a proud testament that an imperious view is empire enough. It offered the perfect seclusion for someone who desperately needed to be less visible for a while, and Lorenzo described Pico as living *a very pious and religious life, almost as a monk* during this period, though this may in part have been an attempt to reassure Pico's critics that the *enfant terrible* had indeed repented of his Roman extravaganza and had reformed his life. It is clear that Pico was not really in solitary confinement, though, as Poliziano's letters from these years show him constantly at Pico's elbow, painting a picture of the two reading together and breaking now and then to tease each other or share some fascinating discovery. Pico has *chosen me as the almost constant companion of his studies*, Poliziano writes to a friend, *and is wont to share with me his sweet attention and now and then indulge in pleasant banter.* One day Pico was telling his friend about the names for musical instruments in Aramaic and Hebrew; on another the pair together were *galloping through* (as one does) *the ancient commentators on the Old Testament, especially the Greeks Diodorus, Philo, Gennadius, Aquila, Origen, Basil, Didymus, Isidore, Apollinaris, Severianus, and many others of the same kind.* Fiesole was a charmed place in which to break open these remnants of the past: whether or not one believed the claims that Fiesole was built by the legendary Atalantus and was indeed the first settlement in Europe, it was certain that pieces of the past seemed practically to float to the surface of the Fiesolan ground. Ficino recounted a day when he and Pico were walking the hills around the villa and speaking about the perfect house, which would be set between the worked land and the forest, surrounded by streams, facing south and east as Aristotle had suggested was best, and high enough up the hill to escape the mists and winds of the Arno, when, turning a corner, they came upon exactly such a place. *Don't stop!* Pico cried out, *as it seems that we are now seeing what we imagined and desired, as commonly happens to dreamers.* It transpired that the dream house was once the dwelling place of none other than Boccaccio, and was now owned by Pier Filippo Pandolfini – a fitting owner, Pico mused, as *the place was sacred, and dear to the oracles*, just as the name Pandolfino signified in Greek *all-is-Delphic*. Poliziano was to write in these years, in one of the poems that he read as a prologue to his city lectures, that *happy in spirit and like to the gods is he who does not seek the false glint of fame or the lure of evil luxury, but instead passes his days quietly in a humble and blameless life, away from the city and with few demands.* Even the most high gods, as Ezra Pound once put it, cannot boast of more than to have watched such a sunlit hour as it passed.[3]

To be sure, they were not always alone. Among those who also spent time with Poliziano in these years was the young Michelangelo, who recalled to his biographer half a century later how the great scholar had suggested to him the subject for his first sculpture, and

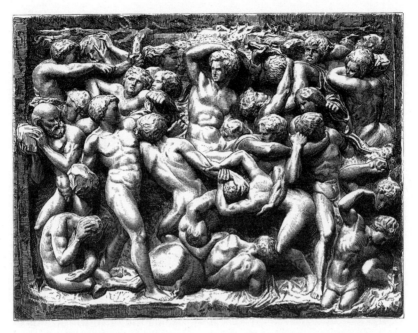

An etching of Michelangelo's first work, 'The Battle of the Centaurs', a topic suggested by Poliziano

had explained to him in great detail the meaning of the myth he was to depict. This frieze depicting a *Battle of Centaurs,* still in Florence at the Casa Buonarotti, is rough-hewn out of the marble and unfinished, though given Michelangelo's later obsession with the relation between stone and subject it is not entirely clear that this is unintentional. For the scene that we encounter in it is one of beings returning to undifferentiated matter, a confusion of body parts from man and horse so bewildering that it is not clear what belongs to whom, each hand and fetlock emerging out of the numinous stone or disappearing back inside it. There is some disagreement about precisely which story Poliziano set the apprentice to create – whether the gruesome battle of the drunken and lustful centaurs described by Ovid or another story in which the centaurs come to the aid of Hercules – but this much is clear: the piece is a masterful evocation of brawling crowds and the fear of them, the struggle of the individual to wrest

161

free of the mass of writhing joints and the vertigo of being sucked back in, indistinguishable from the rest and perhaps from matter itself, a mind without fixed location within the thicket of limbs. The meaning of the story had something to do with the power of wine and lust to make even the most civil lose their minds, but it is hard not to read into it also Poliziano's desperation to emerge from the fulminant city, and a premonition of what was soon to come.[4]

Pico's nephew was to try very hard in his biography to paint his uncle's life after Rome as one of stainless piety, and it is true that Pico focused his efforts more narrowly after that close shave on studies that appeared to be above suspicion. Certainly there was good reason to want to put distance between himself and some of his former associates: in March 1489 his old tutor Mithridates, whose deception or mistake regarding the 'Chaldean' language Pico seems by this point to have understood, was arrested in Viterbo on charges of murder, heresy and sodomy, a sombre warning of how quickly intellectual transgression could become associated with unpardonable felonies. In the end, the campaign to whitewash Pico's life was so successful that it was in some sense this Pico – pious and disdainful of the wisdom of this world – who lived on: Thomas More maintained that Pico was his own model for turning away from the playful virtuosity of his youth to a devout life, and in translating Gianfrancesco's biography of Pico into English More edited out even more of Pico's youthful extravagances. It is hard, however, to change a camelopard's spots, and Pico was never going to remain content with simple tasks for very long, however willing he might have been to dress his actions up as acts of humble faith. *Water will not turn wood into water in a thousand years*, Ficino wrote in a letter from this period, *but fire will turn it to fire in an instant*, and in such a way Pico *consumes immense volumes, but unlike fire converts them not into ashes but into light*.[5]

Anyone who spends all their time reading, as Pico did in this period, is bound to find hidden worlds opening up inside the sentences of the books. During the Christmas season in the year

Pico returned to Florence, Lorenzo was diligently applying himself to the study of Genesis, and prompted by this Pico was soon busy writing a commentary on Moses' account of creation. It may have been a commentary but this was Pico, so before long he was declaring that Moses was a *master of silence* whose account of the beginning of all things only seemed to be a childish fable, when in truth *there is great reason for us to believe that*, in the first chapters of Genesis, *all the secrets of nature are contained*. It had not taken long for Pico to start a new project to explain all things, and to return to his fascination with the ancient knowledge passed from one culture and one sage to another, though now couched in a form that was likely to be more palatable to the Roman Curia. Did it not after all say right there in the New Testament that Moses was *learned in all the wisdom of the Egyptians, and was mighty in words and deeds* (Acts 7: 22)? Pico contended that Moses had buried all that Egyptian knowledge within the language of his writings, primarily in Genesis, which *if any such, is a book marked with the seven seals and full of all wisdom and all mysteries*, citing Augustine's assessment that the purpose of the simple language of the creation story was *to mock the proud with its loftiness, to terrify the studious with its profundity, to feed the great with its truth, to sustain the humble with its courtesy*. Pico set himself to draw out from the seven days of Moses' creation a new description of the known and unknown world, a version if anything denser and stranger than what he had proposed in Rome. As he launched into his task, he quoted the words of the ancient poet Propertius as his motto: *in great things it is enough to have tried*.[6]

It is said that if a bird is brought up in seclusion and without others to imitate, it develops its own unique and unusual call, known as an *isolate song*, and Pico's *Heptaplus* is just such an expression of his increasing apartness from the world. The treatise begins from the same premise as his Roman debate: that reality exists on many levels and that Genesis tells the story of each of these levels, and though they can be described separately the different levels are in another sense part of the same thing, bound together by the *chains of concord. There is no multiplicity*, Pico pronounces, *which is not a unity, and they are linked together by a certain discordant concord and bound by many kinds of interwoven chain.* The angels live at a higher stage of this reality, their minds capable of encountering ideas and concepts not as vague and evanescent things, as they are for us, but, rather, as a solid and graspable stuff, and these angels themselves are both multiple and single: like the oceans they can be named as separate things, but from another perspective they all flow together and there is no boundary between them. Summoning the strength to describe them, Pico quotes from the Psalms: *Who will now give me the wings of a dove, wings covered with silver and yellow with the paleness of gold?* Our greatest felicity, Pico suggests, is to attain this fluid and angelic state, *just as it is plainly the final happiness of drops of water to reach the ocean, which is the fullness of the waters; so for our happiness . . . we must be joined some day to the first intellect and the first mind of all, which is the fullness and totality of all understanding.* As he had hinted in Rome, Pico felt that the route to achieving this dissolution was to recognize the presence already within us of the traces of all things, like the Taoist *perfect man* who resonates with all possible chords.[7]

Towards the end of the book, Pico's argument moves into new dimensions of density and eccentricity. Travelling even further down a spiralling and fractal path of shrinking proportions, Pico claims that he no longer needs a whole book filled with 900 theses to explain the universe, nor even the simple fables of the Book of Genesis: indeed, the roots of all necessary knowledge are contained in the very first word of the first chapter of the first book of the Mosaic writings, the Hebrew word *beresit* – 'In the beginning'. As this passage suggests, Pico had not entirely forsworn his mentor Mithridates, and indeed he was trying in this period to gain access to the books Mithridates had left in the Vatican. However dangerous the source, Pico was clearly captured by the idea of truths lying hidden in plain sight. In this word *beresit*, he announces, there are unimaginable treasures, *which presented themselves to me as I skirted the shore of this sea without even entering its depths ... Beyond my hope and expectation I found what I myself did not believe as I found it, and what others will not believe easily: the whole plan of the creation of the world and of all things in it disclosed and explained in that one phrase.* He proceeds to pull apart the letters of the word and recombine them, much like the Vedic chanters inserting syllables between the words of their mantras, before announcing the resulting phrase:

bab bebar resit sabath bara rosc es seth rab hisc berit thob.

Though he is able to provide a rough translation of this phrase – saying it means that *The Father, in the Son and through the Son, the beginning and the end or rest, created the head, the fire, and the foundation of the great man with a good pact*, which (he claims) not only proves that the coming of Christ was predicted in the first word of the Bible but also confirms his theory of multiple layers to reality – much of the power is lost in the translation of the formula from its original Hebrew, which not only removes the power of the First Language, but also the rhythms of this cryptic string of syllables. Though Pico had always claimed that there was a wide gulf between his intellectual investigations into the powers of language and those base sorcerers who produced and used magical incantations, it is in some ways difficult to see the difference between the dark magic he rejected and the hypnotic repetition of sounds as we see it here.[8]

It remains unclear whether Pico ever sought to use the power of this language on others, or if he cautiously remained a speculator upon such angelic grammars rather than a practitioner of their forces. While Poliziano attested that he was as attached to Pico *as Plato's iron rings are upon the magnet*, and said that *Pico rains down into me a certain secret power, a kind of divine possession*, which caused him to *rhapsodise* – to speak in dithyrambs as Socrates had done during his seance with Phaedrus – it is never clear whether he is simply exaggerating for effect, putting his admiration for his soul's companion in the terms of their beloved Greeks. There is evidence, however, that what Poliziano was describing was no mere metaphor, and that in addition to their researches into these secret languages the pair of them were taking what they had learned beyond the confines of the library, seeking out people who wielded these powers and perhaps attempting to do so themselves. We learn that during the year after Pico's return to Florence he and Poliziano occasionally broke their seclusion to seek out the charismatic preacher Mariano da Genazzano, who is *able to attract people by the charm of his words, to suspend them using the gravity of his phrases, and direct them by the force of his oratory.* In describing his experience of hearing the preacher speak, Poliziano remarked how it made him *prick up his ears*, become intensely aware of the sound of the speaker's voice, the flow of his sentences, the rhythm of his words, and how the man when preaching seemed actually *to grow in the pulpit*, not merely to unfold himself but to enlarge beyond the scale of a normal human being, and how the words did not fade in the listener's mind but remained fresh and if anything more powerful the next day.[9]

For all Pico's attempt to remain on the sidelines and observe but not use the spellbinding power of language, the reports of contemporaries suggest he could not restrain the effect that he had upon those around him. One man who had been to the library at San Marco to hear Pico speak in a debate in defence of pagan learning, and who had fallen under his spell, attempted to describe what it felt like by comparing him to a bizarre and almost grotesque figure from ancient myth, a being described in a text by the Greek author Lucian, which had only recently been recovered. Lucian was the darling of the Renaissance humanists, admired for the way he trained his savage wit on pretenders of all stripes, in stories and dialogues that shone a light upon the many factions of the ancient world. One sketch of his tells of a figure Lucian claimed he had come across in Gaul, a local version of the demi-god Hercules, complete with his customary club and bow and lion-skin mantle. This French Hercules, however, has a remark-able difference: rather than being a paragon of physical strength, he is old and decrepit, though this did not mean he was powerless. Far from it: rather, he draws after him an immense crowd of people, each of them bound by a slender chain of gold or of amber, which ties them by the ears to the demigod's tongue. Perhaps most troublingly, the crowd seem untroubled by their captivity: *From this flimsy bondage they make no attempt to escape, though escape must be easy. There is not the slightest show of resistance: instead of planting their heels in the ground and dragging back, they follow with joyful alacrity, singing their captor's praises the while; and from the eagerness with which they hurry after him to prevent the chains from tightening, one would say that release is the last thing they desire.*[10]

During the hundreds of years that lapsed between Plato and Lucian, the hypnotic power of speech described by the Greek phil-osopher seemed to have given birth to this unsettling and chimeric monster: the metaphor of the Hercules Stone and its magnetic power has become Hercules himself, and the flexible yet unbreakable chain-like links that bound the speaker to the listener have become actual chains binding the crowd resistlessly to the godly tongue. This figure, called the Hercules Ogmios, was to become ubiquitous in later Renaissance culture, being painted on the walls of palaces and espe-cially libraries as well as appearing in large numbers of illustrations, even finding its way into the collections of hieroglyphs as a modern addition to the secret knowledge of the ancient Egyptians. To some the Hercules Ogmios was merely an emblem of the superiority of persuasion over force, of words over brute strength, but in most instances there was also a darker undercurrent, drawing on Lucian's description of a crowd who colludes in their own captivity and mind-lessly follows the figure to whom they are bonded, a spectre of one being stitched together from many. The swift and frequent reproduc-tion of this chain-gang Hercules across the Continent suggests that many recognized in it a powerful emblem of what they had always

Hercules Gallicus or Ogmios, copied from a fresco on the exterior wall of a building near the Piazza Navona in Rome, in Geoffroy Tory, *Champfleury*, 1529.

known but never been able to name. Many other such symbols were to be encountered across the world.[11]

Pico may have been the first to be compared to this divine and macabre figure at the head of a crowd who were pierced and bound and entranced by their figurehead, this speaker or demagogue or dictator, but it was Pico's opponent in the debate on pagan learning at San Marco who was to become eternally associated with the enraptured mob. This was Girolamo Savonarola, *Il Frate*, the Friar, who was to lead Florence into a period of frenzied theocracy culminating in displays of zeal that were to become the stuff of legends, such as the Bonfire of the Vanities. Pico seems to have known Savonarola from his days in the Dominican friar's hometown of Ferrara, and to have been the one who, through his influence with Lorenzo, had the increasingly celebrated preacher summoned to Florence and installed at San Marco. Pico evidently admired Savonarola, though as suggested by the debate at San Marco – in which Pico attempted to convince Savonarola that the Mosaic books of the Bible contained the same truths as were found in ancient Egyptian and Greek texts – Pico was to be one of the few in Florence who continued to keep his own counsel as Savonarola grew in power. Nevertheless, Pico's lobbying on Savonarola's behalf was an act that was to have profound implications for Florence and for Pico himself, and in a sense for the future of Western Christendom. For in Savonarola, Florence would not only find an orator even more powerful than Mariano da Genazzano and a master of the hypnotic rhythms at the heart of Pico's thought, but also, and more alarmingly, someone willing to test to the very limit the ways in which this power could be used.

This storm cloud still lay at some distance from Pico and Poliziano's halcyon days in San Marco and in Fiesole, though it seems that three years of staying close to home had driven Pico stir crazy and made him eager for the wider world once more. *The Creator of the World rested from his labours on the Sabbath, but our Pico*, Ficino wrote, referring to the recently completed *Heptaplus*, *finished the creation of the world and still attempts to do I know not what other great thing – perhaps, like Democritus, he would make a whole new world.* Pico's plan for solitary confinement in a library was perhaps always doomed to failure: books call out to other books, tempting us with their mention of stories that continue else-where and titles that might have the answers sought, so powerfully indeed that each volume seems a wormhole to others, sucking the reader into an endless quest for the next lost thing. It was in this spirit that two voyages started in the summer of 1491. Pico and Poliziano headed to Venice, where the trade links to Greece and beyond made for unrivalled collections of rare manuscripts. And at the same time Lorenzo followed through on his promise to spare no expense in building his friends' dream library, dispatching his agent Janus Lascaris on a trip to the Eastern Mediterranean in search of missing pieces from the limitless puzzle. Both voyages would involve many wonders and startling discoveries, including another piece in the puzzling search for the secrets of hypnotic language; and when they were all finally reunited in Florence it was a city changed beyond recognition.[12]

XIII

Above My Dukedom

*I*n 1491 on the third day of June at the seventeenth hour after the last sunset we left, the Count Giovanni Pico della Mirandola and I, from Florence, and that evening we lodged at Scarperia. On the Saturday we left from there, we dined at Fiorenzuola, and we arrived at Pianoro both wet and muddy, and that is 32 miles. So begins the travelling book-diary that Poliziano kept during the pair's tour of northeastern Italy, a curious document that variously records where they ate and with whom as well as making highly recondite annotations on obscure texts they were delighted to have found in other libraries. In Bologna on the way to Venice they received two parties of humanist men and a group of ladies; during one of the dinners they discussed a passage in the Roman historian Lucan where some manuscripts read differently from others, and the barbarous habit of swapping the letters d and z in the pronunciation of Latin, as if instead of saying *today* I said *tozay*; they watched a production of a play by Plautus, and visited several libraries, making lists of the manuscripts they read and bought. We might be tempted to divide these lists into books that aligned with Poliziano's interests, texts of legal history and more perfect manuscripts of ancient authors, and the signs of Pico's cosmopolitan curiosity, the books of Arabic dream-interpretation and Hebrew kabbalah from which he was supposed to be weaning himself. But Poliziano makes no such distinction, blending the account of their browsing and reading together in an act of quite irreversible intimacy. By 20 June they had passed through Ferrara and arrived in Venice, a veritable archipelago of libraries in which they were to ensconce themselves for the months to come.[1]

At the same time and following the same route, Lorenzo's Greek book agent Janus Lascaris set out from Florence and passed through Ferrara to Venice, but not stopping there he boarded one of the frequent convoys across the Adriatic, stopping at Corfu and then continuing towards the heart of the Ottoman empire, moving through the Dardanelles to Arta and on to Galata, the European merchant post near the Sublime Porte at Istanbul, where the dawn chorus now mingled monks and muezzins. These were the same trade routes along which Italian travellers had been hitching lifts for almost a century, driven by the growing fascination with Greek culture and feeding it in turn, returning with notebooks of copied inscriptions and sketches of dilapidated monuments, often dilapidating them further by bringing back stonework for Italian collections. So at Arta in the 1440s the merchant-antiquary Cyriac of Ancona had described the Temple of Proserpina with its wondrous façade, and how the builder had placed a golden thread in each of the joints of the masonry, though Cyriac lamented that it was much decayed since his visit fourteen years previously, a decline for which he blamed the Turks. The implied disdain of the Ottomans for antiquities was given the lie by visits to Istanbul, where the marvels of Byzantium were still very much revered, from the Hagia Sophia to the monolithic Numidian obelisk festooned with hieroglyphs, which sat amid the hippodrome. Indeed, so attached were the Ottomans to the Byzantine relics they had captured that one Sultan refused a Venetian offer of 100,000 ducats for a marble block reputed to be the manger in which Jesus was cradled.[2]

Opposite: Cristoforo Buondelmonti, Map of Constantinople, from the *Liber Insularum Archipelagi*

Mare ponticu~

Grecia

Pera

Constantinopolis

A sixteenth-century image of the Ottomans entering Constantinople

These wonders were kept in the treasury of the Topkapı Palace, an edifice that also housed the extraordinary library of the Ottomans. Indeed, we know that the books and the relics were kept side by side because a scandal was created when one free-thinking librarian, a man named Molla Lufti, used the same cradle of Jesus as a step-stool to reach a book on a high shelf. There were in truth many objects that could have been placed either in a library or with the wonder-working holy relics, such as the copy of the Gospel of St John written in the hand of St John Chrysostom, which was reputed to be capable of performing miracles. But Lascaris had not come to Istanbul to deal with the Ottoman Sultan for Christian or even Turkish or Arabic rarities, though this is perhaps more the pity, given that the Ottoman libraries contained such extraordinary volumes as al-Biruni's accounts of Indian culture and Avicenna's autobiography. Instead, Lascaris was using his descent from one of the most prominent Byzantine Greek families as leverage to fulfil the wishes of his patron Lorenzo – namely, to bargain for goods from the last great repository of Greek treasures in Ottoman lands, the fragments of the ancient world that were shored up in the clifftop monasteries of Mount Athos. After the fall of Constantinople to the Ottomans in 1453, and their capture of much of Greece shortly afterwards, the most precious surviving remnants of the ancient world suddenly fell from Christian into Muslim hands. Those textual traditions of Greek and Latin antiquity, and many unique manu-scripts containing materials relating to the early Christian Church, were now in the possession of the enemy, and Western Christendom feared losing for ever the vestiges of its cherished cultural ancestry. In the aftermath of the Ottoman conquest, many prominent Byzantine Greeks had, like Lascaris, kept their heads above water by serving as courtly ornaments, the last representatives of this vanishing past, and treasure hunters, agents who for a price could move along the pathways of the now-defunct Byzantine empire and return with armfuls of its relics. Lascaris was the perfect emissary for Lorenzo, as he was able to move within these surviving, fragmentary networks of the Byzantine nobility, many of whom were playing the same game while hoping that some day the Greeks would once again be an independent people.[3]

Lascaris was evidently successful in his petition to Sultan Bayezid II, as he was soon backtracking from the Bosporus towards Salonica, the embarkation point for the peninsula at whose point sat Mount Athos. Half a century earlier, writing from the island of Thasos, Cyriac of Ancona had recorded a fragmentary statue of a man wrestling with a lion in its death-throes, a giant oracular throne carved into the living rock and decorated with fauns and satyrs, and the view of the peninsula across the water: this *religiously sacred mountain, remarkable, the highest in all Macedonia*, he wrote, was littered with *numerous eremetical monasteries consecrated to God*, and Cyriac did his best to investigate these, *insofar as it was permitted*. Another description by Cristoforo de Buondelmonti called Mount Athos the *palace of angels* for its beatific and unearthly way of life, noting that many of the monks there had reached a state of such serenity that if a great wall collapsed next to them they would not so much as turn their heads or eyes to take notice. Cyriac described the varicoloured marbles and tessellated floors at the monastery of Vatopedi, as well as tantalizingly ancient manuscripts of Homer, and Greek translations of Ovid; at Pantocrator a volume of Dionysius the Areopagite, expert on angels, including an early list of the author's works; at Iveron, letters from Euripides to Sophocles, Hippocrates to Artaxerxes, and from Pythagoras and Brutus, as well as many books in Georgian. Moving from one of these mountain eyries to the next was slow going, with Cyriac being guided between them overland by poor drudges assigned the task by their superiors, but the circumstances were often not uncomfortable once the destination had been reached: at Iveron, Cyriac recorded *three ancient winecasks, huge in size*, each of which was full of wine and twenty feet long by ten in diameter, capable of holding perhaps 40,000 litres of the local vintage. Perhaps more intoxicating than the wine, however, was the local practice of *hesychasm*, a technique of meditation that led the practitioner to encounters with the *energiai*, or power of God, in the form of an enveloping light. This tradition emerged from the early Desert Fathers, hermits who practised in isolation techniques for producing spiritual ecstasy, though similar practices were found elsewhere, as in the Sufi arts of *dhikr* and in the yogic arts documented in India by al-Biruni. In all these practices, the central aim was to dissolve the boundaries of the individual and effect their immersion in a greater Being. A'isha al-Ba'uniyyah, a great authority on Sufi mysticism writing in Damascus during this same period, gorgeously recorded her experience of these mystical practices as *the witness of one who roamed in the desert of singularity and drowned in the ocean of oneness.*[4]

Continuing on his journey, Cyriac finally reached *the greatest monastery of them all*, the Grand Lavra, *at the foot of the highest peak of Mount Athos, not far from the sea, constructed at the very farthest shore of the promontory and fortified by turreted walls.* Despite or perhaps because of the difficulty in accessing the site, it had taken custody of a number of marvels during the five centuries since its foundation, including an immense urn carved from a single piece of marble and a library of unparalleled magnificence. Yet for all his enthusiasm, Cyriac was wholly unqualified to make much of what he found, seemingly only being allowed glimpses of the library holdings, and even when he was given fuller access to the books he often bungled his handling of them. Presented at Grand Lavra with a mouth-watering copy of the *Dionysiaca* of Nonnus, detailing the ancient rites of the god Bacchus, Cyriac proceeded to copy out only the odd-numbered lines, failing to notice that the verses continued across the facing page of the book and producing a nonsensical mishmash as a result. This mangled text, later painstakingly reconstructed by

Poliziano, describes a man driven mad by the sound of the Dionysian chants, *the buzzing of Pan's saturnian whip in his ear.* The poem as Cyriac should have read it describes the manner of this long-lost ritual:

> Bring me the fennel, rattle the cymbals . . . Put in my hand the wand of Dionysus whom I sing; but bring me a partner for your dance in the neighbouring island of Pharos, Proteus of many turns, that he may appear in all diversity of shapes, since I twang my harp to a diversity of songs . . . If as a lion my god shakes his bristling mane I will cry *Euoe!* . . .

In contrast to Cyriac, Lorenzo's Greek agent was much better equipped to infiltrate the monasteries and, moreover, had come armed with a warrant from the Sultan. Far from having to beg for a glimpse of their treasures, Lascaris had brought with him a shopping list of those manuscripts most highly desired by Pico and Poliziano for the Medicean library.

Back in Venice, the pair were engaged in their own odyssey among the islands, making their way through a city broken into pieces by water, each new discovery punctuated by boats. Poliziano's diary mingles notes about how he and Pico returned from San Nicolò in the Lido to the Grand Canal in the late afternoon with the transcribed fragments of an unknown Byzantine hand, records a poem by Petrarch found in manuscript at Santa Maria della Carità (first shelf on the right), lists books on the kinds of poetic rhythm seen at the Duke of Ferrara's house. The visits with books were interspersed with visits to and from people, including with a young Aldus Manutius, whom the Picos were shortly to set up as the greatest printer of that or perhaps any age, a man who would put the erudite contents of the great libraries into the hands of vast numbers, sending pocket-sized editions of Poliziano's most treasured books out into the world as guides for living that would spread across the globe. Manutius' easily identifiable volumes, with their characteristic red bindings, palm-sized format and printer's mark of dolphin and anchor, were key to the Renaissance project of making library knowledge into something that could work upon the world. But the most intriguing new acquaintance Pico and Poliziano made on this voyage was with a new prodigy whom Poliziano suggested might even threaten to rival Pico in his admiration – a young woman named Cassandra Fedele.[5]

As with a great many brilliant female minds of the age, we are heavily reliant on the word of male contemporaries for what we know about Fedele and her accomplishments – her letters to and from the great male celebrities of the day, including Pico and Poliziano, were preserved, but most of her own works have been lost, including a treatise on the overarching structure of knowledge, a problem on which Poliziano was working at the same time. Fedele was from a modest Venetian family but had risen to prominence for her extraordinary precocity in learning ancient tongues, and a few years earlier in her early twenties had written to Pico and Poliziano in hopes of obtaining their patronage. The pair duly arranged to meet her during their stay, and Poliziano writing to Lorenzo afterwards reported in rapt terms that *she is a miraculous thing, whether in Italian or Latin – most modest, and to my eyes also beautiful – and I left stupefied.* Poliziano promised that Fedele would visit Florence one day and expected that she would prove a great success in the Medici household, though Ferdinand and Isabella of Spain were also lobbying her to come and join their court, at that time encamped outside of the last Spanish Muslim stronghold at Granada; still another tradition held that the Doge of Venice had actually forbidden the export of this *ornament of the state* from Venetian territory. With a kind of tragic inevitability, very little came of the great promise shown by the young Fedele. Though Poliziano continued to correspond with her, praising her in overblown terms and excusing his long silences between letters as being struck dumb by her brilliance, the truth was that the

Ætatis An. XVI.

CASSANDRA FIDELIS VENETA
LITERIS CLARISSIMA.

Portrait of Cassandra Fedele

fifteenth-century intellectual world had no place for women: all its structures, posts and rituals had been created with men in mind, and the requirements for solitary travel, public demonstrations of wit, and intimate meetings in which patronage was extended amid much drinking, effectively excluded Fedele and her like. A few years later, in her early thirties, Fedele was to marry and the records of her achievements fall silent after that.[6]

For all that Fedele's writings have been mostly lost, her letters, which were gathered together and published a century and a half later, give some sense of her trenchant mind, and among them we find her to be one of the few who understood and openly addressed the obvious question that hung over the fascination of Pico and Poliziano with what Milton called *resistless eloquence*, speech so powerful that its effects could not be withstood. Responding to a great scholar at the University of Padua, who was trying to recruit her on behalf of Isabella of Spain, Fedele praised his persuasiveness by saying that *the force of sweet speech is so great (Immortal Gods!) that it makes that which seemed most difficult to do seem easy.* Unlike her male contemporaries, however, Fedele does not let the matter rest at mere niceties, but continues down the line of thought. *Is the will of man able to refuse good ideas when they are put across in powerful speech? If that is conceded, the will could be led to choose bad as well as good, which I think no one will dare to affirm. If this is impossible, then who could deny free will?* Into this conventional exchange of compliments, the young prodigy has inserted an unusually clear statement of the only question that mattered: if the rhythms and harmonies of powerful speech could lead the listener, like those attached by golden chains to the tongue of Hercules Ogmios, to good and to evil alike, then what was the meaning of sin, and what of free will? When the vicious and the virtuous act were not of an individual's particular choosing, there is no sense in praise or blame; indeed, it scarcely makes sense to consider the listener a separate entity from the speaker. Fedele signs off with a deferential remark that is also a provocation: *if it is a beautiful thing to seek the unknown and be instructed in it by the learned, I will happily be instructed by you.* There was as far as we know no response to her question about free will, though it would become an increasingly fraught one in the years ahead.[7]

At the monastery of Grand Lavra at the foot of Mount Athos, Janus Lascaris was to acquire a manuscript that contained the greatest statement of this power ever written, and which was to become entirely central to European philosophy in the years to come. There is no reason to believe that Lascaris set particular store by this manuscript among the 200 odd that he collected for Lorenzo's library on this expedition, but there is reason to believe that Pico did – because the manuscript, an unremarkable copy in plain Greek script now held in Paris, is littered with Pico's characteristic reader's mark, the two-headed meteor that he etched in the margin next to passages that particularly excited his attention. The text in question was the *Peri Hypsos,* which was attributed to one Dionysius Longinus, a classical Hellenic author once believed to have been a disciple of Plotinus, and which came later to be known as the treatise *On the Sublime.* In this book Longinus attempts nothing less than to provide a practical guide for how to produce this hypnotizing speech, a step-by-step manual for mesmerizing an audience and putting them under the control of the speaker. The author admits that it is no simple task, that it is easier to put one's finger on the things that break the spell than those that create it, that make the speech (in words marked out by Pico) *transcend mere persuasion.* Still, Longinus is determined to try, to pin down or distil whatever it is that makes the audience of Homer shiver when he speaks of how the Titans *threatened to give battle to the sky and all the gods, piling Mount Ossa on Olympus, and on Olympus leaf-strewn Pelion, so to make a road to heaven, and would have made it too had they but lived.* Longinus suggests that it is not the words alone that have this effect, and the effect depends upon the place, the manner of speaking, the circumstances and the motive, but it also has something to do with the piling of one idea, one image upon the other, like the Titans building a ladder to the heavens, with rhetorical questions one after the other, asked and answered with no time to stop and think, with no pause for breath, *for the onward rush of passion* (Pico marks) *has the property of sweeping everything before it; it does not allow the hearer leisure to consider the number of metaphors, since he is carried away by the enthusiasm of the speaker.* At the crescendo of the account, in a long passage along which Pico's mark streaks like a meteor, Longinus tells his reader that this mode of speech *is a kind of harmony of the words that are implanted in man at his birth, and which affect not his hearing alone but his very soul. And it is my belief that it brings out manifold patterns of words, thoughts, deeds, beauty, and melody, all of them originally born and bred in us; moreover, by the blending of the myriad tones it brings into the hearts of the bystanders the actual emotion of the speaker, and without fail forces them to share it.* It is madness, Longinus says, to dispute the existence of something that we all of us have experienced at one time or another. *Are we not to believe that by these means it casts a spell on us, and draws our thoughts towards what is majestic and dignified and sublime, and towards any other potentialities which it embraces, gaining a complete mastery over our minds?* In Longinus as in the writings of Cassandra Fedele, the matter of these *other potentialities* of sublime speech is left hanging, the implications unthinkable – for if there is nothing to guarantee that this effect can only be wielded by those with high thoughts and noble intentions, a crack in the teacup opens that leads in worrying directions.[8]

Most historians of Western philosophy would mark out the rediscovery of *On the Sublime* as a pivotal moment in the history of modern thought. As religious conviction slowly ebbed away among European intellectuals, this treatise was to offer a non-theological means of understanding those ecstatic feelings that were unquestionably central to human experience but which seemed to resist rational explanation. From the late eighteenth

183

century onwards, experience of the Sublime offered reassurance that our ideas about the world were indeed connected to a greater framework – a *metaphysical* realm – though one not thought to be populated by a society of supernatural beings or accessed by divine revelation or mysticism. Instead, Romantics fixed upon encounters with the arresting grandeur of the natural world as evidence that certain sensitive individuals – those in possession of *genius*, now transformed from an attendant spirit to a quality of mind – acted as conduits through which the majesty of the great and ineffable beyond was channelled to the rest of mankind.

The impact of Longinus' treatise, extraordinary as it was, would be curiously played out in slow motion and also characterized by efforts to contain what it suggested: it was half a century after Lascaris' trip before the first printed edition was published, and a century after that before a French translation brought the text into the mainstream, and it was another century again before it became central to Romantic thought. While over the course of this period the Sublime became a useful counterweight to Enlightenment rationalism – helping to explain apparently irrational impulses, and to reconnect human activity to something beyond the merely here and now – what was lost was the sense shared by Pico and his contemporaries that the Sublime was also a tool, one tool among many half-remembered from across the course of history, which had potential to unlock new elements of human existence, and to reveal truths about what lay beyond the thinkable. As suggested by the fact that the text was commonly paired in manuscripts with Aristotle's *Problems*, Longinus' text was seen for much of its history as a practical manual for stimulating a physical effect, though constantly hanging over the text was the implication that this phenomenon could simply be provoked by certain rhythms, sounds, cadences and patterns of speech. As the prominence of the Sublime grew in European culture, there seemed to be a general impulse to avoid what could be extrapolated from this common experience, and to assume that the Sublime must be tied inalienably to the good and the virtuous and the holy – the major argument for this, even if often unspoken, being that any other conclusion was literally unthinkable, so immense and annihilating in its consequences would it be. For on the other side of this cliff's edge all the central pillars that upheld European thought fell away – the existence of the individual as a meaningful entity, capable of making its own decisions and facing the consequences for them, and the possibility of a hereafter in which justice would be done to each in their turn.

Lascaris returned from Mount Athos via Crete and Apulia with a haul of some 200 manuscripts destined for Lorenzo's library, but he was never to have the chance to present them to his patron. During the Greek's absence, death had come for The Magnificent: he had taken to bed in his villa at Correggio and, racked with pain in his stomach and intestines, had asked a grief-stricken Poliziano whether Pico was around and might be available. Poliziano assured him that Pico was indeed in Florence, and had only not visited so as not to be a nuisance, but Lorenzo had asked Poliziano to summon Pico without delay – as long as the journey to the villa wasn't too much of a bother. Poliziano describes how Pico sat on the bed and Lorenzo, after saying that he would depart the easier for having set eyes one last time on his dear friend, had in a gesture of exquisite tenderness joked with Pico that he would have preferred for death to have delayed its touch *till that day when I had fully completed your library*. Poliziano commented that it seemed as if everyone else in the room were dying, and Lorenzo alone was in good health. Lorenzo left off building his library on 8 April 1492, rumoured to be hastened to his death by a doctor who administered powdered jewels to him as a rich dose befitting such a magnate, and Tuscany expressed its grief by recording the catalogue of marvels which registered this seismic event. A bright star fell at the moment of his death. Brunelleschi's Dome, crowning the Florentine skyline, was struck by a lightning bolt, opening the roof lantern (according to one observer) *like a pomegranate*, shattering the marble of the cupola, and knocking one of the golden orbs from the Medici arms, an event all the more marvelled at in that the bolt struck from a clear sky – though others distinctly remembered a storm. Lights were seen descending over the Medici tombs at Fiesole; lights appeared over the castle at Arezzo, and a she-wolf howling; a pair of lions in the Florentine menagerie attacked each other. The suspected doctor killed himself. At Santa Maria Novella, where Lorenzo and his friends looked on from the frescoes of Ghirlandaio, a woman rose to her feet among the churchgoers and ran possessed through the church in a frenzy, shouting at the top of her voice, *Look! Look! Citizens! Don't you see the raging bull that knocks this massive temple to the ground with his flaming horns?*[9]

Another of Poliziano's friends compared the death of Lorenzo to the melting of mountain snows, a silent event that turns into floods for those in the valleys beneath. For Florence this flood was to take the form of the man who visited Lorenzo's bedside just as Pico was leaving – Girolamo Savonarola, who told the dying man to live a blameless life and turned to leave without giving him his blessing.

XIV

The Shudder

All Florence was mad for preachers, and soon the crowds to hear Savonarola could no longer fit in San Marco and his sermons had to be moved to the cathedral, where by one report 15,000 gathered every morning to hear him speak. The young Machiavelli, who attended Savonarola's sermons with everybody else, in later decades marvelled how *the people of Florence were persuaded that he spoke with God*, and that *an infinite number believed him, without having seen anything extraordinary to make them believe it.* Entering the Duomo past the various angels in the architecture, the *cittadini* dangled and twitched upon his every word. *As to do good works with merit is above the power of creatures, who cannot succeed without charity and grace, without which there is no hope of salvation*, Savonarola said in his Sermon on Prayer, *so must every man entirely throw himself down in the face of God's majesty, throw himself down and prostrate upon the ground, to ask not only for that ineffable blessing which comes to all who love Him wholeheartedly, but also to beg him that he should deign to bestow the grace through which it is obtained. And so much the more ready must we be to beat upon the door of his mercy, as much the more we see the danger of its loss: and most when we see Times of Danger, and Men of Perversion multiply upon the earth, as we manifestly see in our own days, of which speaking sadly the chaste eyes of men and women zealous for the Honour of God bathe their faces with bitter tears, seeing the whole world turned upside down, all True and Living Lights of Virtue now being extinguished, and not finding other in Christ's church than Iniquity or else Pretended Holiness. For which reason Our Merciful Lady in Christ, mother and son, if it were ever necessary to pray continually and with tears and sighs to keep beating at the door of the sweet saviour Jesus Christ for our own salvation and that of others, I believe that most in this Blind, Miserable, Adulterous, Leaden and Exhausted State we have the more need as our faith is the more spent and totally dead, every impiety abounding upon the earth. O miserable and tearful state of the spouse of Christ our mother, who does not remember the blood of her sweet husband, and as if delirious does not value such a treasure; O that we should be born in these Worst and Most Dangerous of Times, in which many of us doubt our salvation, goodness now being taken as a sin and sinfulness as a good.*[1]

Few were able to deny in later years the power of Savonarola's speech. Writing to the College of Cardinals in the aftermath of the Friar's ascendency to beg forgiveness for an entire city that had been drawn into ecstasies of spiritual extravagance by this preacher, Ficino was to claim that there were *many proofs* that *this prince of hypocrites, led by a spirit not so much human as diabolic, has seduced us, not merely setting traps for us but even sapping our vital energies.* The instrument of this vampiric hold upon his audience, Ficino writes, was *the face, the voice, the speech frequently lightning fast while declaiming, carrying his listeners along not so much by voluntary persuasion as by violence. For often in the midst of disputation he would suddenly cry out, take fire, and thunder forth, being carried away exactly like those possessed by demons, or the Furies, as the poets are wont to describe it.* The Pope himself was said to have immediately recognized the Friar's style in his writing. Savonarola was to boast of the mysterious influence of his voice, which had (he claimed) among other things made Pico's hair stand on end. The novelist George Eliot, who drove herself to distraction attempting to recreate Savonarola's Florence for her novel *Romola,* imagined her heroine *vibrating to the sound* of his voice, trembling and following the commands of *that subtle mysterious influence of a personality by which it has been given to some rare men to move their fellows.* Eloquent testimony of the power Savonarola wielded over Florence came as well from the methods used to try to make him stop, as when a group of dissenters at the height of Savonarola's influence broke into the cathedral where he was to preach the next day and daubed the pulpit with shit, drove nails up through the lectern from underneath, and covered it all over with the putrescent skin of a donkey. The violence of this act, the offence of the materials used, and used upon the heart of the greatest temple of the city, was an act of self-harm designed to interrupt the invasive and pervasive words of the Friar. All the while Savonarola toyed with the people of Florence, showing his power by speaking untruths they were powerless to deny, claiming that he, poor he, had no eloquence, *at least of that mundane kind that sounds in the ears rather than the mind.* He even wrote a treatise denying the

Image of Savonarola preaching, from his 1495 *Compendio di Rivelazione*

power of rhyme and metre, all the while stringing the people of Florence along using what Roger Bacon had called the *hidden song* (cantus occultior) of his speech.[2]

Pico and Poliziano should have been ready for Savonarola, and indeed in many senses had prepared the way for him. In the first volume of his *Miscellanies*, Poliziano had written of a goddess called the *Peitho* or else the *Suadela* who sat upon the lips of great speakers such as Pericles of Athens, and who was understood *to leave behind, as it were, certain goads in the minds of those who had listened.* Europeans would shortly encounter something similar in

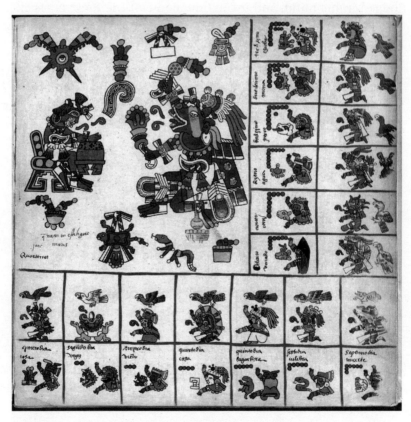

A page from the Mixtec Codex Borbonicus, showing the speech scrolls representing overpowering speech.

190

the *teocuitlaquauhtentetl* or *golden eagle lip plug*, worn by Aztec rulers, a symbol of their ability to wield power over others by transferring their *tonalli*, or life-force, through speech, an experience also rendered in their manuscripts, where speech is shown emerging from certain people like tentacles reaching towards the listener. The idea of a goad that remains in the mind, sometimes imagined as a barb or a sting or a hook like that by which the Hercules Ogmios draws the crowds behind him, is also found widely among those straining to describe the sharp and irresistible experience of such voices: Michelangelo was to tell his biographer decades later that the sound of Savonarola's living voice remained lodged in his mind, and indeed the name of the foremost spell-book of the age, the *Picatrix*, is thought to derive from the verb *picar* or *to bite*, evoking the venom left behind by these words upon their victims. So powerful was this force – also known as *psychagogos* and *flexanima* ('soul-wielding') – understood to be that many of the earliest law codes contained passages levelled at regulating the exercise of this power, as in the Twelve Tables of the Roman law in which a fragmentary passage prescribes measures against *whoever casts a magic spell . . . or wields a song in enmity . . . or composes a song . . .* and the Prophet Muhammad took steps to silence poetic voices other than his own, considering them to be the means by which the *jinns* worked upon the world.[3]

For all that Pico had played a central role in bringing Savonarola to Florence, however, his relationship with the Friar during his ascendency was an altogether more ambivalent affair. During these years Pico passed on his estates to his nephew for a fraction of their real value, and even distributed much of the proceeds among the needy, keeping for himself only enough to support a small household. Moreover, his nephew said that however serene and angelic Pico continued to appear, he had seen upon his uncle's body the mark of the lash – though given his early flirtations with Poliziano, it may be hard to tell where for Pico erotic flagellation gave way to the mortification of the flesh. He was finally pardoned for his outstanding offences by the new Pope Alexander VI, though this was more of a matter of renewed Medici influence at the Vatican than evidence of Pico's reformation. Our knowledge of these later years is also complicated by the fact that Pico's nephew is more or less the only witness to this radical turn in his uncle's behaviour, and his credibility is deeply questionable given the image of Pico that he attempted to construct in the years following his death, a portrait of the prodigal son who, after a tempestuous and impious youth, had seen the error of his ways and ended his life in sanctity. As part of this strategy most of Pico's strange and troubling works were pushed into the background and a great many may have been destroyed altogether, and instead a small selection of devout letters and poems, which cast the *enfant terrible* in a very different light, were pushed to the fore. But there is evidence that Pico remained on much the same path during these years, ignoring letters from his pious nephew in order to indulge as he always had in orgies of reading, as when in the months after Lorenzo's death he wrote that he had for twenty days and nights been buried in certain Hebrew books that had been brought to him by another Sicilian Jew he had found to replace Mithridates and feed his appetite for obscure truths.[4]

More importantly, Pico never seems to have become a confirmed follower of Savonarola's, one of those acolytes known as *piagnoni*, or 'wailers', for their howls of self-abnegation, for all that his nephew Gianfrancesco and his best friend Girolamo Benivieni certainly did. Pico turned a deaf ear to Savonarola's urgings that he join the Dominican Order, and while Savonarola was to try to wrest Pico's genius to his own ends there is little evidence that the attachment was mutual. Savonarola claimed that Pico treated him as a confidant and confessed to him a wish to join the Order, but the Friar only made this claim after Pico's death, when he was no longer able to confirm or deny it. A number of Pico's works survive copied out in Savonarola's hand or annotated by it, and the Friar seemed particularly interested in a tract of Pico's *Against Astrologers*, which

Savonarola hoped could be used to silence accusations that he was a false prophet and was using astral magic to make his predictions. Pico's arguments are an extension of the vision he had outlined in various forms before, of a universe of multi-layered realities in which there were equivalences between things on one level and another, which allowed in certain transcendent circumstances the transformation of things into their counterparts higher up the chain. But Pico didn't believe that the same worked in the other direction: the power of the celestial was muddied as its influence percolated down into the gross matter of the physical world, meaning that it would be impossible to make specific predictions about what happened upon this fallen earth by analogy with the perfect motions of the heavenly bodies. Astrologers, then, were nothing more than charlatans, and later ages were to credit this as Pico's greatest achievement; his arguments suggested that humans should no longer consider the paths of their lives determined by heavenly bodies, opening up the possibilities of self-determination and free will. Savonarola, for his part, seems to have leapt upon Pico's tract both to quash rumours circulating in Florence that the rise of false prophets at that time, and even Savonarola's specific inclination towards heresy, had been read in the stars; at the same time Savonarola argued that Pico's disproof of astrology demonstrated that his own predictions, which seemed to have been borne out by events, must therefore be true, divinely inspired prophecies.[5]

There exists the same uneasy relationship between Pico's last great work and the path upon which Savonarola was leading the people of Florence. Still wrestling with his unified field theory, still attempting to reconcile Plato and Aristotle, Pico was in his final years engaged in trying to puzzle out a central sticking point between the two schools, namely the question of what came first, the One (identified by Christians with God) or existence itself. This is likely to strike many as a hollow or even meaningless question, but it was a key point of contention given that all things necessarily followed from whatever came first. If the principle of existence, that quality which all existing things share, came first, that would seem to make it superior to God, as it could exist without him but not the other way around; if, on the other hand, God came first, it was not quite clear in what way God could be said to have existed before existence. Pico addressed this matter in a treatise called *On Being and the One*, which he said was composed at Poliziano's urging, as a bringing to completion of the great task that Pico had set himself in his youth. Pico's solution to the problem is characteristically slippery. He argues that the One does not exist in the same senses as other things, but is in itself the principle of existence, whereas of all other things 'existence' is a quality they are said to possess. One way to think of this is by comparison to other qualities: just as the concept of 'whiteness' is not in itself understood to be white, or 'tallness' to be any more tall than other ideas, so the One does not exist so much as being the very concept of existence. Another way to think of this, Pico argues, is in relation to the number one itself: while all other numbers exist by virtue of being multiples of number one, the number one itself (known in mathematics as 'unity') does not rely on this relationship but is instead the principle on which the rest of the system is based. Pico's reference to numbers is telling here, alerting us to the fact that we are back in the realm of Parmenides and the logic-paradoxes of the ancient Eleatic philosophers, where all things threaten to collapse back into a vertiginous and undifferentiated oneness in which no distinctions can be made nor any stable and separate entities identified.[6]

Later in the treatise Pico comes at this again in a different way, confronting the problem of prime matter – that is, raw matter, in its most basic state, before it takes on the property of being anything in particular. The question is, then, how is *this* not one, how is *it* not a primal unity, which could be said equally to encompass and unite all things? Pico's answer to this is that prime matter is infinitely multitudinous, in that it can be divided indefinitely, and that *an infinite multitude does not have the nature of the one, as it does not have the nature of a limit.* That is to say, because no bounds can be set on matter, it has no claim to being one single thing. But it is also the case that, as matter is infinitely divisible, and division destroys things, the universe requires God or the One as a principle of being to stand outside the system of matter and guarantee their existence. God, then, is to be seen as what saves us from the vertiginous fate of utter undifferentiation, of existing in a quagmire where the bounds of one thing and another cannot be found. In a virtuosic turn, and having leant over the edge into an abyss where meaning ceases to matter, Pico leaves an escape ladder for those wishing to climb back out: God, here, is nothing more than the necessary guarantor of a world in which individual objects exist and their actions matter, the gold standard of the idea of unitary and independent existence. In this sense God is also like the law, which in pronouncing one man to be guilty of something creates a useful fiction in which individuals are capable of acting alone and being independently guilty of things. Just as the law sets a limit to the abyss of an undifferentiated world where the buck never stops, turning away from man's internal divisions and his place within wider social groupings to isolate him as a guilty individual, so God makes the universe stable by guaranteeing the existence of discrete, separate, real things.[7]

The shaky, unstable nature of this arrangement is obvious, and even in Pico's own philosophy this stability which God provides to the universe is counterbalanced by the deep yearning of things to slide back towards oneness, to coalesce with others in love or ecstasy. In a similar way, the confidence of theology or the law that people do really exist individually was also called into question by the great many rituals and folk traditions that drew attention to the opposite. Pico would have known of the ancient Athenian ceremony of *Bouphonia*, an annual event which centred around the sacrifice of a sacred ox. As the killing of the sacred ox was at once central to the ritual and a terrible crime, a ceremony was constructed in which it was difficult to identify the guilty party: three virgins were to draw water from a well, which others use to wash the axe, handing it to still others to sharpen, and more to carry, before it is handed over to one who strikes the ox and another who cuts its throat, after which the ox is roasted and the whole community partakes of the feast. As it is unclear who was ultimately guilty of the terrible crime of killing the ox, a ceremonial trial is held in which each group accuses the next in turn – the water drawers and the sharpeners, the bearers and those who struck and ate – until guilt is finally pronounced upon the axe itself, which in punishment is thrown into the sea. A ritual that seems to make a mockery of the law, by pinning the blame on a mere accessory to the crime, in fact creates a community by making them all collectively guilty of the crime. A similar game is played by the Jewish nursery rhyme 'Chad Gadaya', in which father's goat is eaten by a cat, which is bitten by a dog, which is hit by a stick, which is burned by a fire, which is quenched by water, which is drunk by an ox, which is killed by a slaughterer, who is slain by the Angel of Death, who is destroyed by God. It is not clear where father should seek redress for his lost goat, and the attempt to pin down the guilt instead seems to fan out to include all things, ending only with God, that One by whom all infinite series are contained.[8]

It was just such a game that was being played by Savonarola, who used the power of his pulpit to draw the Florentines into an ecstatic community, working upon their yearning to be part of something greater, using a shared sense of guilt and outrage to yoke them together in such a way as would make it difficult later on to know where or how to assign responsibility for what had happened. While Pico's argument may have vanquished the power of the stars to determine the course of our lives, what wasn't clear is what happened if the influence came from much closer at hand, as from a charismatic speaker holding his audience under his sway: in such a case, free agency would become a zero-sum game, gained by one person only by depriving other people of their own. Shakespeare's hesitant Prince Hamlet would later dream of possessing this kind of power, of a voice that would *drown the stage with tears, And cleave the general ear with horrid speech, Make mad the guilty and appal the free, Confound the ignorant and amaze indeed The very faculty of eyes and ears.* At the heart of his perfect evocation of sublime speech Shakespeare has placed perhaps the greatest contronym in English – the word 'cleave', which means both to join together and to tear apart – and so encapsulated the very experience of listening to such mesmerizing words, attempting to live within the paradoxes and keep one thing and its opposite in mind at once, feeling as though torn apart and also clumped together with the world around. One way of understanding how exactly this influence worked was the *power of suggestion*, which was documented as early as the medieval Islamic encyclopaedist Ibn Khaldun, who noted that *a person who walks upon the ledge of a wall or upon a high tightrope will certainly fall down if the idea of falling down is strongly present in the imagination.* This idea was later formalized by the psychologist William James, who emphasized the ways in which religious experience primed listeners for this kind of implantation, as implied by the very notion of 'suggestion', a word that originates in the idea of *something received from on high: an idea, to be suggestive,* James writes, *must come to the individual with the force of revelation.* An illustration of Savonarola in the heat of preaching, published at the height of his powers, seems to show just this: the man himself in the *adlocutio* stance, a symbol of speech that is wielded like a sword, his crowded listeners merging into a single, solid mass.[9]

As these accounts of suggestion imply, key to this influence being exerted is the impression that the idea is not coming to the listener from an external source but instead emerges from within – the words of the preacher merely echoing something that has been there all along. In his sermons Savonarola drew upon the same intuition as Pico, of the deep yearning of people to be dissolved into union with greater entities, a dissolution that was felt in the very sublime speech through which he described it, urging silent prayer so that his was the only voice that could be heard, and having his sermons printed and distributed for greater impact. *What kind of a thing is prayer then if not the rational creature and his maker speaking together, heaving breath together, sweetly bewailing his griefs and begging that inestimable Grace with the hopes of receiving it? Joining his intellect with that incomprehensible light and his feelings through that sweet bond shared with the immense goodness, and so raising the mind above all created things, and finally becoming one and the same with his creator, God. O sweetest of commands, O softest of bonds, O most lovely of chains: who would not wish to be tied up with this sweet rope? Who would not wish to be strangled by this delicious strap? Who would not want to be forever in a tight embrace with his sweet saviour Jesus?* Savonarola's sermons, which both describe the experience of becoming enchained to a greater entity and make that idea a reality, were to prompt a reckoning with the power of speech that was to echo down the centuries.[10]

XV

Life Unbound

I t seemed to many that since the death of Lorenzo life had been nothing but a procession of marvels, dark forebodings of the stormhead to come. One of the Florentine diarists noted that *a belly* was pulled from the River Tiber in Rome and inside it a baby still alive, which had been rescued and christened 'Tiberino' by the Pope. There was also found in the walls of Santo Cataldo in Taranto, the land of the *tarantella* spider dance, a book with leaden covers upon which were punched the letters *CJD*. The book had been taken in secret to the King of Naples and its contents were revealed to none, but there were those who said that the cryptogram on the book stood for *Cito Judicium Dei* – God's Judgement Is Swift. Almost lost among these records is the news that came to Florence in May 1493 that certain young men sent out by the King of Spain beyond where the Portuguese had sailed came across new islands in which the men and women lived naked and wholly given over to nature, and the Spaniards celebrated more lavishly even than when they had defeated the last Islamic kingdom in Iberia the year before, though there were others who said this so-called New World was already to be seen on the ancient maps brought to Italy by Cardinal Bessarion.[1]

It was in this moment fraught with signs that the waters around Florence began to rise, with rains so heavy in the summer of 1494 that the Florentines brought the statue of Our Lady from Santa

Maria Impruneta, the oldest Virgin in Italy, inside the city walls in hopes that this would bring some relief from the constant downpours. For a moment it seemed that the trick may have worked and the rains stopped, but they were falling elsewhere and on 10 June in the evening the waters of the Arno began to rise and covered the fields above and below the city, destroying the crop. It was the worst flood, writes one, that anyone could remember, and another says that *because of this it was foretold that the greatest evil would overcome the city and change would come of it.* Savonarola by this time was taken by many as a prophet, something (the diarist notes) he never denies in his sermons, saying only in response *as the Lord says . . .* It would not do, of course, to claim this power openly: as Deuteronomy commands, *when a prophet speaketh in the name of the Lord, if the thing follow not, nor come to pass, that is a thing the Lord has not spoken but the prophet hath spoken it presumptuously: thou shalt not be afraid of him* (18: 22). But the Friar knew all too well how to draw from the innumerable moments of the past such strands as seemed to connect them to the present. *Do you not remember how often I said to you, 'Though it looks like fair weather now, soon it will be cloudy,' and that I used to say* Qui habet aurens audiendi audiat, *that is, 'He who has ears to hear let him hear'? You have seen how it turned out for any who did not want to hear.* The city of Florence was poised upon a tightrope, and needed only a suggestion of which way to fall.[2]

Though all of Italy had gathered in condolence of Lorenzo de' Medici, it soon became clear that his son, Poliziano's student Piero, had none of his father's instincts, and before long a challenge was upon the city that would have put even Lorenzo to the test. The French king had long been looking for a reason to invade the peninsula and now found a ready partner in the Milanese regent Lodovico Sforza, who promised to support Charles's claim to Naples in hopes of gaining the Duchy of Milan for himself. As the waters of the Arno rose and the French approached, Piero's attempt to play the balance of powers as his father had seemed little more than cowardly indecision: first he pledged allegiance to Naples, then declared that Florence would be neutral, and all the while his cousins were offering their support to France and the Signoria of Florence were backing slowly away. As the French army passed Pisa, Piero tried the only thing he hadn't yet and without the approval of the city government gave way to Charles on each and every demand. The powerless and indignant Florentines could smell a scapegoat and Piero's entourage was barred from entering the Signoria to report this shameful capitulation. Soon after, Lorenzo's sons left Florence with the movable treasures, including all the library books they could carry, and the French began to swarm the city. The arrangement was supposedly that the French would come in peace and pay for their lodgings in the city before moving on, but one diarist notes that the troops were as those who *paid for the horns and ate the ox.* All the while Savonarola's power grew, and while Piero's capitulation was seen as treachery the Friar's messianic aura was only strengthened as he greeted Charles with open arms: *At last* (he was reported as saying), *you have come, O King.* Was this not the Sword of God of which he had so often spoken?[3]

In the middle of these tempests Angelo Poliziano suddenly took fever and, after lingering for a few weeks, died. He seems to have remained faithful to his former student even as Piero de' Medici dug his own grave, so much so that Poliziano was caught up in the hatred felt by the city for the failed Medici heir. He died, one diarist recorded, *with as much infamy and public vituperation as one man could bear,* a brutal scorn occasioned *not so much by his own vices as the hatred of Piero de' Medici his student, whom as they were unable to remove him the populace hated and even more his friends.* It seems that between the hatred of the world and the fever, Poliziano lost his mind in his final days. *Fortune wishing to show her power,* the diarist writes, *made it so that this man, being so lettered in Latin and Greek, with so much knowledge of history, rites and customs, so learned in dialectic and philosophy, died insane and out of his mind from illness.* Another, more scurrilous letter of the time suggests that at his end Poliziano called Pico by the name of Peter and also believed himself to be God and demanded worship. This last would have given those hearing it a dark foreboding, as it was the mark of the antichrist. Pico did not record a response to the painful end of his closest companion, though his silence is perhaps a more eloquent testimony of grief. He could not have remained unbroken by the loss of half his soul. Pico's favourite poet Cavalcanti describes heartbreak in these words: *I go as one by life unbound, who seems, to those who look, a man made out of copper or of stone, or pine moved by machinery alone – and in his heart a wound, which is of this his death an open sign.*[4]

Whether it was heartbreak or otherwise, Pico was never to speak publicly again after the death of Poliziano, and it soon became apparent that his own final days might soon be at hand. He seems at some point to have moved into the monastery of San Marco, the inner sanctum of Savonarola's followers, but also near the decimated remains of the Medici library. A prophetic nun was said to have foretold that this move of Pico's to San Marco would happen *in the time of lilies*, which only later was seen to betoken the approach of Charles of France with his fleur-de-lys standards. Some accounts suggest that Pico had succumbed to an illness – perhaps the same fever that had bereaved him of his friend – that lasted for thirteen days and responded to no treatment, even when King Charles sent his best physicians, and that Pico may have moved to San Marco for the better health of his body and soul. Certainly it is comforting to think of Pico spending his final moments in the friars' cells of San Marco, where the murals of Fra Angelico pick out the moments of the Gospels most touched by transcendence.[5]

Pico's decision to take up his final residence within the precinct of San Marco also meant that when he died his papers were in the hands of Savonarola, with whom they remained for some time before passing into the possession of Pico's nephew Gianfrancesco.

In the biography he wrote two years after his uncle's death, Gianfrancesco mentions a great many unpublished works that he intended to bring out to add to his uncle's fame, though in the event he released precious few of these and only those that would help to bolster a narrative of Pico turning away from a misspent youth towards repentance and piety. Pico once said that only the loss of these writings could possibly disturb his seraphic calm and provoke him to anger, but by the time they went missing he was no longer capable of that. His nephew's failure to publish these writings may not have been entirely down to a desire to rewrite his uncle's story: in Gianfrancesco's telling of it, Pico's hand during his last days, tracking the pace of his thought as it raced across all knowable things and a few besides, *was driven so fast that he could hardly control it*. His writings were so haywire, crossed out and written over, patched together and confused, that he left a *thicket and a farrago* impossible to untangle. It is in some way fitting that Pico's final writings should have metamorphosed into a sort of sublime gibberish, the illegible and incomprehensible in hot pursuit of the unthinkable. Whatever the reason, most of the works mentioned by Gianfrancesco or by Pico himself in his published writings simply vanished.[6]

There emerged, in the following years, more sinister accounts of Pico's final days. In the dying throes of Savonarola's theocracy, after Rome had excommunicated the Friar and banned him from preaching in an attempt to contain what they could no longer control, a man named Cristoforo Casalmaggiore, who had once been Pico's secretary, confessed under torture that he had hastened his master's death by poison at the command of Piero de' Medici. Casalmaggiore's arrest and torture was part of a move by Savonarola's allies to purge the remaining Medici loyalists in hopes of staving off the collapse of their regime, so the confession was probably extracted with a view to pinning yet another crime upon the Medici, and it seems unlikely that Pico would have been a target of his former patrons. This does not mean, of course, that there was no foul play involved in Pico's death during his thirty-second year, and it seems at the very least suspicious that he should die under the watchful eye of Savonarola on the very day and almost at the hour at which his old protector, Charles VIII, rode into Florence. Savonarola was to admit in a sermon days after his death that he had often *threatened Pico with the lash*, but protested that he *did not seek his death – it was not my idea*. To what these defences responded is not clear. A follower of Savonarola's also reported having had a vision of Pico in Purgatory surrounded by fires, confirming the Friar's claims that he had died without God's grace. There is great temptation to give into suspicions and so fall into the trap, to try to make Pico's death another proof of Savonarola's evil, to use it to mark the end of Renaissance Florence, to be followed by an age of war and schism, just as the Savonarolans tried to use the loss of this bright star to damn the Medici clan. Just as the omens at his birth were meant to prove that the course of Pico's life was shaped by fate, so the circumstances of his death should tie up his life and make it meaningful. We are story-making beings, and our discomfort at loose ends, at the gratuitous and the arbitrary, is intense. Perhaps this is in part because, without a firm beginning and end, each individual is in danger of simply melting into the crowd, like a wave that for a moment crests above the water but never had a real identity to call its own.[7]

A few weeks before Poliziano's death, Ficino wrote what he did not know would be his final letter to the two, with whom *he had in all his life been of the same soul*. He wrote to celebrate Pico's triumph over the astrologers, and to distance himself from anything in his own works that had suggested that the course of man's life might be read in the stars. Pico and Poliziano were, he says, like Athena and Hercules, conquerors of giants, or better still like Jove, who also once turned back the Titans' vain and impious assault from heaven. Rather than having the course of their lives laid out by the stars, Pico and Poliziano's deeds would after death be written upon the heavens like the heroes of old. Though Pico's curious legacy was in tatters and would remain for the most part misunderstood for half a millennium, one clear lesson was taken from his life by those who came after: that the rules of the game are not fixed, that the limits of our aspirations should be far higher than they normally are, that within the span of even a foreshortened life there was an infinitude of density so great as to make each moment pregnant with all that there is, and that a life should be lived in the awareness that we see only one scale in a series of layers, but that our every act is framed by its connection to the most fundamental and the most universal things, and indeed that these are the same. Ficino wished that Poliziano *nonetheless should live long upon the earth, and be happily well,* but the old philosopher remained after the young had died – just as he had been there before their arrival – like the astonished witness of a thunderbolt.[8]

On the day of Pico's death, 17 November in the year 1494, Florence was preparing to receive the triumphal entry of the French king. Charles was to be lodged in the Medici palace, where columns bearing the French arms were erected at the entrance: the chief residence of the city was both the obvious billet for the conquering hero and a symbol of the changing of the guard. In demonstration of their loyalty to this strange bedfellow, the Florentines brought out the trappings of their holidays. The *edifizi*, theatres on wheels in which were acted miraculous scenes from the Bible and the lives of saints, were pulled through the streets as they were on feast days. The particular play chosen for this occasion was the Annunciation, which was also the masterwork of Fra Angelico's murals in the cells where Pico probably lay. So through the Florence streets and in San Marco a scene played out over and again of an angel whose words stirred in the belly of a young woman a life, and not just any life but one whose beginning and end were not really a beginning or an end but a begetting and resurrecting, a mystery whereby the One or Word by becoming flesh assures for all others an eternity as individuals. Among the crowds welcoming the French king that day to Florence were also the *spiritegli*, performers on stilts who represented the angel-like beings from ancient art, into whom the souls of the recently departed were transformed, drawn upwards like the spirit at the sound of a song and yet not dissolved, for ever young and bodily the same as when in life they had been most themselves. Everywhere on that day were signs of a struggle, between the yearning to remain individual and the equally powerful lure of the opposite.[9]

XVI

Epilogue: Sublime and
Superorganism

In 1529, or by some accounts 1530, a Gascon friar called Jacobo de Testera arrived in the former Aztec empire to spread the word of God. Frustrated at the difficulty of acquiring the local language of Nahuatl, Testera hit upon the novel idea of having the central professions of the Christian faith written out in the pictograms used by the local scribes. These 'Testerian Codices', which soon became widespread and tremendously popular, borrowed from the Aztec script to produce guides to the Ten Commandments, the Seven Sacraments, and *indeed* (it was claimed) *the whole of Christian doctrine*. Translating the mysteries of the faith into the language of a culture so wholly different was challenging, but there were some aspects for which these picture-gospels found a ready vocabulary. When it came to the matter of angels, and the miraculous powers of speech and song given to them by God, the translators simply used the speech scrolls that they found in Aztec manuscripts, the very curling, sinuous tentacles by which the Mixtec people believed their world was sung into being. These scrolls are shown emerging from the mouths of powerful speakers, those gods and kings and even animals whose voices seem not simply to emerge from their mouths but also to curl back around, pulling the listener towards them. In the most potent cases, in a design that the Testerian codices borrow for their angels, the scroll unfolds at its periphery into blossom, like

207

a flowering tendril binding together mouth and ear, an idea also found in the Nahuatl name for sublime language – *in xochitl in cuicatl*, which means 'flower and song'. In the earliest versions of this, the speech scrolls are found emerging not from the mouths of people but of birds, birds that seem to be conferring their powers upon kings.[1]

In the centuries after Pico's death Europeans were to encounter in a great many places evidence of beliefs in the sublime nature of language, of its ability to enrapture the listener and force them to render themselves up to the control of something outside of them. The French traveller Jean de Léry, witnessing in Brazil a two-hour Tupinambá ritual that he could only describe as a 'Sabbath' or a 'Bacchanal', recorded *the rhythm and repetitions of their song –* which he wrote down as best he could as *heu, heuaüre, heüra, heüraüre, heüra –* which drove the female listeners into ecstatic trance, as well as his own reaction to it: *I was left entirely ravished, and every time I recalled them my heart shivered and it seemed to me that they were still in my ears.* Another Portuguese account reported that the indigenous people of Brazil understood their sovereigns to be the same as the bird that led the dawn chorus. Leo Africanus was to tell his European readers of a certain holy man in the North African province of Tlemcen who had accrued an immense following, though Leo was convinced he was a magician as he wielded little more than incantations made up of certain secret names of God. A Jesuit missionary to the Algonquin peoples recorded how their songs were often made up of just a few words layered over one another in patterns of tonal repetition, and they told him that *we imitate in our songs the chirping of birds, and do not seek to improve upon them,* an effect that seemed highly unpleasant to the Jesuit, though their songs drove the Algonquin into fits of enthusiasm. The hybrid Vodun and Candomblé religions

Opposite: A page from the Codex Testeriano Bodmer, showing the use of Mixtec speech scrolls to portray angel-speech

that developed in the Atlantic world during the centuries of slav-ery, mixing West African rituals with those the captive peoples encountered in the Caribbean, involved the learning of secret languages, riddles and chants that contained no actual words but nevertheless produced sublime effects in the listener. The most powerful of the Candomblé chants, used to initiate new members into the mysteries of the cult, is called the *Ingolosi,* or 'Angel Song'.[2]

Any hope that this would provoke in European observers a recognition of a common experience, of the shared ground that sublime speech provided to the most cherished beliefs of so many cultures, was dashed by the reaction that had begun to set in against these experiences within Europe itself. In the aftermath of Savonarola's theocracy, and of similar episodes in which charis-matic preachers turned their multitudinous listeners into a single unity – at Münster in Germany and among the Covenanters in Britain – the mood turned against those who toyed with these ecstatic operations. The prophet Giovanni Mercurio da Correggio had been able to lead a following through Rome in 1484, but when he attempted to return in 1499 his entrance to the Vatican was barred by a Church wary of such provocateurs.

Before long European philosophers began to elaborate new understandings of the world centred on the idea of the rational individual. According to these philosophies, the only acceptable ideas and decisions were those arrived at by the rational individual themselves, with all others being dismissed and condemned as superstition and mob mentality. Long-standing traditions that drew upon ecstatic experiences to speculate upon other forms of being that lay just beyond our grasp now became the subject of ridicule and bigotry: the attempts by Pico and his predecessors to peer over the cliff edge of thought and imagine the structures of the universe beyond our perceiving, where the apparent existence of individual objects gave way to a more fundamental level at which they were united by the shared essence of all matter – an experience they seemed to glimpse when sublime speech eroded their sense of separation from the world around them – were treated with contempt, derided as mere arid wranglings about the number of angels that could fit upon the head of a pin. Though some continued to speculate upon the strange effects that could be worked upon people at a distance – with the likes of Giordano Bruno still searching for the *vinculum vinculorum*, or 'bond of bonds', that could be created between things, and of which the power of sublime speech was the ultimate example – these things were increasingly confined to the occult, as matters that could not be subjected to measure and so proof. Bruno was burned at the stake in Rome for his views, a little over a century after Pico's death; like Pico, his thought blended observation of the world and ideas drawn from the widest ambit to reconsider some of the most fundamental Christian beliefs, in ways that posed an immense threat to established Church doctrine. Demonstrations that at least some of the key documents in this mystic heritage were forgeries, such as the proof by Isaac Casaubon that the *Pimander* did not show the ancient origins of Platonic thought but, rather, came long after and borrowed from Platonism, shattered confidence in these traditions, causing the ideas they contained to be thrown out along with them. 'The conceit of scholars' – the Neapolitan historiographer Giambattista Vico's derisory term for the belief that our most vital ideas have existed since antiquity and can be recovered from there – was slowly replaced with a pride in triumphant modernity, and an assumption that the insights of the past were irredeemably tarnished by their association with primitivism and superstition. The disreputable nature of ecstatic thought was reinforced by its association in popular culture with those who attempted to summon spirits and force them to do their bidding, and any interest in the powers of chanting or sublime rhythms was increasingly tarred with the brush of devil-worship or crankery, with fables about the likes of Roger Bacon and Doctor Faustus warning people of the disastrous consequences of dabbling in these ideas.[3]

Observations about the power of rhythmic sound continued to emerge from time to time – as in the thought of the seventeenth-century Jesuit Athanasius Kircher, who developed a theory of *musurgia universalis* in which the effects of harmony were the key to understanding the connection of all matter, and the notion of 'animal magnetism' outlined by the German physician Anton Mesmer, who used *moving tunes* on his piano to provoke trances that bonded people together – but these ideas provoked stern responses and were made the subject of public mockery. Jonathan Swift, in an early and very funny satire called *A Discourse of the Mechanical Operation of the Spirit* aimed at the likes of Kircher as well as at Methodist and Baptist preachers, traced the entire history of *fanatic auditory* from Dionysus to the Puritans and jestingly described how in this art *the skill and influence lie entirely in the choice and cadence of the syllables*, creating a musical nonsense that can *divert, bind up, stupefy, fluster and amuse the senses, or else justle them out of their stations*, so putting the listener under the speaker's power. Mesmer's belief in the power of music led him to support the career of the young Mozart, who nevertheless repaid him with a series of merciless caricatures including the magnet-wielding quack philosopher Don Alfonso in *Così Fan Tutti* and the village witchdoctor Colas in *Bastien and Bastienne*, who attempts to hypnotize a young woman using an incantation of nonsense words – *Diggi, Daggi, Schurry, Murry!* – in an aria that, in a grand historical irony, continues 300 years later to raise the hairs on the back of many a neck. Ritual chant fell into disrepute, written off as no more than hocus-pocus (a corruption of the transubstantiating formula 'Hoc est corpus' from the liturgy of the Mass). It remained largely the province of lullabies sung to quieten crying infants, using the magic of rhythm and the trick of rhyme, which makes words jink and folds back time, to bring the children into line.[4]

Not only was great effort expended to eradicate these lines of thought from Europe, turning them from sublime to grotesque, but also to stamp them out where they were found elsewhere. The sixteenth-century Jesuit missionary Matteo Ricci, confronted with the fundamental and highly problematic Buddhist belief that *heaven, earth, and all phenomena share one material energy* – an intuition deeply tied to the practice of reciting mantras – and that *the human body may simply appear as a physical body, but both within it and outside of it there is a material energy of heaven and earth*, and that *whether things are large or small, their basic natures are organically one*, would have known well that there were many traditions within European thought that had reached much the same conclusion. He nevertheless chided his Chinese interlocutors for these beliefs with undiluted vitriol: *The error in what you have just said is greater than any I have previously heard*, he stormed, *How dare I hold a similar view?* He went on to say that the writings of the Buddha should be banned for making people *infected with his poisonous words*, and that the very suggestion of one angel that he was made of the same stuff as God was what led to the creation of Hell. *To say that what is created is on an equal footing with the creator is to use the arrogant words of the Devil*, and this crime is of the same nature as a citizen or an insect in a ditch saying to the Emperor of China, *You are I and I am you.*[5]

An increasingly common distinction began to be made between rational, Western individuals and those outside who were drawn to precisely this *tincture of enthusiasm*: Swift's satire, in fact, is aimed precisely at shaming Englishmen who were drawn to these ecstatic practices, which had *been able to produce revolutions of the greatest figure in history, as will soon appear to those who know anything of the history of Arabia, Persia, India, or China, of Morocco and Peru.* The enlightened European was to be distinguished from all barbaric others precisely by his rejection of any ecstatic practice that might threaten his rational individualism, and (as the anthropologist Claude Lévi-Strauss observed) any inclination towards these behaviours was increasingly cordoned off from the rest of society as a form of madness.

Only after centuries of bullish confidence in the European Enlightenment, which enshrined the Individual as a thinker and a voter and a holder of rights, did anthropologists begin to consider how anomalous the idea of a bounded, unitary self is in the context of world history and culture. In its rush to isolate people as individuals who could be counted, surveyed, taxed and subjected to laws, Western cultures had cut themselves off from a whole variety of feelings and experiences that had always been central to human culture and which could be found across the world and throughout the historical record. Pico's nephew rightly lamented his passing as a lost moment at which the warring factions of thought could have been reconciled – uniting in one person *Thales with his vapour, the fires of Heraclitus, Democritus' atoms*, bringing together Orpheus and Pythagoras with Plato and Aristotle, reconciling Averroes, Avicenna and Aquinas – as Pico was also one of the last people to attempt a truly global philosophy, reconciling the thoughts of other cultures with traditions he recognized as his own; before long, European thought increasingly defined itself by how it differed from that of other cultures, rather than on the basis of what it shared.[6]

The *Treatise on the Sublime* by Longinus, a rare copy of which had been found by Janus Lascaris on Mount Athos and marked up by Pico, did eventually make it into the mainstream of European culture, and the notion of the Sublime was to be central to the pan-European cultural and philosophical movement known as Romanticism, though not as a universal phenomenon that connected European thought to its own mystical past and to broader global culture, as it would have seemed to Pico. The new ideas of the Sublime received their most important expression in the works of the German philosopher Immanuel Kant, who attempted to explain the relationship between our physical experience of the world and the realm of abstract truths in a way that avoided the need for mystical experience, moving away from Plato's account where sublime

214

experiences of love and rhythm give us a glimpse into a meta-physical elsewhere, above the messy and imprecise world of everyday objects. At the centre of Kant's system is the idea that what we experience as 'beauty' is really *the free interplay of reason and imagination*, meaning that the cyclical process of looking at something and trying to understand it and then looking at it with fresh eyes, and so forth, creates in us a pleasurable 'aesthetic' feeling – the stimulation of the senses, which we call 'beauty'. In certain circumstances, however – such as looking at a mountain or into deep space or at the soaring lines of a Gothic cathedral, or listening to certain music – the feedback loop between what we see or hear and what we are able to understand cycles beyond our ability to grasp it, filling us with awe in our attempt to imagine the infinitude of space or complexity of which we have had a glimpse, and to understand orders of existence beyond our ability to comprehend: this is the Sublime. In a masterful expression of this idea, the poet Wordsworth described the experience of walking a path in the Alps and feeling the landscape provoke him into transcendent experience:

> The immeasurable height
> Of woods decaying, never to be decayed,
> The stationary blasts of waterfalls,
> And in the narrow rent, at every turn,
> Winds thwarting winds bewildered and forlorn,
> The torrents shooting from the clear blue sky,
> The rocks that muttered close upon our ears,
> Black drizzling crags that spake by the wayside
> As if a voice were in them, the sick sight
> And giddy prospect of the raving stream,
> The unfettered clouds and region of the heavens,
> Tumult and peace, the darkness and the light –
> Were all like workings of one mind, the features
> Of the same face, blossoms upon one tree,

Characters of the great Apocalypse,
The types and symbols of Eternity,
Of first and last, and midst, and without end.

The Romantic account of the Sublime given here by Wordsworth does not seem that different from what the Florentine Neoplatonists would have understood; it simply focuses on explaining the individual experience rather than saying too much about what might exist beyond our grasp – there are no angels or spirits involved here. There is, however, a significant difference, in that Kant is careful to separate out from his account of sublime experiences provoked by nature anything that too strongly affects the emotions or fixes an object in the mind during the experience, something that he writes off as *fanaticism*. To Kant's way of thinking, the Sublime is only sublime when it leaves intact the freely judging individual at the end of it; anything else is *an undermining disease*. The anxiety surrounding the potential dangers of a sublime that could implant ideas in people's minds is easier to understand in the context of the French Revolution, which was ongoing as Kant wrote, and whose excesses were felt by many to have been provoked by just such enrapturing speech. In order to save the idea of the Sublime from being tarnished by association with revolutionary zeal, Kant proposed as sublime only those solitary experiences of natural things that gestured to the infinite beyond without any attempt to use the power this created over the person experiencing it. By framing this *egotistical sublime* Kant hoped to keep this ecstatic power safely within the realm of personal, individual experience, and firmly away from the spectre of crowds chained to a speaker, losing distinction between one another as they are swept up in the rhythm of the voice and feel as if they are speaking it themselves.[7]

This version of the Sublime has continued to exercise considerable power over modern culture, which routinely celebrates experiences of rapture at natural or musical beauty – albeit usually more sedate and polite ones than those discussed in this book – but is deeply uncomfortable with the spectre of crowds being whipped into ecstatic states by powerful speakers. Hitler's speeches and the spectacle of vast crowds being merged into a single entity by the power of his rhythmic utterances remain for the contemporary West one of the most potent emblems of pure evil, and Charlie Chaplin's immortal parodies of these speeches in *The Great Dictator* get right to the heart of the matter, recognizably retaining the Führer's voice even when the words spoken are meaningless gibberish. The idea of hypnotic chant turning people into automatons remains at the centre of our cultural imagination, the stuff of innumerable horror films from *The Wicker Man* and *Rosemary's Baby* to *Indiana Jones and the Temple of Doom* and *The Manchurian Candidate*.

The extraordinary energy invested by our culture in inoculating us against enrapturing speech is understandable, given the traumas with which it has been associated in the past; but this suppression is not without cost. At the very least, it has made us turn away from a full understanding of a profound human experience, shared widely across the world, which may hold significant clues to the deeper nature of our existence, simply out of discomfort at the implications of where this line of thinking led. The fierce insistence on the sacrosanct nature of the individual has also left us ill-prepared to understand other cultures, past and present, who are not so invested in enshrining individuality, and not so horrified at the thought that humans are drawn by certain experiences to form group bonds, and to put their own interests below those of the group. Despite the fact that this has been the case in the vast majority of cultures for almost all of recorded history, Western culture still professes shock at societies that expect people to put the group ahead of themselves, and nightmarish visions of Communist conformity and cult indoctrination still haunt our collective imagination. This lack of individual identity is haunting despite the fact, of course, that the market forces of capitalism lure or propel people in the West into remarkably similar lives, albeit ones apparently of our choosing and with some token external differences.

The violent rejection of anything that might dissolve the individual in the multitude has created problems not only in our understanding of other cultures which have not severed their connection to widespread traditions that actively seek to dissolve the individual in greater structures, but also in attempts to coordinate responses to shared problems faced by our own societies. Many of the most serious problems of the world today – from environmental destruction to global poverty, pandemics to tax evasion – necessarily require collective action, but efforts to create shared plans of action often run aground over different cultural attitudes to the matter of individual freedom, with those in the modern West reacting with horror at the thought of coming under the control of the group. While the desire to place checks and balances in the way of tyrannical control is understandable given historic traumas, this feeling often extends to a discomfort with the idea of collective action more generally, something that should be seen as a legacy of the wholesale rejection of earlier notions of the self and the negative association between self-annihilation and barbarism or superstition.

During recent decades biologists have come to understand more about the ways in which certain species coordinate their group actions in such a way as to be acting effectively as a single entity, as is the case with ant colonies, in which the use of chemical signals directs each ant to focus its energies on the tasks prioritized by the group. This 'superorganism' may be made up of individual entities, but it is acting as if it were a single being. We may again look at this with deep anxiety, as a version of that collective of automatons that haunts our cultural imagination, though it seems likely that from the perspective of the individual ant these are tasks they are willingly undertaking – that is, that the pheromones that are directing it create a sensation of desire, and so it experiences the collective action as the fulfilment of those desires. There is a striking similarity between this and the widespread cultural record of sublime experience, of the most heightened experiences of feeling coinciding precisely with an experience of the loss of the boundaries of the self, a feeling that the voice outside is actually coming from within us. Modern neuroscience has also made discoveries that suggest that the ancient pioneers of sublime speech were onto something: the existence of *cryptophasia*, in which pre-verbal twins develop languages of nonsense words that nevertheless allow them to communicate; the evidence that the structure of our brains is deeply impacted by the rhythms that we hear as infants; the phenomenon of 'mirror neurons', which cause us to mimic the emotions and even actions that we see in others. The internet is awash with videos promising to excite autonomous sensory meridian response (ASMR), or 'brain tingles'. We are left with the provocative and (to many) troubling possibility that our most profound and exquisite experiences are remnants of a mechanism that was developing towards our integration in a superorganic entity – a step towards that One in which Pico and so many others were interested.

This idea is perhaps less disturbing if we consider the fact that the vast majority of us are already, in important ways, fast becoming part of a superorganism. The internet has created a digital central nervous system to which an increasing majority of humans are connected, through which an increasing number of exchanges (verbal and economic) are conducted, and disconnection from which increasingly makes many people uncomfortable. Far from being something we have been forced into by tyrannical powers, this coordinating entity is something people feel strongly compelled to be part of, and behaviours are increasingly shaped by trained responses to the collective will, with desired behaviours being rewarded by positive reinforcement and undesired ones being punished (as with the viral hits and cancellations of social media). As surely was the case in the formation of ant colonies,

219

there will be those with whom this does not sit well, but if it works for and upon the vast majority, then these outcasts will be (at best) irrelevant.

One response to this realization may be to break determinedly away from the forming organism, to go off-grid and resist assimilation, and, given the centrality of individualism to the culture that has developed in 'modernity', this is quite understandable. Yet the history of the search for self-annihilation as told in this book may give one pause before doing so. For one thing, the story suggests that the desire to dissolve the individual in larger groups or structures is far more 'natural' and profoundly central to who humans have been than individualism, and we may stop to wonder precisely why we in the modern West have become so attached to individualism and the belief that it must be preserved at all costs. Given the evidence that humans have throughout history and across the world been drawn in one way or another to submerge themselves in collective entities, we might also wonder whether we shouldn't be more active in choosing the form that these superorganisms take. Is a collective shaped by constant short-term gratification – the visual stimulation of pictures, the emotional rewards of approval, the gratification of various appetites – really so much better than one that is shaped by ecstatic experience? Perhaps by better understanding these experiences, rather than writing them off as primitive delusions, we will be better able to shape our collective future.

If nothing else, Pico's life should remind us that discoveries are not only made by explorers or in laboratories, but, rather, that each of us is ourselves an uncharted territory and an array of instruments for peering beyond the boundaries of the known. Advances in modern medicine have often had the effect of demystifying us to ourselves, turning us into little more than machines whose workings can be explained as biological processes or chemical reactions. But there are many aspects of our existence – perhaps the most important ones – that are still far beyond the reach of science: how the manifold physical operations of brain and body produce consciousness, indeed how life itself emerges out of inert matter, and the consequences of these questions for how we live in the world or beyond it are almost limitless, as they hold the key to understanding our relation to the everything of which we are a part. Clues to these questions might even lie in our everyday experiences, or in the records of cultures who for thousands of years conjured from nothing the wherewithal to preserve their most daring intuitions, their most profound experiences and the means that they had found to share these ideas and feelings, in writing and art but also in recitation and ritual tradition. It was just such an intuition that the Vedic priests left behind when they put at the head of their pantheon of gods *Prajāpati*, or *Ka*, which is nothing more than the elusive and unresolvable heart of existence, that horizon seen by all who grasp at thoughts and words just beyond their reach. Prajāpati is according to this line of thought the one indispensable entity, because a world without it would eventually become entirely fixed, known and without mystery. And who would wish to live in such a world?

ACKNOWLEDGEMENTS

My first debts of gratitude go to the John Simon Guggenheim Foundation, which provided me with a Guggenheim Fellowship in 2023–4, during which much of this book was written, and to the Warburg Institute for hosting me as a Visiting Fellow during that year, and so providing access not only to their extraordinary library but also with the perfect community within which to think and write about this subject. As ever, I am also grateful to the Master and Fellows of Sidney Sussex College, Cambridge, for allowing me to take leave during the period of the Fellowship, and for their continuing support and friendship.

Once again, I am immensely grateful to Arabella Pike and her team at William Collins for their trust, care and thoughtfulness; and to Isobel Dixon and the team at Blake Friedmann Literary Agency, who have continued to be a delight to work with and a source of great support.

Pico's thought covers an extraordinary range of areas and in my attempts to understand it I have benefited from conversations with a large number of people whose expertise in these areas is much greater than mine, which it is a pleasure to acknowledge here, though I am sure that many others worthy of thanks have been omitted. Important steers as well as practical assistance were given at various stages in this project by Vanessa Paloma Elbaz, Almut Hintze, Julia Lovell, Rob Macfarlane, Chris Page, Renato Pasta,

Aarushi Punia, Bill Sherman, Craig Stephenson and Clive Wilmer. I have greatly enjoyed and benefited from my various conversations with Carina Johnson, Joe Moshenska and Ayesha Ramachandran about anthropology, many of which have crept into my thinking about this book. Drafts of the typescript were read at various stages by Charles Burnett, Brian Copenhaver, Emma Gilby, Alberto Manguel, Joe Moshenska, Clive Wilmer and, as ever, Kelcey Wilson-Lee. Such errors and imperfections as remain throughout the book are the result of my failure to heed the excellent advice given by these generous people.

As always, I am grateful for the patience, good humour and love of Kelcey, Gabriel and Ambrose, who put up with many absences, both physical and mental, during the writing of this book.

NOTE ON SOURCES AND
SUGGESTIONS FOR FURTHER
READING

While the reader will find the source of specific quotes and assertions in the endnotes, this section is designed to provide the non-specialist reader with a brief sketch of the immense scholarly terrain that has grown up around Pico and his world as a starting point for further reading. As these materials become familiar, the reader will quickly see that my account has focused on certain aspects of Pico's work in order to situate him on a through-line in the history of thought – namely the ecstatic experience of sublime language, the ontological problems posed by this, and the metaphysical systems developed to respond to these problems – at the expense of many other areas which may have equal or perhaps greater claim to being at the centre of Pico's writings. The reader interested in pursuing these matters – centrally the importance of Hermeticism, Kabbalah and classical Neo-Platonism in late-fifteenth century thought and its aftermath, will find some starting points here, as well as other readings designed to guide the reader towards further materials on Pico's life, on his milieu, and on ecstatic experience and sublime language.

If interest in Pico has never really disappeared since his early death, the modern history of Pico studies begins in earnest with the central place accorded him in late-nineteenth century accounts of the Renaissance, as in Jacob Burckhardt's *Civilisation of the Renaissance in Italy* (1860) and in Walter Pater's essay on him in his *Studies in the Renaissance* (1873). While earlier accounts of Pico may have taken too much at face value his nephew's attempt to fashion for him a pious life in which a prodigal youth was followed by repentance and orthodoxy, the focus now turned to certain specific sections of Pico's works – primarily the *Oration* intended to precede his debate in Rome, which by then was widely known as the *Oration on the Dignity of Man* – in order to position him as a herald of a new, proto-existentialist order, in which the human emerged from under the shadow of religion in order to assert his own transcendent capabilities. This framing of Pico, which drew attention away from the deep commitments of his work to late-scholastic thought and the centrality of occult philosophy to his way of seeing the world, was further enshrined by the popular anthology on *The Renaissance Philosophy of Man* (1948), edited by Ernst Cassirer, Paul Oskar Kristeller, and John Herman Randall, Jr, in which many students (including the author) first encountered Pico from the post-war period onwards. At the same time, however, Pico studies was benefitting from foundational work on his texts and contexts from the likes of Kristeller and Eugenio Garin, who edited a wider selection of Pico's writings for modern readers and began to map his network of intellectual commitments and social connections. This fuller version of Pico gave way to a wholesale re-evaluation in the nature of his thought, perhaps most famously in Frances Yates' *Giordano Bruno and the Hermetic Tradition* (1964), which accorded Pico an important place in its argument that the textual and magical traditions associated with Hermes Trismegistus formed a vital but unrecognised undercurrent in European philosophy from the late-fifteenth to late-sixteenth centuries. While later scholarship has questioned the pre-eminent place that Yates accorded to Hermetic thought in the period, her intervention marks a watershed after which interest began to centre around the esoteric intellectual commitments of Pico and his contemporaries, as in Edgar Wind's studies of Orphism (*Pagan Mysteries in the Renaissance*, 1958) and importantly in

the work of Moshe Idel and Chaim Wirszubski on the deep influence of Hebrew mysticism and of Kabbalah on Pico's thinking
(culminating in Wirszubski's *Pico della Mirandola's Encounter with
Jewish Mysticism*, 1989).

Those working on Pico today are fortunate enough to have
access to a wide range of excellent publications which build upon
these textual and contextual foundations, including new editions
of Pico's *Oration* and his nephew's biography edited by Brian
Copenhaver (*Life of Giovanni Pico della Mirandola*/Gianfrancesco
Pico della Mirandola; *Oration*/Giovanni Pico della Mirandola,
2022) and a forthcoming new edition of Pico's *Theses* in the same
iTatti Renaissance Library series. As this edition was not yet
available for use in preparing this book, references are given to S.
A. Farmer's *Syncretism in the West: Pico's 900 Theses* (1998),
which is at present the most accessible version of that text for
English-language readers. Copenhaver has also provided authoritative new accounts of the afterlife of Pico's works and reputation
(*Magic and the Dignity of Man*, 2019), and of the controversy
surrounding Pico's *Theses* and the proceedings against him in
Rome in 1487 (*Pico della Mirandola on Trial: Heresy, Freedom
and Philosophy*, 2022). An interesting recent intellectual biography of Pico can be found by French readers in Louis Valcke's
Pic de la Mirandole: Un Itinéraire Philosophique (2005), while
English-language readers might start with Copenhaver's entry on
Pico in the online *Stanford Encyclopedia of Philosophy*. The recent
bibliography of works on Pico's life, thought, context and afterlife
is immense and cannot be summarized here, though English
readers will particularly benefit from consulting the works of
Michael J. B. Allen, Giulio Busi, Christopher Celenza, M. V.
Dougherty, Amos Edelheit, Anthony Grafton, Jill Kraye and
Denis J-J Robichaud, as well as the comprehensive online bibliography of English-language translations of and scholarship on
Pico maintained by Dougherty ('Pico in English: A Bibliography',
http://www.mvdougherty.com/pico.htm).

As the fullness of even this very preliminary account of scholarship on Pico alone would suggest, the field of study which includes his close associates Poliziano and Ficino and the broader milieu of Renaissance Italian thought is of even more staggering size and resists even preliminary attempts to summarize. English readers will enjoy access to some of the most important texts in excellent editions and translations in the iTatti Renaissance Library (such as Poliziano's *Miscellanies*, by Dyck and Cottrell, *Letters*, by Butler, *Silvae*, by Fantazzi, and Ficino's *Commentaries on Plato*, by Allen, and *Platonic Theology*, by Allen and Hankins), as well as authoritative and accessible overviews of the social, material, and intellectual contexts in publications such as Christopher Celenza's *Intellectual World of the Italian Renaissance* (2018) and Grafton's *Magus: The Art of Magic from Faustus to Agrippa* (2024).

If this book has taken its own idiosyncratic path through Pico's thought and intellectual milieu, the same is also true of its treatment of the Sublime and of magical language, on each of which a vast and complex field of scholarship exists, even if the two are rarely treated together as they are here. The expansive field of writings on the Sublime in its classical form and in its later artistic and philosophical guises is particularly tricky to navigate given the lack of agreement on what precisely constitutes the Sublime, which can be seen as anything from a synonym of sorts for grandiosity in aesthetic style to an aesthetic-metaphysical nexus which was always leading up to and away from the Romantic sublime; readers can get an overview of this trajectory and ideas for further reading in volumes such as Philip Shaw's *The Sublime* for the New Critical Idiom series and Costelloe's *The Sublime: From Antiquity to the Present*. This account has chosen, however, to focus on those ontological and ethical problems posed by the experience of the Sublime as described by Longinus, a topic more often associated with treatments of magical language, theurgy, and necromancy, and angel-magic, about which readers may discover more in the works of (among many others) Charles Burnett (*Magic and Divination in the Middle Ages*), Anthony Grafton (*Magus*), as well as in non-elite contexts in Stephen Wilson (*The Magical Universe: Everyday Magic and Ritual in Early Modern Europe*), as well of course as in Keith Thomas's classic *Religion and the Decline of Magic*. There is, however, good reason to focus on the overlap between these two areas, and one good example of this is in Jenny C. Mann's *The Trials of Orpheus: Poetry, Science, and the Early Modern Sublime* (2021), which centres on the English context, and which came to my attention too late in this long-gestated project to be integrated into its foundations. In my own attempt to conjoin the interest in the sublime and the magical powers of language, in order to provide a way into thinking about these questions for those who might struggle with any account centrally reliant on a belief in supernatural agents, I have of course failed effectively to digest either, though I hope it has helped the reader to share some of my fascination with the deep ontological and ethical issues prompted by these still-common experiences, and encouraged them to engage with the ways in which cultures separated from them in time and space have thought through such questions.

This account set itself a further task of connecting the various traditions available to Pico with those that existed in the many other cultures of which Pico and his immediate successors were only slowly becoming aware. The global, comparative study of this Sublime and related concepts is still a work in progress, and most accounts come from the field of anthropology (such as Mircea Eliade's *Shamanism: Archaic Techniques of Ecstasy* and Gilbert Rouget's *Music and Trance: a theory of the relations between music and possession*), and from intellectual formations (in the case of Rouget) which make for reluctance to draw cross-cultural links between these phenomena. While this book has managed to be no more than suggestive in this regard, it is to be hoped that further work linking these traditions will soon be produced.

LIST OF ILLUSTRATIONS

In-text Images

Statue of the Virgin and Child Commissioned by Giulia Boiardo for the Palazzo della Ragione, Miranola, unattributed photograph. (author's collection)

Woodcut of a wryneck from Andrea Alciati, *Emblemes d'Alciat, de nouveau translatez en françois* (Paris: H. de Marnef, 1561). (Public Domain)

Italy, Ferrara, View of Castello Estense. (Getty Images / DEA / A. DE GREGORIO / Contributor)

Image of the Orphic god Phanes, owned by Ercole d'Este, now in Galleria Estense, Modena. (Alamy)

Leonardo da Vinci's designs for a production of Poliziano's *Orpheo* (Alamy)

Vishnu's avatar Matsya recovering the Vedas from the belly of a fish and returning them to Brahma. (Public Domain)

Mosaic inlay portraying Hermes Trismegistus, from the floor of Siena Cathedral (Alamy)

Rhythmomachia board from Jacques Lefevre d'Etaples, *Arethmetica et Musica* (Paris: Joannis Higman, 1496), sig. [i8^r]. (Public Domain)

Arabic talisman to protect against scorpion bites, 10th century, Louvre. (Public Domain)

A depiction of the discovery of the *Tabula Smaragdina*, 1602. (Alamy)

A page from Flavius Mithridates' *Sermo de Passione*, Vatican Library Barb. Lat. 1775, fol. 102r. (By permission of Biblioteca Apostolica Vaticana, with all rights reserved)

A psalter in the language of Geʿez, possibly used by Mithridates to teach
   Pico: Vatican Library, Vat.et.20, fol. 3ʳ. (By permission of Biblioteca
   Apostolica Vaticana, with all rights reserved)
An etching of Michelangelo's first work, 'The Battle of the Centaurs', a
   topic suggested by Poliziano. (Alamy)
Hercules Gallicus or Ogmios, copied from a fresco on the exterior wall
   of a building near the Piazza Navona in Rome, in Geoffroy Tory,
   Champfleury, (Paris: Gilles de Gourmant, 1529), fol. 3ᵛ.(Public
   Domain)
Cristoforo Buondelmonti, Map of Constantinople, from the *Liber
   Insularum Archipelagi*, Universitäts- und Landesbibliothek,
   Düsseldorf, MS-G-13, fol. 66ʳ. (Public Domain)
Ces Moeurs et fachons de faire de Turcz (Customs and Fashions of the
   Turks) after Pieter Coecke van Aelst, published by Mayken Verhulst,
   1553 (Public Domain)
Portrait of Cassandra Fedele from Giacomo Filippo Tomasini, *Elogia
   virorum litteris et sapientia illustrium* (Padua: Sebastiano Sardi,
   1644), p. [344]. (Public Domain)
Image of Savonarola preaching, from his 1495 *Compendio di
   Rivelazione* (Alamy)
A page from the Mixtec Codex Borbonicus, showing the speech scrolls
   representing overpowering speech, Bibliothèque de l'Assemblée
   Nationale, Paris (Public Domain)
A page from the Codex Testeriano Bodmer, showing the use of Mixtec
   speech scrolls to portray angel-speech, Cod. Bodmer 905, fol. 3ᵛ.
   (The Martin Bodmer Foundation, Cologny (Geneva))

Plate Section
Paul Delaroche, 'The Childhood of Pico della Mirandola', 1842, Musée
   des Beaux Arts, Nantes. (Alamy)
'April' from the frescoes at the Palazzo Schifanoia, Ferrara. (Alamy)
Domenico Ghirlandaio, 'The Annunciation of the Angel to Zecharias',
   Tornabuoni Chapel, Santa Maria Novella, Florence. (Bridgeman
   Image Library)
Golden lip plug in the form of an eagle head (teocuitcuauhtentetl),
   before 1521, Saint Louis Art Museum
Cosimo Rosselli, detail from the 'Miracle of the Sacrament'
   showing Pico clasped by two figures traditionally associated

with Poliziano and Ficino, Sant'Ambrogio, Florence. (Bridgeman Image Library)

Detail from Raphael's *School of Athens*, showing an unidentified figure looking out of the picture, identified by some as Pico. (Alamy)

Botticelli, detail from 'The Trials of Moses', Sistine Chapel, Vatican, portraying the Ethiopian ambassadors from the 1481-2 embassy. (Alamy)

Portrait of Girolamo Savonarola, *Il Frate*, by Fra Bartolomeo della Porta, from the Museo di San Marco. (Bridgeman Image Library)

ABBREVIATIONS USED

IN THE NOTES

Commento – Eugenio Garin, ed. and trans., *De Hominis Dignitate, Heptaplus, De Ente et Uno, e Scritti Vari* (Florence: Vallechi Editore, 1942)

Miscellanies – Angelo Poliziano, *Miscellanies*, 2 vols, ed. Andrew R. Dyck and Alan Cottrell (Cambridge, MA: I Tatti Renaissance Library, 2020)

Opera – *Opera Omnia Ioannis Pici, Mirandulae Concordiaeque comitis* (Basel: per Heinricum Petri, 1557)

Oration – *Life of Giovanni Pico della Mirandola & Oration*, ed. Brian C. Copenhaver (Cambridge, MA: I Tatti Renaissance Library, Harvard University Press, 2022)

Theses – *Syncretism in the West: Pico's 900 Theses (1486) with Text, Translation and Commentary*, ed. S. A. Farmer (Arizona: Arizona Center for Medieval and Renaissance Studies, 2008)

NOTES

I. The 900

1. *Diario della città di Roma di Stefano Infessura scribasenato*, ed. Oreste Tommasini (Rome: Forzani, 1890), pp. 216, 217–18, 220–21, 222–3, 224–5; *Diario Romano dal 3 maggio 1485 al 6 giugno 1524 di Sebastiano di Branca Teddalini*, ed. Paolo Piccolomini, in *Rerum italicarum scriptores: raccolta degli storici italiani dal cinquecento al millecinquecento* (Città di Castello: S. Lappi, 1907–11), p. 316. The quotes from Pico's letters to his nephew Gianfrancesco are here taken from Thomas More's translation of the life and letters, *The Lyfe of Johan Picus Erle of Myrandula* (London: William Rastell, 1510), and have been lightly modernised.

2. Giovanni Pico della Mirandola, *Conclusiones DCCCC publice disputandae* (Rome: Eucharius Silber, 7 December 1486). References to this text will henceforth be given to the edition by Farmer (as the edition most accessible to English-language readers) under the short title *Theses*; see here introduction, p. x, and Louis Valcke, *Pic de la Mirandole: Un itinéraire philosophique* (Paris: Les Belles Lettres, 2005), p. 155. *Miscellanies*, I.484–5. Unless otherwise noted I have made my own translations from this volume, though guided by the translation given there.

3. *Theses* 2>40, 7.25, 2>49, 22.4–8, 28.7, 9>21. Quotations from the life of Pico by his nephew Giovanni Francesco and from Pico's *Oration* are taken from the Copenhaver edition under the short title *Oration* (here pp. 116–17, 139); again, unless otherwise specified I

have made my own translations, though guided by Copenhaver's and other previous translations.

4. Gugliemo Raimondo Moncada, *Sermo de Passione Domini*, ed Chaim Wirszubski (Jerusalem: Israel Academy of Arts and Sciences, 1963); the sermon survives in Vat. Lat. Barberini 1775, fols 90–126. See also Grafton, *Commerce with the Ancients* (Ann Arbor: University of Michigan Press, 1997), p. 94.

5. Valcke, *Pic*, pp. 152–3.

6. *Oration*, pp. 120–23; *Theses*, p. 42.

7. *Oration*, pp. 118–121, 175, 86–7, 80–81.

8. *Oration*, pp. 86–7; 98–9; 100–103.

9. Of course, a great many of the theories of action at a distance relied on theories of astral influence, occult sympathy between objects and theurgy or the summoning and control of spirits, though those will not be treated in detail here in order to preserve the focus on the specific traditions to do with the experience of sound and voice, which I posit here not only to be central (though by no means isolated and exclusive) and to provide a broad connection between such ideas throughout the world and throughout history. The scholarship on astral magic, theurgy, necromancy and divination is immense, and cannot possibly be summarized here, but key studies for the medieval and early modern period include Frances Yates's classic *Giordano Bruno and the Hermetic Tradition* (Chicago: Chicago University Press, 1964); Richard Kieckhefer, *Magic in the Middle Ages* (Cambridge: Cambridge University Press, 1989); Charles Burnett, *Magic and Divination in the Middle Ages: Texts and Techniques in the Islamic and Christian Worlds* (Aldershot, UK: Variorum, 1996); and Claire Fanger, ed., *Conjuring Spirits: Texts and Traditions of Medieval Ritual Magic* (University Park, PA: Penn State University press, 1998). For a recent and accessible overview of the ideas most relevant to Pico's period, see Grafton, *Magus: The Art of Magic from Faustus to Agippa* (London: Allen Lane, 2024).

10. *Commento*, p. 556. The translation of Isaiah is here taken from the English Standard Version of the Bible, following Valery Rees, *From Gabriel to Lucifer: A Cultural History of Angels* (London: I. B. Tauris, 2013).

11. The story of Pico's later reputation has recently received a compelling and comprehensive account in Brian Copenhaver's

Magic and the Dignity of Man: Pico della Mirandola and his Oration in Modern Memory (Cambridge, MA: Harvard University Press, 2019); I am indebted here and elsewhere to Copenhaver's many works on Pico. The painting by Paul Delaroche is in the Musée des Beaux Arts in Nantes, Inv. # 902.

12. *Oration*, pp. 128–9; 138–9.

II. Ring of Fire

1. *Oration*, pp. 10–11. *Picatrix: A Medieval Treatise on Astral Magic*, trans. Dan Attrell and David Porreca (University Park, PA: Penn State University Press, 2019), p. 44; *Commento*, pp. 505–6. Plotinus, *The Enneads*, trans. Stephen McKenna, ed. John Dillon (London: Penguin Classics, 1991), I.6, pp. 48–9.

2. *Oration*, pp. 10–13.

3. References to Plato's works, unless otherwise stated, relate to *Plato: Complete Works*, ed. John M. Cooper (Indianapolis: Hackett, 1997), under the name of the particular work and giving both the page number and the standard reference, here *Symposium*, trans. A. Nehemas and P. Woodruff, p. 490 (207d–e). The 'Ship of Theseus' received its classic formulation in Plutarch's life of Theseus in his *Lives of the Noble Greeks and Romans*.

4. L. Dorez, 'Lettres inédites de Jean Pic de Mirandole, 1482–1492', in *Giornale storico della letteratura Italiana*, 85 (1895), 352–61, 356. *Oration*, pp. 12–13.

5. Valke, *Pic*, 87. The question of whether the building exists first in the mind of the architect or in physical form, central to Pico's thought, responds to the terms of debate laid down by Aristotle in *De Anima* 403a–b, and taken up in Plotinus, *Enneads* I.6 (p. 48); for Pico's use of it, see *Commento*, p. 467, *Heptaplus*, in Pico della Mirandola, *On the Dignity of Man/On Being and the One/Heptaplus*, trans. Charles Glenn Wallis, Paul W. J. Miller, and Douglas Carmichael (New York: Hackett, 1998), pp. 86–7.

6. *Oration*, pp. 12–13. Sac. F. Ceretti, 'Intorno a P. Francesco Ignazio Papotti ed ai suoi Annali della Mirandola', *Memorie storiche della città e dell'antico ducato della Mirandola* III, (Mirandola: Gaetano Cagarelli, 1876), p. XXVI.

7. Dante, *De Vulgari Eloquentia*, ed. and trans. Steven Botterill (Cambridge: Cambridge University Press, 1996), pp. 2–3, 34–7. Giovanni Pontano, 'Naeniae', in *Varia Opuscula* (Naples:

Sigismondo Mayr, 1505), Fii^{v}–[Fv]^{r}. The question of whether the Romans themselves learned Latin as a grammatical language or a vulgar tongue was a subject of lively debate in the period; see, for instance, the third part of Poggio Bracciolini's *Historia disceptativa convivialis*, which also discusses Bruni and Biondo's views.

8. (Ps.?-)Plato, *Halcyon*, §8, trans. Brad Inwood; Cavalcanti, 'Fresca Rosa Novella' in Guido Cavalcanti, *Complete Poems*, ed. and trans. Anthony Mortimer (London: Alma Books, 2012), pp. 2–3; I have used the Italian from this edition for ease of reference, but made my own translations. On Sigurd and Fáfnir see, for instance, 'Fafnismal', in *The Poetic Edda*, trans. Carolyne Larrington (Oxford: Oxford University Press, 2014). Jacobus de Voragine, *The Golden Legend*, ed. Richard Hamer and trans. Christopher Stace (London: Penguin Books, 1998), pp. 263–5. For a recent survey of the treatment of birdsong in culture, see Francesco Santi, 'When and Why the So-Called Chirping of the Birds Pointed out the Harmony of the World', *Micrologus* XXV (2017), 149–67, revising Leo Spitzer's earlier suggestion that this connection in *Stimmung* had been a phenomenon continuously present in European culture. The intuition that the training of the human ear is similar to the method by which fledglings learn birdsong has been confirmed by modern brain science: see, for instance, Bolhuis and Everaert, eds, *Birdsong, Speech and Language: Exploring the Evolution of Mind and Brain* (Cambridge, MA: MIT Press, 2013), esp. Ch. 5.

9. Pindar, Pythian IV. For the play on Pico/Picus, see for instance Poliziano, *Letters* III.xxi; on the Chaldean traditions concerning the *Iynges*/wryneck, see Ruth Majercik, *The Chaldean Oracles: Text, Translation, and Commentary* (Leiden: E. J. Brill, 1989), p. 9. See also Copenhaver, *Magic and the Dignity of Man*, pp. 9–12. On *pico bocciolo* (i.e. *tocciolo*) as an Italian name for the *Iynges*/wryneck, see, for instance, Gessner, *Historia Animalium Liber III De Avibus* (Frankfurt: Ioannis Wecheli, 1585), pp. 520 and 573, citing Augustino Nifo; Gessner assumes that *tocciolo* is a bastardization of *torzicuello*.

10. Ficino discusses the links between Pico and his works on Plato and Plotinus in the preface to his edition of Plotinus, the *Prohemium Marsili Ficini in Plotinum*, in Plotinus, *Opera*, trans. Marsilio Ficino (Florence: Antonio di Bartolommeo Miscomini, 7 May 1492), sig. [aii]$^{r-v}$; see also Valcke, *Pic*, 143.

III. A Light & Winged & Sacred Thing

1. Quotations from the *Phaedrus* and *Parmenides* are drawn from *Plato in Twelve Volumes*, trans. Harold N. Fowler (London: William Heinemann, 1925), with further material from the translation of Benjamin Jowett, 5 vols (Oxford: Oxford University Press, 1888); references are given to the standard notations, so here *Phaedrus* 227ac230e.
2. *Phaedrus*, 267b–d; 228b–c.
3. *Phaedrus*, 230c, 259a–d.
4. Quotations from the *Ion* are taken from *Classical Literary Criticism*, trans. Penelope Murray and T. S. Dorsch (London: Penguin Classics, 1965), pp. 1–4, 5–7.
5. Pliny, XXXIV.42; Evliya Çelebi, *An Ottoman Traveller: Selections from the Book of Travels of Evliya Çelebi*, ed. and trans. Robert Dankoff and Sooyong Kim (London: Eland Books, 2011), II.9; on Thales, see Aristotle, *De Anima* 405a; on the reciprocal relationship between action and passion, see *Physics* III.3, and Sarah Waterlow, 'Agent and Patient', in *Nature, Change and Agency in Aristotle's Physics: A Philosophical Study* (Oxford: Oxford University Press, 1982), pp. 159–203. Petrus Peregrinus, *Epistola de Magnete*, here quoting from an anonymous sixteenth-century English translation found in Gonville and Caius College, Cambridge MS 174/95, pp. 395–441, which can be accessed through the wonderful database of Peregrinus texts maintained by Christoph Sander. The connection between magnetism and song/enchantment continued to be central to sixteenth-century understandings of this phenomenon; for instance see Pietro Pomponazzi, *De Incantationibus*, ed. Vittoria Perrone Compagni (Rome: Olschki, 2011) III.2–3, pp. 17–18; and Sandro Landi, 'The Multitude's Two Bodies: On a key concept of Machiavellian criticism', *Essais: Revue interdisciplinaire des humanités* 19 (2023).
6. *The Iliad*, VIII.25–7, trans. A. T. Murray, 2 vols (Cambridge, MA: Harvard University Press, 1924).
7. Dodds, *The Greeks and the Irrational* (Berkley, CA: University of California Press, 1951), p. 79; the passage suggesting Socrates' insider knowledge of the Corybantic initiation rites is at *Euthydemus* 277d. Aristotle noted that the dithyramb could only be composed in the eastern, Phrygian mode and not in the Greek, Doric one, at *Politics* 1342b; see also Rouget, *Music and Trance: a*

theory of the relations between music and possession, trans. Brunhilde Biebuyck (Chicago: University of Chicago Press, 1985), p. 92.

8. Pierre Clastres, *Le grand parler: Mythes et chants sacrés des Indiens Guarani* (Paris: Éditions du Seuil, 1974), pp. 7, 11, 113.

9. *Parmenides,* 130d–e.; Plotinus returns to the question of mud and hair at *Enneads* VI.7.11–12.

10. *Phaedrus,* trans. Jowett, 250b–c. Importantly, while poetry/music and erotic love may seem to be divergent ways of accessing the transcendent, the understanding of how eros works upon the individual is highly dependent upon analogy with music, as at the end of Agathon's speech in the *Symposium,* where he describes Love as 'singing a song that enchants [thelgon] the thought [phronema]', a line later picked up by Dionysios the Areopagite. see K. Corrigan, 'Pseudo-Dionysios the Areopagite', in *The Stanford Encyclopedia of Philosophy,* from which the quotation from *Symposium* 197C here is taken.

IV. The Philosopher

1. Bernardino Zambotti, *Diario Ferrarese dall'anno 1476 sino al 1504,* ed. Giuseppe Pardi, in *Rerum Italicarum Scriptores* XXIV/vii (Bologna: Nicola Zanichelli, 1937), p. 59.

2. Zambotti, *Diario Ferrarese,* pp. 61–2, 72–3; Thomas Tuohy, *Herculean Ferrara: Ercole d'Este, 1471–1505, and the invention of a Ducal Capital* (Cambridge: Cambridge University Press, 1996), pp. 4, 7.

3. Zambotti, *Diario Ferrarese,* pp. 73, 79. Pico's brother Galeotto was married to Ercole's sister Bianca Maria d'Este.

4. Zambotti, *Diario Ferrarese,* p. 75.

5. Quotations from Aristotle's *De Anima* are taken from the translation by J. A. Smith contained in the *Works of Aristotle,* ed. W. D. Ross, vol. III (Oxford: Clarendon Press, 1931); references will be given in the standard format, here *De Anima* 413a.

6. *De Anima* 414b, 417a; Pico mentions his familiarity with it by 1484 in *Opera,* p. 350.

7. Aristotle's rejection of the multiple-worlds theory of the atomists is given in *De Caelo* I.7; Jacques Lefèvre d'Étaples 9; on the ethical implications of multiple world theory, see, for instance, James Warren, 'Ancient Atomists on the Plurality of Worlds', *Classical Quarterly* 54/2 (Dec 2004), 354–65. The Aristotelian attack on Eleatic monism is found at *Physics* 1.2 184b25–1.3 187. For more recent discussions of modal realism and many-world

theory, see David Lewis, *On the Plurality of Worlds* (Oxford: Blackwell, 1986).

8. The key passage is *De Anima* 430a.

9. See, for instance, the remembrance of Pico by the French humanist Jacques Lefèvre d'Étaples, in Valke, *Pic*, pp. 281–2. Pico, *Heptaplus*, trans. Carmichael, 140. Zambotti, *Diario Ferrarese*, pp. 65–6. I have translated here from *Apuleo volgare tradutto per il magnifico conte Matteo Maria Boiardo* . . . (Venice: Nicolò di Aristotile, detto Zoppino, 1526), sig. A3^r.

10. Matteo Maria Boiardo, *Orlando Innamorato*, ed. Luigi Garbato, vol. 1 (Milan: Marzorati, 1970), I.42, p.48. Cavalcanti, 'Chi è questa che vèn, ch'ogn'om la mira'. The probable portrait of Galeotto Pico della Mirandola and his bride Bianca d'Este is in the 'July' section of the *Schifanoia* 'mesi'.

11. The engraving of Pico used in Giambattista della Porta's *Della fisonomia dell'uomo* (Padua: Tozzi, 1623), fol. 172v, appears to be based on a portrait of the Estense style used by Cosimo Tura, and possibly specifically the 'Portrait of a Young Man' by Tura at the Metropolitan Museum of Art (Accession Number: 14.40.649), whose sitter has not been identified, suggesting that there was at one point a portrait in this style believed to be of Pico.

12. On classical and early modern understandings of the Phanes/ Mithra cult, see Simona Cohen, *Transformations of Time and Temporality in Medieval and Renaissance Art* (Leiden: Brill, 2014).

V. Orpheo

1. Poliziano, *Letters*, ed. Shane Butler, vol. I (Cambridge, MA: Harvard University Press, 2006), pp. 34–7, 41. The background and contexts for the *Orpheo* are best laid out in Antonia Tissoni Benvenuti's *L'Orfeo del Poliziano* (Padua: Editrice Antenore, 1986); English readers may consult Corinna Salvidori, Peter Brand and Richard Andrews, *Overture to the Opera: Italian Pastoral Drama in the Renaissance* (Dublin: UCD Foundation for Italian Studies, 2013). Quotations here are taken from Poliziano's *Stanze per la giostra de Giuliano de' Medici* (Florence: Bartolomeo de' Libri, 1494).

2. Poliziano, *Letters*, ed. Butler, pp. 220–22. On the long debate over the nature of Poliziano's argument with Clarice Orsini, see Alan Stewart, *Close Readers: Humanism and Sodomy in the English Renaissance* (Princeton, NJ: Princeton University Press, 1997), pp. 19–28.

3. *Miscellanies*, I.134–6; 186-93; II.144–9. See also the letter to Ermelao Barbaro on the 'Herculean Knot', *Letters*, ed. Butler, p. 41.

4. Poliziano, *Letters*, ed. Butler, pp. 16–25. On the passage on sexual pleasure and pain from the *Disputationes adversus astralogiam*, see Grafton, *Commerce with the Ancients*, p. 121.

5. Poliziano, *Letters*, ed. Butler, I.7, p. 27. Montaigne, 'De L'Amité'. Iamblichus, p. 216. The story about Poliziano's death comes from Paolo Giovio's *Elegia doctorum virorum* (1546), as quoted in Blake Wilson, *Singing to the Lyre in Renaissance Italy: Memory, Performance, Oral Poetry* (Cambridge: Cambridge University Press, 2019); for a discussion of the afterlife of Poliziano's sexuality, and the contexts of late-quattrocento Florentine law, see Alan Stewart, *Close Readers*, Ch. 1.

6. Poliziano, *Stanze*, sigs. E3ᵛ, E[7]ʳ.

7. N. G. Wilson, *From Byzantium to Italy: Greek Studies in the Italian Renaissance* (London: Duckworth, 1992), p. 86. On Ficino's Orphism, see *The Letters of Marsilio Ficino*, translated from the Latin by Members of the Language Department of the School of Economic Science, 11 vols (London: Shepheard-Walwyn,1975–1981), I.67–8, 129 and IV.35; Poliziano, *Miscellanies* I.484/5; Valcke, *Pic*, p. 79.

8. Wilson, *Singing to the Lyre*, p. 193, quoting Lorenzo's *De summo bono*; the letter from Callimachus mentioning the costume brought from Poland is in Ficino, see Ficino, *Letters*, vol. 7, p. 93 (Supplemental Letter E).

9. Plotinus, *Enneads*, p. 327; Charles Le Blanc, 'From cosmology to ontology through resonance: A Chinese interpretation of reality', in *Beyond Textuality*, ed. Gilles Bibeau and Ellen E. Corin (Berlin: De Gruyter, 1995); *Letters of Marsilio Ficino*, I.7, pp. 13–19.

10. Pindar, *Nemean Odes/Isthmian Odes/Fragments*, trans. William H. Race (Cambridge, MA: Harvard University Press, 1997), p. 303; Poliziano, *Stanze*, sigs. F2ʳ–F3ʳ. Poliziano, 'Nutricia', in *Silvae*, ed. and trans. Charles Fantazzi (Cambridge, MA: Harvard University Press, 2004), p. 123. In Pico's *Conclusions*, Bacchus was to come to be associated with the 'purest wine' of the Cabbalists as well as with spiritual intoxication in the Bible; see Pico's seventeenth Orphic thesis; I am grateful to Brian Copenhaver for drawing my attention to this.

11. The two intaglios mentioned here are held at the Metropolitan Museum of Art, New York, both being approximately dated to the second to third century CE: 'Jasper intaglio: Harpocrates seated on a

lotus', accession number 41.160.638; 'Serpentine intaglio: Radiate lion-headed god', accession number 10.130.1392. On the Araweté, see Eduardo Viveiros de Castro, *From the Enemy's Point of View*, trans. Catherine V. Howard (Chicago: University of Chicago Press, 1992), pp. 13, 58, 66, 225–30. On 'talisman', see *Picatrix*, p. 14.

VI. The Studious Artizan

1. William E. Gohlman, *The Life of Ibn Sina: A Critical Edition and Annotated Translation* (Albany, NY: SUNY University Press, 1974), pp. 25, 27–9, 31.
2. Gohlman, *Life of Ibn Sina*, pp. 35–7. Pico, *Oration*, p. 16.
3. Paul Hullmeine, 'Al-Bīrūnī and Avicenna on the Existence of Void and the Plurality of Worlds', *Oriens* 47 1/2 (2019), 114–44; al-Biruni, *Alberuni's India*, trans. Edward C. Sachau (London: Kegan Paul, 1910), pp. 33, 125. Staal, *Discovering the Vedas: Origins, Mantras, Rituals, Insights* (Haryana: Penguin Books, 2008), p. 203.
4. al-Ghazali, Ihya Ulum ad-Din, trans. Duncan B. Macdonald as 'Emotional Religion in Islam as Affected by Music and Singing', in the *Journal of the Royal Asiatic Society* (Apr. 1901), 195–252, 218–19, 229–30; (Oct. 1901), 705–48; (Jan. 1902), 1–28. Leo Africanus, *Descrittione dell'Africa*, in Giovanni Battista Ramusio, *Primo volume delle navigationi et viaggi* (Venice: Giunti, 1550), fol. 44^r.
5. Ficino, *Letters*, I.52–3. The belief in an 'anima mundi' seems to be the sense of the story told in Gianfrancesco's life (*Oration*, p. 62) in which Alberto Pio tried to comfort Pico on his deathbed by having him think of nature following the ideas of Alexander of Aphrodisias, Themistius and Averroes; Pico's response that he only has limited time left to make such mistakes seems to suggest not only that he had previously subscribed to the idea but also possibly that he had brought Pio to that way of thinking as well. On the matter of individual sin, it is important to note that the early Christian church was less concerned with personal sins than with the stain of sin shared by all humans, and that the concept of individual sin was elaborated during late antiquity on the model of Roman law; see Edward Peters, 'Ecclesiastical Discipline: Heresy, Magic, and Superstition', in *The Cambridge History of Medieval Canon Law*, ed. Anders Windroth and John C. Wei (Cambridge: Cambridge University Press, 2022), pp. 511–36, and Gabriel Thome, 'Crime and Punishment, Guilt and Expiation: Roman Thought and Vocabulary',

Acta Classica 35 (1995), 73–98. The idea of the shared intellect appears in the second and third of Pico's *Theses* on Averroes.

6. *Theses*, pp. 59–60; Valcke, *Pic*, p. 40. As Sten Ebbesen explains ('Averroism', *Routledge Encyclopedia of Philosophy: Islamic Philosophy*), there may have been few who openly promoted the idea of something being true philosophically and an alternative thing being true theologically, though the continuing practice of teaching the philosophy as well as the theology amounts to much the same thing.

7. Elia del Medigo to Pico in Garin, *Commento*, p. 67.

8. Chaim Wirszubski, *Pico della Mirandola's Encounter with Jewish Mysticism* (Cambridge, MA: Harvard University Press, 1989), 3–7; Valcke, *Pic*, pp. 96–7, 270–71; see the letter from Elia del Medigo to Pico edited by Giovanni Licata in *Secundum Avenroem: Pico della Mirandola, Elia del Medigo e la 'seconda rivelazione' di Averroè* (Palermo: Officina di Studi Medievali, 2022) II.i, esp. pp. 199–200. The letter suggests that Elia was aware that Pico was learning Arabic, though may well come from after Pico hired Mithridates, whose own disreputability was confirmation of the dangerousness of kabbalah. I am grateful for Brian Copenhaver's guidance on this.

9. An English translation of the letter to Barbaro is available in *Renaissance Debates on Rhetoric*, ed. and trans. Wayne A. Rebhorn (Ithaca: Cornell University Press, 2000), pp. 58–67; Valcke, *Pic*, pp. 110–11.

10. Christopher Marlowe, *The Tragicall Historie of Doctor Faustus*, ed. Roma Gill (Oxford: Oxford University Press, 1990), 1.3,5, pp. 34–6.

11. *The historie of the damnable life, and deserued death of Doctor Iohn Faustus . . . translated into English, by P.F. Gent* (London: Thomas Orwin, 1592). Sig. A2ᵛ; Marlowe, *Doctor Faustus*, 1.pp. 51–62.

VII. Poppysma

1. On the description of Pico's first visit by Antonio Benivieni, see Valcke, *Pic*, p. 95; Ficino's contending version is given in his dedication to Lorenzo in Plotinus, *Opera* (Florence: Antonio di Bartolommeo Miscomini, 7 May 1492), sig. [aii]ʳ.

2. Poliziano, *Letters*, pp. 100–103; *Miscellanies* I.97, p. 469.

3. Poliziano, *Miscellanies*, pp. 202–5. The two manuscripts Poliziano cites appear to be BML Plut.20 sin.1, fol. 316ʳ, and Plut. 82.2, fol. 91ᵛ. Giovanni Pontano, *Dialogi Charon et Antonius* (Naples: Mathias Moravus, 1491), sig. fiiᵛ–fiiiʳ.

4. *Opera*, p. 348; Kristeller, 'Giovanni Pico and his Sources', in *Studies in Renaissance thought and Letters*, 4 vols (Rome: Edizioni di Storia e Letteratura, 1956–1996), vol. III, 227–321, 233.

5. Poliziano, *Letters*, pp. 262–5 (IV.vii), 205 (III.xx). Vasari, *Le Vite de' piu eccellenti pittori* (Florence: Guinti, 1568), vol. I, part II, p. 438. See Brian Copenhaver's discussion of possible portraits of Pico, and the history of finding Pico in paintings, in *Magic and the Dignity of Man*, pp. 300–308. As Copenhaver points out, many of these pictures do not resemble the much less flattering Uffizi portrait (integrated into the cover of this edition), though Vasari's comments confirm that shortly after Pico's death there was a tradition of associating this angelic figure with Pico.

6. Gaspar Schott, *Magiae universalis natura et artis*, vol. 3 (Bamberg: Joan. Arnoldi Cholini, 1572), p. 598; see also Michel de Certeau, 'Angelic Speech', in *The Mystic Fable*, ed. Luce Giard and trans. Michael B. Smith (Chicago: University of Chicago Press, 2015), vol. 2, 161–80. Dante, *Paradiso* XXVIII.93. The term 'fe li' used to describe the angel's name in Judges 13: 18 can also be translated as 'secret', 'mysterious' and 'unintelligible'. On the passage from Judges 13: 18, and its importance for Reuchlin and Agrippa, see Grafton, *Magus*, pp. 195–6. On language and silence in Dionysius the Areopagite, see, for instance, *Mystical Theology* 1033C. Note that in the 'Songs of the Sabbath Sacrifice' from the Dead Sea Scrolls, the praise-song of angels is also a kind of divine silence; see Rees, *Gabriel to Lucifer*, p. 21.

7. Hermes appears as messenger and psychopomp at the end of *The Iliad* (24:153, 182, etc.), and then widely in *The Odyssey*; see Wolfgang Speyer, 'The Divine Messenger in Ancient Greece, Etruria and Rome', in *Angels: The Concept of Celestial Beings Origins, Development, Reception* (Leiden: Brill, 2006), p. 38. Dante, *Paradiso* XIV.127–9. Dante, *De Vulgari Eloquentia*, p. 4–5. For a recent, wide-ranging study of angel-lore, see Valery Rees, *From Gabriel to Lucifer*. Pico's thoughts on there being a single angel in each class were widely shared among late scholastics; see Jacobus Brutus, *Corona Aurea* (Venice: Giovanni Tacuino, 1496), sig. kii[v]–kiii[v] for a list of authorities.

8. Plotinus, *The Enneads*, trans. McKenna, p. civ; Plato, *Timaeus*, 23a–b. The tradition of Greek knowledge being derived at least in part from Egyptian would have been widely known to Pico's contemporaries through Jerome's 'First Letter to Paulinus', which was frequently used as a preface to the Bible. Ficino to Pier Leone, 3 January 1488 (i.e. 1489).

9. For a modern reconstruction of the Zoroastrian ritual, see the MUYA (Multimedia Yasna) project; I am grateful to Almut Hintze for her guidance on Zoroastrian ritual. Staal, *Discovering the Vedas*, pp. xiv–xv, 70; *Mahabharata*, trans. Carole Satyamurti (London: W. W. Norton & Co., 2016), p. 238.

10. *Enneads*, trans. McKenna, pp. 47–50, 310, 323–4. For an argument that the theory of prayer outlined in Plotinus *Enneads* was central to Ficino's philosophy, see Denis J.-J. Robichaud, 'Ficino on Force, Magic and Prayers', *Renaissance Quarterly* 70/1 (2017), 44–87, and 55, particularly on the importance of the 'synapse' as the manner in which 'prayer brings us in contact with the divine.'

11. N. G. Wilson, *From Byzantium to Italy*, p. 86, quoting Ficino. Ficino had translated the *Pimander* in 1463, but later became aware of the pseudonymous nature of the Hermetic corpus; see Robichaud, 'Ficino on Force, Magic and Prayers', 74. On the contexts of the composition of the Hermetic corpus, see Garth Fowden, *The Egyptian Hermes: a historical approach to the late pagan mind* (Cambridge: Cambridge University Press, 1986).

12. The major documents regarding Giovanni Mercurio da Correggio can be found in Wouter J. Hanegraaff and Ruud M. Bouthoorn, eds, *Lodovico Lazzarelli (1447–1500): The Hermetic Writings and Related Documents* (Tempe, AZ: Arizona Center for Medieval and Renaissance Studies, 2005), which also contains an excellent overview of the scholarship related to Giovanni Mercurio and Lazzarelli; the quotation here is taken from pp. 136–7, with a lightly adapted translation. See also David B. Ruderman, 'Giovanni Mercurio da Correggio's Appearance in Italy as Seen through the Eyes of an Italian Jew', *Renaissance Quarterly* 28/3 (1975), 309–22. I am grateful to Brian Copenhaver for his guidance on Giovanni Mercurio.

13. Ruderman, 'Giovanni Mercutio', 320; Yates, *Giordano Bruno*, Ch. 5.

VIII. Panurge in Paris

1. Jerome's 'First Epistle to Paulinus' appears in the 42-line *Biblia* (Mainz: Gutenberg and Johann Fust, *c*.1454), fol. 1ʳ. Pico's copy of the *Vita Apollonii* of Philostratus is at 43 in Pearl Kibre's inventory, *The Library of Pico della Mirandola* (New York, NY: Columbia University Press, 1936); he seems to have had it copied from the manuscript owned by Baptista of Mantua, as Kibre notes at p. 13. Pico, *Oration*, p. 15.

2. *The Correspondence of Erasmus*, Vol. I, 'Letters 1-141', ed. and trans. R. A. B. Mynors and D. F. S. Thomson (Toronto: University of Toronto Press, 1974), Ep. 64 and 108, pp. 135–6 and 202–3.

3. Pico's thesis on the minima naturalia is 2>34 in *Theses*. Aquinas's response to the 'Universal Mind' problem was that minds are *not* pure form, but *form plus existence*, in that they have added to their form their separate existence (which is what allows us to conceive of them as separate things); furthermore, even if they were immaterial to begin with, they take on material form in embodiment, and even after leaving that material form don't lose this manner of distinction. See, for instance, Aquinas, *Selected Philosophical Writings*, ed. Timothy McDermott (Oxford: OUP, 1993), pp. 104–7.

4. *Oration*, pp. 44–5; Valcke pp. 102–3, 261–3.

5. See Valcke, *Pic*, pp. 44–5, 133–4, and Dag N. Hasse, *Success and Suppression: Arabic Science and Philosophy in the Renaissance* (Harvard, MA: Harvard University Press, 2016), Ch. 5, on the fortunes of Averroes in Paris and late medieval and Renaissance Europe.

6. Aristotle, *Problems*, trans. Robert Mayhew (Cambridge, MA: Harvard University Press, 2011), IV.i, VII.i and v, XIX.xxvii. Frank Kermode, 'Eliot and the Shudder', *London Review of Books* 32/9, 13 May 2010.

7. See Ficino's comment upon this, linking it to Origen and Synesius, at *De Vita* 3.21. Quotations from the *De Radiis* are taken from al-Kindi, *De Radiis*, trans. Charles Burnett and Merlin Cox. I am grateful to Prof. Burnett for sharing a pre-publication version of this translation with me. See also Charles Burnett, 'Powerful words in medieval magical texts', in *The Word in Medieval Logic, Theology and Psychology*, Acts of the XIII international colloquium of the Societé Internationale pour l'Etude du Philsophie Médiévale (Turnhout: Brepols, 2009).

8. *Picatrix*, trans. Attrell and Porreca, pp. 16, 44, 58, 102, 254. Rabelais, *Le Tiers Livre*, XXIII. On the context for Pico's ownership of a manuscript of the *Picatrix*, which also apparently contained Thābit ibn Qurra's *On Talismans*, see Charles Burnett, 'Thābit Ibn Qurra's *On Talismans* Between the Middle Ages and the Renaissance, and Between the Science of the Stars and Magic', in *Bruniana & Campanelliana*, Anno XXVII (2021), 1–2, 23–50.

9. Pseudo-Albertus Magnus, *Liber seu liber secretorum*, Bk III, *De virtutibus animalium*; Kiber, *Library of Pico della Mirandola*, §984.

10. *The Opus Majus of Roger Bacon*, ed. J. H. Bridges, 3 vols (Oxford: Williams and Norgate, 1900), I. pp. 401–2; here quoted in the translation of Robert Belle Burke, *Opus Majus* (Philadelphia: University of Pennsylvania Press, 1928), I. pp. 416–17. The earliest written account of the 1284 event that would serve as the basis for the tale of the 'Pied Piper of Hamelin' appears in the fourteenth-century *Exodus Hamelensis* by Henricus de Hervordia, Lüneburg, Ratsbücherei, Herzog August Bibliothek Wolfenbüttel, Theol. 2° 25, fol. 268r. Amanda Power, *Roger Bacon and the Defence of Christendom* (Cambridge: Cambridge University Press, 2012), Ch. 4; Irène Rosier, *La parole comme acte: sur la grammaire et la sémantique au XIIIᵉ siècle* (Paris: J. Vrin, 1994), Ch. 6. For an excellent summary of the different sides of the debates regarding magic and astrology, see Grafton, *Magus*, pp. 34–9; as Grafton suggests (Ch. 3), Pico's disdain for such 'popular magic' seems not to have been entirely comprehensive.

11. A useful recent edition, translation and summary of this material is available in M. David Litwa, *Hermetica II: the Excerpts of Stobaeus, Papyrus Fragments, and Ancient Testimonies* (Cambridge: Cambridge University Press, 2018), pp. 314–16.

12. *Hermetica II*, trans. M. David Litwa, p. 316. On enormous ancient emeralds, see Theophrastus, *De Lapidiis*, §23–4. The story of the Pillars of Seth is found in Josephus, *Antiquities of the Jews*, Bk I, Chs 2 and 3. On the obelisks and the importance of hieroglyphs to the Florentine intellectual scene, see Karl Giehlow, *The Humanist Interpretation of Hieroglyphs in the Allegorical Studies of the Renaissance*, trans. Robin Raybould (Leiden: Brill, 2015), Ch. 5.

13. James M. Robinson et al., *The Nag Hammadi Library in English* (Leiden: Brill, 1977), pp. 7, 10, 20–21, 271, 362.

14. Pythian VI, in *The Odes of Pindar*, trans. C. M. Bowra (Harmondsworth: Penguin, 1969).

IX. The Death of the Kiss

1. On Mithridates' translation of Maimonides tract on bodily resurrection, see Mauro Zonta, 'Guglielmo Raimondo Moncada traduttore di Maimonide', in Perani, *Guglielmo Raimondo Moncada alias Flavio Mitridate* (Palermo: Officina di Studi Medievali, 2008), p. 185–199.

2. Henri Bresc, 'Le judaïsme sicilien: caractères généraux et particularités', Shlomoh Simonsohn, 'Guglielmo Raimondo

Moncada: Un converso alla convergenza di tre culture: ebraica, Cristiana, e islamica', and Angelo Michele Piemontese, 'Guglielmo Raimondo Moncada alla Corte di Urbino', in Perani, *Guglielmo Raimondo Moncada alias Flavio Mitridate*, particularly pp. 33, 157.

3. The episode is recounted in an undated letter from Ficino to Domenico Benivieni, *Opera* (1561) Sig. Iii 5^{r-v}, but given the various date constraints the debate was likely to have taken place in 1486, during the peak period of Pico's association with Mithridates.

4. Simonsohn, 'Un converso alla convergenza di tre culture', pp. 29–30; Wirszubski, 10–13; *Letters*, p. 113; Pico, *Heptaplus*, trans. Carmicheal, p. 170; for an English translation see Ficino, *Letters*, vol. 7, pp. 90–92 (Supplementary Letter B). Copenhaver, *Magic and the Dignity of Man*, p. 365.

5. Wirszubski, *Pico della Mirandola's Encounter with Jewish Mysticism*, pp. 4–7. Copenhaver, *Magic and the Dignity of Man*, pp. 340–43.

6. Pico to Ficino, September 1486, in Ficino, *Letters*, vol. 7, pp. 90–92 (Supplemental Letter B).

7. Valcke, *Pic*, p. 152; Grafton, *Commerce with the Ancients*, p. 107.

8. A thorough and detailed account of this embassy is given in Verena Krebs's excellent *Medieval Ethiopian Kingship, Craft, and Diplomacy with Latin Europe* (Basingstoke: Palgrave Macmillan, 2021), pp. 126–39, from which this account is drawn.

9. Luca Waddingo, *Annales Minorum*, vol. 14 (Rome: Rochi Bernabò, 1735), p. 243; Krebs, *Medieval Ethiopian Kingship*, pp. 129, 131.

10. Samantha Kelly, 'The Curious Case of Ethiopic Chaldean: Fraud, Philology, and Cultural (Mis)Understanding in European Conceptions of Ethiopia', *Renaissance Quarterly* 68 (2015), 1227–64. The Psalter in Ge'ez is Vat. Eti. 20.

11. Garin, *Commento*, pp. 495, 497, 501–2, 524–5, 557–8, 561.

12. Ficino, *Letters*, vol. 7, Letter 27 (p. 32). Valcke, *Pic*, p. 146.

13. *Oration*, pp. 20–21; *Opera*, pp. 378–9; Wirzubski, p. 16; Valcke, *Pic*, pp. 146–7

14. Garin, *Commento*, pp. 526–7, 530, 553–4, 567.

15. Hanegraaff and Bouthoorn, *Lodovico Lazzarelli*, pp. 33–4. Valcke, *Pic*, p.155.

X. The Language of Birds

1. Poliziano, *Miscellanies*, vol. I, pp. 14–15.

2. Georgius de Drogobyč, *Prognosticon 1483* (Rome: Eucharius Silber, 7 Feb 1483), fols. 2ʳ, 3ᵛ; Lorenzo Buonincontro, *Vaticinium (Prognosticon for 1486/87)* (Rome: Stephan Plannck, between 2 February and 1 March 1486), fol. 7r. *Theses*, p. 46, quoting Kristeller and Garin. Dorez, 'Lettres Inedites', p. 358. Pico was presented with a writ by the papal nuncio 'in domo suo soli[t]e residencie, in quadam camera superiori existentem' the following July (*Pic de la Mirandole en France*, p. 141), but the specific location of his residence is not mentioned. For a fuller treatment of the printing of the *Theses* and their underlying ideas, see Copenhaver, *Magic and the Dignity of Man*, 339 ff.

3. As Valcke suggests (*Pic*, p. 254), Pico's ideas on non-contradiction draw on Plotnius, and qua Farmer, on Nicholas of Cusa (*Theses*, note at 3>12–15).

4. On the persistence of the individual soul, see *Theses* 7.4; it is qualified (or its meaning reversed) at 3>20; see also the Introduction at pp. 113–14. Staal, *Discovering the Vedas*, p. 180.

5. *Theses*, 9>9–21. For an interesting example of how the Indian analysis of these things also revolved around the *minima naturalia*, see the texts by Vasubandhu and related discussion in Sonam Kachru, *Other Lives: Mind and World in Indian Buddhism* (New York: Columbia University Press, 2021).

6. On Kautsa, see Staal, *Discovering the Vedas*, pp. 141–5.

7. Aristotle, *Rhetoric*, III.8–9, *Poetics* §1459b–1460a. The story of al-Khalil is recounted in the treatise on Arabic prosody composed by al-Hassan ibn Muhammad al Wazzan (also known as Leo Africanus) at the request of Leo X; part of the treatise survives as Laur. Plut. 35.36, fol. 54ʳ-61ᵛ, and has been published by Angela Codazzi as 'Il trattato dell'arte metrica di Giovanni Leo Africano', in *Studi orientalistici in onore di Giorgio Levi Della Vida*, vol. I (Florence: Olschki, 1956), pp. 180–98 (here p. 185). On the vocables in the Mixtec *Cantares Mexicanos*, see Gary Tomlinson, *The Singing of the New World* (Cambridge: Cambridge University Press, 2007), p. 56.

8. *Theses*, 9>13. The story of Iambulus and the inhabitants of the Islands of the Sun is preserved in Diodorus Siculus' *Bibliotheca Historica*, II 56. Note that Dante also imagines Empire as a single bird made of many birds in Paradiso XIX.

9. *Oration*, p. 93.

10. *Oration*, pp. 14–17. The Second Register of borrowers from the Vatican Library (Vat. Lat. 3966, fol. 43r) shows that Pico borrowed a

manuscript of Thomas Aquinas's *De ente et essentia* on 24 December 1486 (likely Vat. Lat. 772), returning it on 3 January 1487, and a manuscript of Roger Bacon on astrology on 16 January, returning it on 5 March, as well as a manuscript of Henry Bate on 6 March, which he appears to have returned immediately owing to the loss of his borrowing privileges. See Grafton, *Commerce with the Ancients*, p. 105.

XI. Illumination

1. The papal brief *Cum inunctio nobis*, issued on 20 February 1487, is transcribed in *Pic de la Mirandole en France*, 114–115. *Apologia conclusionum suorum* (Naples: Francesco del Tuppo, after 31 May 1487), fol. 1ʳ.

2. The arguments over Pico's theses have recently been thoroughly and convincingly studied by Brian Copenhaver, in his *Pico della Mirandola on Trial*, and here I largely follow that account, while also drawing on Farmer and Valcke.

3. This is an attempt to translate an anecdote that appears on fol. 45v of Pico's *Apologia*, and which turns on a pun on the word 'testes', which in Latin can mean either 'witness' or 'testicles'.

4. The Papal Bull 'Etsi ex iniuncto nobis' is dated 4 August 1487 but was not promulgated until December of that year, on which see further below. *Bulla 4 Aug. 1487 'Etsi ex iniuncto' condemnatoria libelli Conclusionum DCCCC Joannis Pici Mirandulani* (Rome: Eucharius Silber, after 4 August 1487). On fol. [2r] the Bull notes that the findings of the Comission were 'reiteratu[m] nonnunquam etiam in nostra presentia accuratum & laudabile examen dictarum Conclusionem & contentorum in eis nobis concorditer retulerunt . . .'

5. *Bulla 4 Aug. 1487*, fol 3ʳ⁻ᵛ. The general Bull against printing of heretical volumes was also issued by Silber, on 17 November 1487, as *Bulla S. D. N. Innocentii contra impressores librorum reprobatorum: [(inter multiplices nostrae solicitudinis curas)]*. The British Library's illuminated, parchment copy of Pedro Garcia's *Petri Garsie Episcopi Ussellen . . . in determinatiões magistrales côtra conclusiones apologales J. Pici . . . proęmiũ* (Rome: Eucharius Silber, 1489), is IB.18896. One copy of the Bull survived in the library of Hernando Colón, where it was given the Registrum B number 7961.

6. See discussion of the relevant materials in Bruce Lincoln, *Myth, Cosmos and Society: Indo-European Themes of Creation and Destruction* (Cambridge, MA: Harvard University Press, 1986).

7. See, for instance, Ingrid D. Rowland, 'The Intellectual Background of *The School of Athens*: Tracking Divine Wisdom in the Rome of Julius II', in *Raphael's School of Athens*, ed. Marcia Hall (Cambridge: Cambridge University Press, 1997), p. 156.
8. Pico's letter defending himself to Lorenzo is found in the Archivio di Stato di Firenze, Mediceo Avanti il Principati, Fil. 51, doc. 584, (fols. 686ʳ-687ᵛ). The documents relevant to Pico's time in France are printed in Dorez, *Pic de la Mirandole en France*, pp. 146–62, and discussed on pp. 71–101.
9. Gianfrancesco's life of his uncle recounts an episode in which Pico was promised 'secular titles and a healthy income' by a king if he would only ask it, but does not specify which king, and it is possible that this also refers to the attempt by Ferdinand to lure Pico to Spain: *Oration*, p. 50.
10. Nicholas of Cusa's library catalogue was published by Franz Xavier Kraus in *Serapeum* 24 (1864), 369–83.

XII. The Isolate Song

1. Poliziano, *Miscellanies*, pp. 76–83; *Letters*, p. 127. Lehmann surmises that Piero di Cosimo's giraffe in his *Allegory of Civilization* (Ottowa: National Gallery of Canada) is copied from the sketches made by Cyriac of Ancona on his visits to Egypt, and that Bellini copied from Piero, though she does not consider the fact that there was a live giraffe present in Florence when Piero was painting. See Phillis William Lehmann, *Cyriacus of Ancona's Egyptian Visit and Its Reflections in Gentile Bellini and Hieronymus Bosch* (Locust Valley, NY: J. J. Augustin, 1977).
2. Brian Curran, *The Egyptian Renaissance: The afterlife of Egypt in early modern Italy* (Chicago: University of Chicago Press, 2007), pp. 149–50; Giehlow, *The Humanist Interpretation of Hieroglyphs*; George Boas, trans., *The Hieroglyphics of Horapollo* (Princeton, NJ: Princeton University Press, [2020] 1969), pp. 45–7, 56–8; P. W. Lehmann, *Cyriacus of Ancona's Egyptian Visit*, p. 11. Kibre notes (*The Library of Pico della Mirandola*, p. 14) that Pico wrote to Giorgio Valla in 1492 asking for 'the *Orus* or Sacred Carvings of the Egyptians', and that this copy of Horapollo seems to have been his own, which he was asking for in return.
3. Poliziano, *Miscellanies*, I.461, pp. 484–5 (I have retained Dyck and Cottrell's translation of the latter); *Silvae*, ed. and trans. Charles

Fantazzi, p. 32 (I have made my own translation, though guided by Fantazzi's); Giovanni Villani, *Croniche Fiorentine* (Florence: Bartolomeo Zanetti Casterza, 1537), Aii^{r-v}; Ficino, Letter to Filippo Valori, 27 October 1489, in *Letters*, vol. 7, 69–73; Pound, 'Erat Hora'.

4. A thorough treatment of the materials relating to Poliziano's influence on Michelangelo's *Battle of the Centaurs* can be found in Charles Dempsey, 'Angelo Poliziano and Michelangelo's Battle of the Centaurs', *Mitteilungen des Kunsthistorischen Institutes in Florenz* (2020), 62, 158–79.

5. Ficino to Francesco Gaddi, 11 October 1488, *Opera*, sig. Kkk [6]^{v}.

6. The idea that Moses spoke in riddles (using hieroglyphs or Pythagorean symbols to hide the truth from the uninitiated) derived from Julian the Apostate, and was later taken up (via Cyril of Alexandria) by Urbano Bolzanio and others; see Giehlow, *The Humanist Interpretation of Hieroglyphs*, p. 205. I have followed the translation of Propertius here and in the epigraph from Carmichael's translation of the *Heptaplus*, though the modern standard numbering has the line at Elegy II.x.6, not III.i.6 as given there.

7. *Heptaplus*, pp. 78–80, 105, 145.

8. *Heptaplus*, p. 170.

9. Poliziano, *Letters*, pp. 265–8, 261.

10. Piero Crinito, *De honesta disciplina* 3.2 (Florence: P. de Giunta, 1504), sig. [b.v^{r-v}]; Grafton, *Commerce with the Ancients*, p. 43. Translations from Lucian are taken from F. G. Fowler and H. W. Fowler, *The Works of Lucian of Samosata*, vol. 3 (Oxford: Clarendon Press, 1905), p. 257. On the Hercules Ogmios, see Edgar Wind, '"Hercules" and "Orpheus": Two Mock-Heroic Designs by Dürer', *Journal of the Warburg Institute*, 2/3 (1939), 206–18; Robert E. Hallowell, 'Ronsard and the Gallic Hercules Myth', *Studies in the Renaissance* 9 (1962), 242–55; and Edward W. Wouk, 'Reclaiming the Antiquities of Gaul: Lambert Lombard and the History of Northern Art', *Simiolus: Netherlands Quarterly for the History of Art*, 36 1/2 (2012), 36–65. Valeriano included a discussion of the Hercules Ogmios in his *Hieroglyphica* (Basel: [Michael Isengrin], 1556), fol. 239^{r}, and an emblem was included in the *Emblemata* of Andrea Alciato (Basel: Christian Weschel, 1534), p. 98. Dürer's illustration of the Hercules Ogmios, which is here blended with attributes of Hermes, has been included as the end-papers of this edition.

11. The similarities to Aby Warburg's *Bilderfahrzeuge*, pathos-formulae, and engrams is conscious here, though the polygenesis of the images suggests repeated recognition of the same experience, rather than transmission or inherited memory.

12. Ficino to Roberto Salviati, undated, *Opera* sig. Lll 3ᵛ–Lll4ʳ.

XIII. Above My Dukedom

1. 'Diario odeporico-bibliografico inedito del Poliziano', first published in the *Memorie del R. Instituto Lombardo di Scienze e Lettere*, Milano 1916, repr. in Poliziano, *Opera*, ed. Ida Maïer (Torino: Bottega d'Erasmo, 1971), vol. III, pp. 155–65 (229–39).

2. Lascaris' list of desiderata for his book-hunting expedition, as well as those books he encountered, is preserved in Vat. Gr. 1412, and has been transcribed by K. K. Müller as *Neue Mittheilungen über Janos Laskaris und die Mediceische Bibliothek* (Centralblatt für Bibliothekwesen, Sept–Oct 1884). See also Graham Speake, 'Janus Lascaris' visit to Mount Athos in 1491', *Byzantine Studies* 34 (1993), 325–30. Gülru Necipoglu, Cemal Kafadar and Cornell Fleischer, eds *Treasures of Knoweldge: An Inventory of the Ottoman Palace Library (1502/3–1503/4)* (Leiden: Brill, 2019), pp. 10–11.

3. Manuscript J of the life of Ibn Sina was in the Topkapı Palace library, and survives as Ahmet III MS 3447(6); see *The Life of Ibn Sina*, p. 3, and Necipoglu, Kafadar and Fleischer, *Treasures of Knowledge*, 164n.12, and on al-Biruni's Tarikh al-Hind, p. 590.

4. Cyriac of Ancona, *Later Travels* ed. and trans. Edward W. Bodnar, with Clive Foss (Cambridge, MA: I Tatti Renaissance Library, 2003), pp. 113, 120–35; Buondelmonti, *Description des Iles*, trans. Émile Légrand (Paris: E. Leroux, 1897), p. 250. On *hesychasm*, see Peter Adamson, *Byzantine and Renaissance Philosophy* (Oxford: Oxford University Press, 2022), pp. 123–7. *The Yoga Sutras of Patañjali*, ed. and trans. Mario Kozah (New York, NY: Library of Arabic Literature, NYU Press, 2020). Al-Ba'uniyyah, A'ishah, *The Principles of Sufism*, trans. Th. Emil Homerin (New York, NY: Library of Arabic Literature, NYU Press, 2016), pp. 2–3. The continuity between Yogic and Sufi practices of self-enchantment was first noted by Louis Massignon in his *Essai sur les origines du lexique technique de la mystique musulmane* (1922); see Rouget, *Music and Trance*, p. 8.

5. Poliziano, 'Diario odeporico-bibliografico', p. 162 [236].

6. A selection of Fedele's writings in translation can be found in
Cassandra Fedele, *Letters and Orations*, ed. and trans. Diana Robin
(Chicago: University of Chicago Press, 2000); see also the
discussion in Lisa Jardine, "'O Decus Italiae Virgo", or, The Myth of
the Learned Lady in the Renaissance', *The Historical Journal* 28.4
(1985), 799–819, as well as Grafton and Jardine, *From Humanism to
the Humanities: Education and the Liberal Arts in Fifteenth- and
Sixteenth-Century Europe* (Cambridge, MA: Harvard University
Press, 1986), Ch. 2. Poliziano's writings on and to her are found in
Letters, I.325, III.xvii, p. 189.

7. Cassandra Fedele to Aurelio Augurello, in *Clarissimae feminae
Cassandrae Fidelis Venetae epistolae & orationes* (Padua; Francesco
Bolzetta, 1636), letter 10, pp. 15–16.

8. Lascaris notes the MS of Λογγίνου περὶ 'ὑψους on p. 411 of Müller's
transcription. Müller associates the manuscript located by Lascaris as
BML MS 28.30, though Speake also notes that many of the
manuscripts brought back by Lascaris were not intended for Lorenzo;
Paris Gr. 2974 is identified by Carlo Maria Mazzucchi as having been
in the possession of Lascaris in the late fifteenth century; see *Dionisio
Longino: Del Sublime* (Rome: Università Cattolica, 2010), Intro., pp.
xxxv–xxxviii. Pico's characteristic reading mark, two side-by-side dots
above a long trail, was identified by Wirszubski (*Pico della Mirandola's
Encounter with Jewish Mysticism*, p. 23; see, for instance, Vat. Ebr. 190
fol. 84^r or 101^v for examples of the mark in MSS prepared for Pico by
Mithridates); the mark can be seen throughout the Paris Gr. 2974 MS
of *Peri Hypsous*. The particular examples quoted here are on fols 23^v,
24^v, 26^{r-v}, 37^r, 46^r; the last mark is slightly unclear as it is smudged at
the top, but seems to be consistent with the other marks, and is not
like any other readers' marks in the MS. Pico's reader's mark can also
be seen in the BNF copy of Aspasius' *Commentary on Aristotle's
Nichomachean Ethics*, Paris Gr. 1902, which has been identified as
Pico's; see for instance fol. 11^v. Translations of Longinus here are taken
from *Classical Literary Criticism*, trans. Penelope Murray and T. S.
Dorsch (London: Penguin Classics, 2004).

9. Poliziano, *Letters*, p. 247. Landucci's diary makes clear that the
lightning actually struck the cathedral on the night of 5 April, three
days before Lorenzo's death, while the *Ricordanze* of Tribaldo di
Rossi (*Delizie degli eruditi toscani*, vol. 23, pp. 273–4) suggest that a
storm had been raging all night. See also Piero di Marco Parenti,

Storia Fiorentina, ed. Andrea Matucci, 2 vols (Florence: Leo S. Olschki, 1994–2018), vol. I, pp. 21–2.

XIV. The Shudder

1. Landucci, *A Florentine Diary from 1450 to 1516*, trans. Alice de Rosen Jervis (London: J. M. Dent, 1927), p. 53; Machiavelli, *Discorsi*, I.xi. Savonarola, *Sermone dell' oratione* (Florence: Antonio Miscomini, 20 October 1492), sig. aii^{r-v}.
2. Ficino, in Savonarola, *Selected Writings*, pp. 355–6. George Eliot, *Romola* (London: Oxford University Press, 1975), pp. 165–6. Lauro Martines, *Fire in the City: Savonarola and the Struggle for the Soul of Renaissance Florence* (Oxford: Oxford University Press, 2006), pp. 168–9; Savonarola, *Sermone dell' oratione*, sig. aii^{v}.
3. Poliziano, *Miscellanies*, pp. 425-7; I have followed Dyce and Cottrell's translation here. On the Aztec speech scrolls, see Elizabeth Hill Boone, 'Pictorial Talking: The Figural Rendition of Speech Acts and Texts in Aztec Mexico', in *Sign and Design: Script as Image in Cross-Cultural Perspective (300–1600CE)*, ed. Brigitte Miriam Bedos-Rezak and Jeffrey F. Hamburger (Washington DC: Dumbarton Oaks, 2016); Tomlinson, *Singing the New World*, p. 64. Crawford et al., *Roman Statutes*, vol. 2 (London: Institute for Classical Studies, 1996), pp. 580–81, 677–9. Johann Christoph Bürgel, *The Feather of Simurgh: The 'licit magic' of the arts in medieval Islam* (New York: New York University Press, 1988), pp. 8–9.
4. Pico, *Opera*, p. 360.
5. On the *Disputationes adversus astrologiam*, see Grafton, *Commerce with the Ancients*, pp. 118–29; *Theses*, pp. 38, 138–43, 172–3; Valcke, *Pic*, pp. 102, 176.
6. An accessible English translation of Pico's *De ente et uno/On Being and the One* is available in *On the Dignity of Man/On Being and the One/Heptaplus*, trans. Charles Glenn Wallis, Paul J. W. Miller, and Douglas Carmichael, which is cited here for ease of reference.
7. Pico, *On Being and the One*, pp. 53–4.
8. The Greek and Hebrew notion of a *scelus* or crime of which the stain could spread by contagion evolved in Roman law into culpable involvement (being an 'accessory' to a crime); see Thome, 'Crime and Punishment', p. 77.
9. Ibn Khaldun, *The Muqadimmah: An Introduction to History*, trans. Franz Rosenthal (Princeton, NJ: Princeton University Press, 2015), p. 394.

10. Savonarola, *Sermone dell' oratione*, sig. Aiii^v.

XV. Life Unbound

1. Parenti, *Storia Fiorentina*, vol. 1 , pp. 45, 79. Landucci, *Diary*, 5 November, pp. 59–60. Tribaldo di Rossi, *Ricordanze*, p. 281.
2. Landucci, *Diary*, 19 May, 10 June. Selected *Writings of Savonarola*, p. 142.
3. Landucci, *Diary*, p. 59.
4. Parenti, *Storia Fiorentina*, p. 100; for the wider tradition, see Stewart, *Close Readers*, pp. 10–11; Cavalcanti, 'Tu m'hai sì piena di dolor la mente'.
5. Pico, *Oration*, pp. 72–3; as Copenhaver notes, the prophetic nun was Camilla Ruccellai.
6. Pico, *Oration*, p. 34.
7. Marin Sanuto, *I diarii di Marin Sanuto*, ed. F. Stefani (Venice: F. Visentini, 1879), vol. I, col. 726; Farmer, *Theses*, pp. 177–8.
8. Ficino to Poliziano, 20 August 1494, *Opera* Sig. Ooo [7]^v.
9. Landucci, *Diary*, p. 65.

XVI. Epilogue: Sublime and Superorganism

1. The use of pictogram-catechisms by Testera and others is described in Géronimo de Mendieta's *Historia eclesiástica Indiana*, which was written contemporaneous to Testera's mission but not published until 1870 (Mexico: Antigua Libreria, 1870), p. 665 particularly on Testera, but also pp. 246–50. On the Nahuatl *diphrasis* for poetry, see Tomlinson, *The Singing of the New World*, p. 24, and p. 36 on the Olmec speech-scroll at Xochicalco (*c*.650 CE).
2. Jean de Léry, *Histoire d'un voyage fait en terre de Brésil, autrement dit d'Amérique* (La Rochelle, 1578). p. 276/ Sig S2^v; Fernão Cardim, *Tratados da terra e gente do Brasil* (Rio: J. Leite, 1925), p. 167; *Navigazione et viaggi*, 65^v-66^r; Paul le Jeune, *Relation de la Nouvelle France, en l'année 1634*, in *Relations des Jésuits* (Québec: Augustin Coté, 1858), p. 18; Rouget, *Music and Trance*, pp. 39, 59–60. See also Gary Tomlinson, *The Singing of the New World*. The Algonquin formula for producing music existed in very similar fashion in Europe, in the circular 'chace' compositions, which often imitated birdsong. For later examples, see Michel Leiris's *La langue secrète des Dogons de Saga*, and G. Lienhardt, *Divinity and Experience: The Religion of the Dinka* (Oxford: Clarendon Press, 1961), p. 236–44.

See also Serge Gruzinski, *Quand les Indiens parlaient latin* (Paris: Fayard, 2023), 139, for an example of the opposite–the use of European musical training to teach indigenous peoples foreign poetic metres and rhythms.

3. Hanegraaff and Bouthoorn, *Lodovico Lazzarelli*, p. 38. Giambattista Vico, *New Science*, trans. David Marsh (London: Penguin Classics, 1999), p. 77. Giordano Bruno, 'On Magic', in *Cause, Principle and Unity and Essays on Magic*, ed. Richard J. Blackwell and Robert de Lucca (Cambridge: Cambridge University Press, 2012), p. 141.

4. Jonathan Swift, 'A Discourse Concerning the Mechanical Operation of the Spirit', in *Major Works*, eds Angus Ross and David Woolley (Oxford: Oxford University Press, 2003), pp. 167–74.

5. Matteo Ricci, SJ, *The True Meaning of the Lord of Heaven (T'ien-chu Shih-i)*, trans. Douglas Lancashire and Peter Hu Kuo-chen, SJ (Taipei: Institut Ricci, *Variétes Sinologiques*, n.s. 72, 1985), pp. 199, 203–5; on p. 227 it is clarified that the organic unity imagined is similar to belonging to a single body. Ricci's tract was designed to attack Buddhist practices in favour of Confucian ones, which were considered more compatible with Christianity. See also p.189 for Ricci's attempt to introduce Aristotelian categories into the discussion to prevent the collapse into monism by the equation of 'material energy' with 'spirits'.

6. Claude Lévi-Strauss, *Introduction to the Works of Marcel Mauss*, trans. Felicity Baker (London: Routledge and Keegan Paul, 1985), p. 14–16. Pico, *Oration*, pp. 32–4. See the concluding paragraph of Lévi-Strauss's own *Tristes Tropiques*, as well as Marilyn Strathern's 'dividuality' in *The Gender of the Gift*, and Clifford Geertz: 'the Western conception of the person as a bounded, unique, more or less integrated motivational and cognitive universe, a dynamic center of awareness, emotion, judgment, and action organized into a distinctive whole and set contrastively both against other such wholes and against a social and natural background is, however incorrigible it may seem to us, a rather peculiar idea in the context of the world's cultures'. Geertz, 'On the Nature of Anthropological Understanding', *American Scientist* 63 (1975), 47–53, p. 48.

7. Kant, *Critique of Judgement*, trans. James Creed Meredith, rev. and ed. Nicholas Walker (Oxford: Oxford University Press, 2007), §275, pp. 102–5. See Copenhaver, *Magic and the Dignity of Man*, p. 30.

INDEX

Illustrations are denoted by the use of *italic* page numbers.